Japanese Capitalism in Crisis

Is Japan totally exceptional or is it a typical market economy? Is the poor macroeconomic performance of the nineties down to archaic institutions or short-term monetary and budgetary policies? Is the Japanese manufacturing system based on solid ground or does the bursting of the bubble highlight fundamental structural weaknesses? Should the Japanese authorities preserve the main tenets of their post-Second World War economic institutions or should they do more to embrace market-led capitalism?

The contributions to *Japanese Capitalism in Crisis* show that there can be a middle ground between these extremes and deliver two benefits: a deeper understanding of long-term development and an extension of existing theory. A regulationist approach is used to examine how the periods of growth and crisis can be attributed to the institutions which govern capital accumulation.

This book should prove to be invaluable to students and researchers studying the economies of Japan and other east Asian countries as well as all those interested in patterns of boom and recession worldwide.

Robert Boyer is Professor at the École des Hautes Études en Sciences Sociales, Senior Researcher at the National Centre of Scientific Research and Economist at CEPREMAP, all based in Paris. **Toshio Yamada** is Professor of Economics at Nagoya University.

Routledge Advances in International Political Economy

Japanese Capitalism in Crisis

A regulationist interpretation

Edited by
Robert Boyer and Toshio Yamada

London and New York

First published 2000
by Routledge
11 New Fetter Lane, London EC4P 4EE

Simultaneously published in the USA and Canada
by Routledge
29 West 35th Street, New York, NY 10001

Routledge is an imprint of the Taylor & Francis Group

© 2000 Robert Boyer and Toshio Yamada for selection and editorial matter;
individual contributors for their contributions

Typeset in Garamond by
MHL Typesetting Ltd, Coventry
Printed and bound in Great Britain by
MPG Books Ltd, Bodmin

British Library Cataloguing in Publication Data
A catalogue record for this book is available
from the British Library

Library of Congress Cataloging-in-Publication Data
Boyer, Robert, 1943–
      Japanese capitalism in crisis: a regulationist interpretation /
      Robert Boyer and Toshio Yamada.
      p. cm. – (Routledge advances in international political economy)
      Includes bibliographical references and index.
      1. Japan–Economic conditions–1989–2. Japan–Economic policy–
      1989– I. Yamada, Toshio, 1942–II. Title. III. Series.

      HC462.95.B69 2000
      338.952–dc21   99-053107

ISBN 0-415-20559-X

Contents

Figures

Tables

Contributors

Robert Boyer (Introduction, Chapter 7, Conclusion) is professor at *Ecoles des Hautes Etudes en Sciences Sociales*, senior researcher at National Center of Scientific Research (CNRS) and Economist at CEPREMAP. In the domain of institutional and historical economics, he has been active in building and extending *Régulation* theory. His recent publications include *States Against Firms* (with Drache, D. eds), Routledge, 1996. *Contemporary Capitalism* (with Hollingsworth, R. eds), CUP, 1997. *After Fordism* (with Durand J. P.), Macmillan, 1997. *Between imitation and innovation* (with Charron, E., Jürgens, U. and Tolliday, S.), OUP,1998. *Régulation Theory: The state of the Art* (with Saillard, Y.) Routledge, 2000.

Benjamin Coriat (Chapter 10) is professor of economics at Paris 13 University and Director of CREI. His research deals with labour issues, work organisation, firms management of technology, theory of organisation and institutions and he is a contributor to *régulation* theory. His publications include *L'Atelier et le Chronomètre*, Paris: Bourgois 1978. *L'atelier et le robot*, Paris: Bourgois 1990. *Made in France* Paris: Livre de Poche Hachette, 1993. He has analysed the Japanese production and management style in *Penser à l'envers. Travail et organisation dans l'entreprise japonaise*, Paris: Bourgois 1991.

Akira Ebizuka (Chapter 2) is professor of political economy at Osaka City University. He has published on political economy and the social structures of the post-war Japanese economy. On political economy, his recent publications include *The Institutional Analysis of Socio-economic Systems*, Nagoya University Press, 1998 (in collaboration with H. Uemura and A. Isogai, in Japanese). On the Japanese economy, his articles include 'Incentives & flexibility in the hierarchical market-firm nexus' (with H. Uemura), in *Japon Extenso*, no. 31, mars-avril 1994, and 'L'hypothèse de la relation hierarchisée marché-firme et l'économie japonaise d'après-guerre' (with H. Uemura and A. Isogai), in *L'Année de la régulation*, Vol. 1, Paris: La Découverte, 1997.

Patrice Geoffron (Chapter 10) is associate professor of Economics in Paris 13 University and he is member of CREI. His fields of research are the contemporary transformation of financial systems and the analysis of Japanese financial and economic trends. Among his publications is *La crise financière du modèle japonais*, (with Rubinstein, M.) Paris: Economica 1996.

Masanori Hanada (Chapter 5) is professor of Social Policy in the Department of Social Welfare Studies at Kumamoto Gakuen University. His current research interests are two areas: the economics of wage determination and work organisation, and the economics of social security (with special reference to pension systems and the welfare state). His publications include *Teamwork in the Automobile Industry* (co-author), London: Macmillan Press, 1999, and *One Best Way: Trajectories and Industrial Models of the World's Automobile Producers* (co-author), New York: Oxford University Press, 1998.

Yasuro Hirano (Chapter 5) is professor of labour economics and social policy at Fukuoka Prefectural University. His current research is on the socio-economic effects of aged society, specially related with employment systems and with public and private pension schemes. His recent publications include *Japanese Institutions and Economic Growth*, Tokyo: Fujiwara-Shoten 1996 (in Japanese). He also wrote numerous articles on Japanese economy from the point of institutional economics, including 'Relation industrielle et système de salaire au Japon', in *Mondes en Développement*, Tome 20, no. 79–80, 1992 and 'Une économie de partage à moyen terme et son altération', in *Japon in Extenso*, No. 31, mars-avril 1994.

Yasuo Inoue (Chapter 9) is professor of economics at Nagoya City University. His main field of interest is Asian and European economies with special reference to trade, finance and internationalisation. His recent publications include *Reading the Great Transformation fin de siècle*, Tokyo: Yuhikaku 1996 (in Japanese), 'Trajectoires nationales d'industrialisation de la Corée du Sud et de Taiwan', *Japon in Extenso*, No.32/33, juin-septembre, 1994 and 'East Asian capitalism and the *régulation* approach', in R. Boyer and T. Yamada eds, *Recomposition of International Regime* (in Japanese), Tokyo: Fujiwara-Shoten, 1997.

Akinori Isogai (Chapter 2) is associate professor of economics at Kyushu University. His main field of interest is the economics of institutions and evolutionary economics. In this field, his recent publications include a Japanese book, *The Institutional Analysis of Socio-economic Systems: Beyond Marx and Keynes*, Nagoya University Press, 1998 (in collaboration with H. Uemura and A. Ebizuka, in Japanese). He has also written numerous articles on the post-war Japanese economic issues, especially on changes in the differential structures of the labour market, the flexibility of wages and employment, and the structures of incentive mechanism in the post-war Japanese corporate system, in Japanese, English and French.

Michel Juillard (Chapter 7) is associate professor of economics at Paris 8 University. His main fields of research are the analysis of the long-term American growth, the econometric methods for detecting structural change, the institutional and econometric studies of labour markets in an international comparison perspective. His publications include *Un schéma de reproduction pour l'économie des Etats-Unis: 1948–1980*, Bern: Peter Lang 1993, 'Une Analyse Économétrique Des Changements De Régime De Croissance Aux Etats-Unis', *Revue Economique*, Mai 1995. 'Le rapport salarial japonais a-t-il atteint ses limites?', (with Boyer, R.), *Revue Economique*, vol 48, no. 3, Mai 1997.

Naoki Nabeshima (Chapter 6) is associate professor of economics at Toyama University. His research and publications are principally in the areas of Kaleckian and post-Keynesian economics, particularly theories of money and finance. His articles include 'Kalecki's theory of effective demand and the endogeneity of money supply' (*Economic Review*, 1993, in Japanese), 'Minsky paradox: the range of the financial instability hypothesis' (*The Bulletin of Japan Society of Political Economy*, 1997, in Japanese), and 'La transformation du système financier et la crise contemporaine: le mode de régulation financière dans le capitalisme japonais' (*Revue d'économie financière*, 1997).

Marianne Rubinstein (Chapter 10), is associate professor of Economics at Paris 13 University and member of CREI. Her field of research concerns labour market analysis and financial theory. Among her publications: *La crise financière du modèle japonais*, With Geoffron, P.) Paris: Economica 1996.

Hironori Tohyama (Chapter 4) is associate professor of political economy at the University of Shizuoka. He has published on wage-labor nexus, wage-bargaining systems and power on the shopfloor in Japanese. His recent articles include 'Wage bargaining system and evolution of compromises between capital and labor', in T. Yamada and R. Boyer eds., *Post-war Japanese Capitalism: An Analysis of 'Régulation' and Crisis*, Tokyo: Fujiwara-Shoten, 1999 (in Japanese).

Hiroyasu Uemura (Chapters 2 and 8) is associate professor of economics at Nagoya University. He has published widely in the field of the economics of institutions and macroeconomic dynamics. His recent publications include *The Institutional Analysis of Socio-economic Systems: Beyond Marx and Keynes*, Nagoya University Press, 1998 (in collaboration with A. Isogai and A. Ebizuka, in Japanese). He has also written numerous articles, especially on the institutional analysis of the Japanese employment system and the macroeconomic analysis of growth, distribution and structural changes, including 'L'hypothèse de la relation hierarchisée marché-firme et l'économie japonaise d'après-guerre' (with A. Ebizuka and A. Isogai), *L'Année de la régulation*, Vol.1, Paris: La Découverte, 1997.

Hiroyuki Uni (Chapter 3) is associate professor of economics at the Graduate School, Kyoto University. His main fields of research are economics of structural and technological change, Marxian economics and Japanese economy. He is the author of *Structural Change and Capital Accumulation*, Tokyo: Yuhikaku, 1998 (in Japanese). He has also written numerous articles on economic growth in post-war Japan, especially on structural changes in consumption, the structure of export-led growth, and the Japanese innovation system.

Toshio Yamada (Introduction, Chapter 1, Conclusion) is professor of economics at Nagoya University. He has published extensively on economic theories, Japanese capitalism and history of political economy in Japan. His recent publications include *The 20th Century Capitalism*, Tokyo: Yuhikaku 1994 (in Japanese), 'Japon: Démythifier la régulation' (with Y. Inoue), in R. Boyer *et al*. eds, *Théorie de la Régulation: L'état des savoirs*, Paris: La Découverte 1995, and 'Economic development and economic thought after World War II', in S. Sugihara *et al*. eds, *Economic Thought and Modernization in Japan*, Cheltenham/Northampton: Elgar, 1998.

Abbreviations

ASEAN	Association of South East Asian Nations
ASEAN 4	Indonesia, Thailand, Philippines and Malaysia
BIBF	Bangkok International Banking Facility
BIS	Bank of International Settlements
BOJ	(Central) Bank of Japan
CEPREMAP	Centre d'Etudes Prospectives d'Economie Mathematique Appliquées à la Planification (Center of Prospective and Mathematical Economics Applied to Planning)
CNRS	Centre National de la Recherche Scientifique (National Center for Scientific Research)
CREI	Centre de Recherche en Economie Industrielle (Center of Research in Industrial Economics)
CUSUM	Statistical Test of stability
EPA	Economic Planning Agency
EU	European Union
FDI	Foreign direct investment
GATT	General Agreement on Tariff and Trade
GDP	Gross Domestic Product
HMFN	Hierarchical market-firm nexus
IDL	International Division of Labour
IMF, JC	International Metal Workers Federation, Japan Council
JDB	Japanese Development Bank
JES	Japanese Employment System
JETRO	Japan External Trade Organisation
JWLN	Japanese Wage Labour Nexus
MBA	Master in Business Administration
MBS	Main Bank System
MFN	Market-Firm Nexus
MIT	Massachusetts Institute of Technology
MITI	Ministry of International Trade and Industry
MOF	Ministry of Finance

NIE	New Institutional Economies
NIEs	Newly Industrialising Economies
OECD	Organisation for Economic Cooperation and Development
OJT	On the Job Training
R&D	Research and Development
RCA	Relative Comparative Advantage
UK	United Kingdom
US	United States
USA	United States of America
WLN	Wage Labour Nexus
WTO	World Trade Organisation

Glossary

The terms defined in this glossary are identified with an asterisk on their first mention in the text

Chaebols	South Korean large conglomerates, vertically integrated
Domei	Japanese Confederation of Labour
Gensaki	Repurchase agreement bond market
Heisei Boom	Begins in 1989
implication incitée	Induced commitment
Izanagi Boom	Boom of the late 1960s
Kaizen	Continuous improvement
keiretsu	Horizontal and/or inter-company relations
kousei nenkin	Private-sector retirement scheme
Nikkeiren	Japan Federation of Employer's Association
Okurasho	Ministry of Finance
Rengo	Japanese Trade Union Confederation
Salaryman	Regular employee of the large company
satei	Assessment of worker by the direct supervisor
shokuno	Task-performing competence
shokuno-shikaku	Ranks in the competence-based grade system
Shukko	Dispatch of workers during recessions
shunto	Spring Labour Offensive
Sohyo	General Council of Trade Unions of Japan
taishokukin	Retirement payment paid by the firm when the worker leaves the firm
Tekko Roren	Federation of Steel Workers Unions
yendaka	High yen
Zaibatsu	Financial group in prewar Japan

Introduction

A puzzle for economic theories

Robert Boyer and Toshio Yamada

One more book on Japan; why? Actually, back in the 1980s and early 1990s, Japanese studies used to be a sunrise mass-production industry: not any one was a bestseller but at least the market was buoyant. Since the early 1990s, the situation has drastically reversed. Japan is no more a model and any economists or social scientists have an immediate opinion about the reasons for such a poor performance. Basically, for many analysts, the Japanese institutions are perceived as archaic and obsolete and they should be replaced as quickly as possible by American-style management, economic and political institutions.

This book argues that this interpretation is drastically flawed, since it derives from the use of neo-classical theory as a normative tool, not at all as a positive contribution to the understanding of the unfolding of an unprecedented structural crisis, generated by the very success of the so-called 'Japanese model'. By contrast, all the contributors to this edited book share the same concern for institutional economics; institutions matter and they differ significantly from one country to another. Therefore, the Japanese crisis of the 1990s cannot be easily compared with the boom of the American economy during the same period.

It is important to describe briefly some methodological problems raised by the analysis of Japan, then show how and why most contemporary interpretations are unsatisfactory, in order to propose five core principles and capture both the common features and the specificity of Japanese capitalism. The so-called *régulation* theory has adopted these principles for analysing American and European long-term history. This book is extending this theory in order to capture the flavour of the Japanese trajectory since the Second World War. It can be read basically as a novel interpretation of the contemporary problems facing the managers, political leaders and citizens. But it provides too a new development in *régulation* theory. First, it stresses the role of institutional complementarity in the emergence of path dependency properties. Second, it argues that a major shift in the hierarchy of institutional forms has taken place and plays a role in the genesis of the structural crisis of the 1990s.

Three perplexities about research on the Japanese economy

The vast literature about the Japanese economy raises at least three major difficulties, that are far from being settled.

Is Japan totally exceptional or is it a typical market economy?

On one side, the field of Japanese studies is built upon the implicit or explicit hypothesis that any understanding of this country has to rely on typically Japanese concepts, given the strong and original flavour of the culture and history of this country. At the extreme, none of the teaching from social sciences originating from the study of Western society would be relevant. On the other side, many Western scholars think that any of their concepts, theories or models can be applied without restriction or amendment to the Japanese case. If, unfortunately, they do not, the reason is simple; some irrationality or archaism would prevent the theory to be true and therefore should be removed by a bold political action by government enlightened by the adoption of the theory put forward by the scholars.

Clearly none of these strategies is satisfactory. The first one would dissolve social sciences into a pure description of all the observed configurations, without any general result. Still more, it would imply that the Japanese crisis of the 1990s is the outcome of a kind of cultural clash of civilisations that is far from representing the essence of the evolution of economic activity in Japan. Neither is the second option satisfactory. Why does a unique economic model display such contrasted trajectories between the US, EU and the various East Asian countries? This vision has been seriously challenged during the East Asian crisis initiated in 1997. The South Korean pattern does not follow the Mexican track, nor does Japan follow the American trends. Not by a long way!

Mono-causal theories deliver too many conflicting interpretations

In order to reply to these criticisms, many analysts have proposed theories in order to understand why and how the Japanese economy is specific. The interpretations are ranked between two extremes. On one side, Japan would be a clear example of the success of a development State (Johnson 1995), and of planning as an alternative or at least a complement to pure market mechanisms. The so-called administrative guidance would be quite essential to the functioning of the Japanese economy. On the other side, an opposite interpretation stresses that the governments have followed pro-market proactive policies and this would be at the core of the fast catching up of the East Asian economies, including Japan (World Bank 1993; Aoki and Okuno-Fujiwara 1998). Therefore, Japan would blend at an original mix between market and non-market mechanisms, even if theoreticians disagree about the exact position of Japan. One solution in order to reconcile these interpretations would be to diagnose a shift from active State policies, back to the 1950s and 1960s, to the leadership of large corporations in the 1980s with a possible evolution toward stronger market mechanisms during the 1990s.

There are still other oppositions. Some economists think that the cultural values embedded in Japanese society, such as confucianism, have been quite instrumental in promoting hard work, respect for authority, a taste for learning and the propensity to save (Morishima 1982). Others reply that the Japanese economy is a quite typical capitalist one, therefore all the concepts and theories can be applied without restriction. This idea is quite common among Keynesian, classical or Marxist economists. For instance, the 1990s would be clear evidence of the tendency of competition to trigger over-capacity, profit rate decline and financial instability (Itoh, M. 1990).

At the firm level, many authors have been investigating the nature of organisation of Japanese firms and a large consensus tends to conclude that the Japanese configuration is quite or rather specific (Imai and Komiya 1994). But the leading Japanese economists disagree about these specificities. For some, human resources management is the key explaining factor (Koike 1988, 1995), for others, it is the internal flow of information and their relations with the incentive mechanisms built into the wage and promotion systems (Aoki 1988). Still others think that the nature of competition among large corporations is at the origin of innovation, competitiveness and growth (Odagiri 1992) but experts in technical change argue that the emergence of a genuine innovation system is the main source of Japanese success (Kodama 1991). Similar opposition may be found about the nature of the large Japanese firm. Is it the result of a typical capitalist process, via the interaction of managerial strategies and workers' struggles (Nishiguchi 1994) or on the contrary, does it represent the modern expression of a nearly self-managed firm (Komiya 1987), or even a new configuration for a human capitalist enterprise (Ozaki 1991)?

The ideal would be to elaborate a more general and systemic analysis including as sub-components these partial hypotheses, test them in order to diagnose that factors are crucial and possibly reconcile these alternative interpretations. Alas, this is rarely done and this lacuna impairs our understanding of Japan.

A surprising shift from appraisal and admiration to Japanese bashing

The comparison of the contemporary analyses with those made back in the 1980s delivers a major puzzle. Whereas during the 1980s, the vast majority of authors were praising the coherence and dynamic efficiency of Japanese institutions and organisations, the 1990s have experienced a complete and brusque U-turn. Any feature that was perceived as a trump card for Japan is then portrayed as clear evidence of archaism, irrationality and inadequacy for the new trends of the world economy. For instance, experts in industrial organisation had forecast a Japanisation of Western productive systems

(Womack, Jones and Roos 1990; Elger and Smith 1994). The poor performance of the Japanese economy during the 1990s, and by contrast the booming American economy, have totally shifted the appraisal of Japanese production methods. Everybody stresses the organisational inertia, the difficulty in coping with information technologies and the lag of Japanese corporations in science-led innovations by comparison with their North American competitors.

The same shift from overoptimism to dire pessimism takes place concerning the Japanese Employment Systems (JES). It was supposed to be a treasure and a competitive asset since it was synchronising on-the-job training, competition for promotion and the ideal of employment stability under the supervision of enterprise unions. Given the poor macroeconomic context of the 1990s, these features are now perceived as hindering structural adjustment and the adoption of new production methods (Yoshikawa 1994; Geoffron and Rubinstein 1996). Again it remains to be explained why such a drastic reappraisal took place; was the whole interpretation inaccurate? Was it the result of a poor representation of real practice? Or, alternatively, has the changing international context triggered such a shift from success to failure?

Similarly, some observers were praising the wise and honest Japanese bureaucrats and extending this feature to most East Asian countries (World Bank 1993). The recurring examples of corruption at all levels of the Japanese administration throughout the 1990s have totally eroded this rosy picture of Japanese society. By contrast, most American scholars perceive that a quick transition to more transparent market mechanisms is the only solution to overcome the creeping structural crisis and possible financial meltdown (Dornbusch 1998). Was corruption already present during the Golden Age and then how to explain the relative success of Japan? Or is it a novel phenomenon typical of the crisis period?

A final example relates to the synergy between Japanese and East Asian dynamism. In the early 1980s, most experts were convinced that the pace of the world economy would derive from Asian development and that Japan was to be the core of the most dynamic region of the triad (Hatch and Yamamura 1996). But after the Asian crisis in 1997, the picture is strictly the opposite: the recovery of Japan is made more difficult by the adjustment process in Korea, Indonesia, Thailand, and conversely, the uncertain Japanese evolution is hindering the deepening of the international division of labour previously observed within Asia. Few theories address the basic question underlying all these puzzles: why does success finally turn into failure and crisis? By contrast, this is one of the major themes of this book.

The Japanese crisis: still mysterious!

All these difficulties are adding up within the analyses of the evolution of the Japanese economy during the 1990s. There is a clear feeling that one prosperous period is over and that a financial crisis is creeping, whereas unemployment climbs to unprecedented levels. Is it not symbolic that in July 1999 the unemployment rate in Japan is higher than in the United States: 4.9 versus 3.9 per cent (*The Economist* 1999b: 84)?

Too many imprecise meanings

Therefore, the word 'crisis' has permeated in journals, newspapers, government reports, and even economists' analyses. Unfortunately, quite a few economic theories exhibit a clear concept for crisis. For Keynesians, it is mainly the question of the persistence of an under-unemployment equilibrium, with no clear evidence of crisis. For neo-classical economists, the hypotheses of rational behaviour, market equilibrium and rational expectations usually prevent any crisis, in the sense that any evolution, however complex, is basically forecast by economic agents, at least for its determinist component. Only stochastic disturbances, the so-called 'surprises', may explain some deviation of the long-term equilibrium. For financial analysts, a sudden collapse of the stock market Nikkei index is considered to be a crisis, with the fear that the same economic depression of the 1930s may take place. For growth theorists, any slowdown in GDP annual rate is interpreted as an exception to long-term trends, but the term crisis cannot be properly used in such a case. Finally, the persistence of a large public deficit (in Japan) or of a large external deficit (in the US) is sometimes perceived as the evidence, or for some economists, the cause of economic crisis.

Lacking one clear definition and concept of crisis, an understanding of the contemporary Japanese situation is made difficult indeed. At odds with this impressionist interpretation of a crisis, the present book builds upon 'régulation theory' in order to propose a systemic definition of such an episode.

Bad economic policy and adverse shocks?

A second difficulty relates to the fact that each theory is taking into account only a limited number of explanatory variables, most of the time a single one. Thus, the analyst is labelling as 'crisis' any disturbance out of equilibrium but there are as many equilibria as research programmes in economics. For many American economists, the inadequacy of Japanese economic policy is the main culprit for the poor performance observed during the 1990s: a too lax monetary policy during the 1980s promoted a financial bubble; when it burst out, the monetary policy would have become too restrictive and public deficit too small. But this is a quite superficial analysis indeed: how should monetary policy be conducted when the financial system is near to structural instability? It might even be erroneous. In August 1999, the money market interest rate was 0.03 per cent in Japan; and there is no negative interest rate! Clearly, contemporary Japanese economy is not following at all the track of the

American great crisis starting in 1929 (Okina 1999). For other analysts, the mismanagement of the exchange rate between the Yen and the Dollar would be the main culprit (McKinnon 1999), after the clumsy tax increase, decided in 1997, that would have killed the emerging recovery (OECD 1998).

But it might be difficult to explain a whole decade of quasi-stagnation by the succession of adverse events. Thus at the other end of the spectrum, some analysts think that this 'lost Japanese decade' is up to the structural weaknesses of the socio-economic system that were hidden during the Golden Age. The cross-holding of shares among the members of the same *keiretsu** prevents an efficient functioning of financial markets, a poor banking supervision explains the piling up of bad debts, the inability of bureaucrats to run a modern economy, that would be the blocking factors of a strong and long-lasting recovery (Dornbusch 1998). But then, it is difficult to explain why such an archaic institutional architecture has been able to propel the Japanese economy from under- to over-development in less than half a century.

Equivalent criticisms can be directed at most other interpretations of the 1990s: the fact that the Japanese economy exhibits inter-industry instead of intra-industry specialisation, the archaism and the corruption of an elitist bureaucracy, the inability of Japanese managers to master modern managerial tools and principles, the too homogeneous educational system, the lack of intensive links between the academic world and the R&D departments of large corporations, all these factors are again and again pointed out as explaining the gloomy prospects of the Japanese economy. Too many contradictory explanations are not really convincing and this book proposes another vision, based on different epistemological premises.

For an institutional theory of the Japanese economy: five methodological principles

The clear shortcomings of the previous analytical frameworks hint at an alternative set of hypotheses, quite useful in order to put Japan in historical retrospect and international perspective.

From market to capitalism

For most contemporary economists, modern societies are viewed and formalised as a set of interdependent markets, for product, credit, capital, labour, derivatives, polluting rights, etc. Therefore, any economic, financial or social problem has to be related to a malfunctioning of market mechanisms. The only task of the economist is then to defend the 'market viewpoint': the public authorities should organise free access, monitor full transparency of the information, and enforce property rights and private contracts. But modern

---

* Terms followed by an asterisk are defined in the glossary on page xvii.

micro theory, built upon the hypothesis of asymmetric information, provides a more pessimistic view: markets are not self-equilibrating, since rationing upon credit, labour and even product market is the rule (Stiglitz 1987); thus the rationing is shifting from one market to another, generating keynesian, classical or inflationary equilibria (Benassy 1982). In such a context, the precise organisation of the monetary regime, the nature of competition, the process according to which wages are set, all these factors define a complete system, mixing markets with a series of institutions and organisations (Hollingsworth and Boyer 1997). Thus, any significant crisis tends to be systemic.

Therefore, it is more enlightening to use the concept of capitalism, as a complete institutional system with a sophisticated set of core social relations (basically the market relation and the production relation). Consequently, markets are no more and not necessarily the unique mechanism for allocating resources since other mechanisms do exist and thus define many alternative configurations for economic systems. Furthermore, this concept of capitalism exhibits some structural constraints that are binding at any historical period, even if the precise architecture is changing through time, due precisely to the very functioning of this quite dynamic and even contradictory system (Heillbroner 1988).

Systemic complementarity or mismatch of economic institutions?

Thus, the concept of general equilibrium of interdependent markets is replaced by the analysis of the viability of a given set of structural forms (or institutional forms), compatible with the two basic social relations of capitalism. The emphasis is shifted from a static analysis to a historical one: competition among firms and struggles between capital and labour trigger a tendency to capital accumulation, with alternatively booms and depressions or recessions. For some configurations, the price mechanism is sufficient to sustain the structural compatibility of the institutional forms (Boyer 1990a). The system can reproduce itself and there exists a coherent *régulation* mode. Such a system necessarily combines economic forces with the exercise of power, whereas economic activity is inserted into a wider web of social relations, not to mention the relations with the environment.

Only a systemic analysis is able to take into account the property of such a dynamical system. The sources of crises are not limited to the malfunctioning of markets but they may derive from the progressive erosion of the dynamic stability provided by a *régulation* mode. Symmetrically, there is no need for *a priori* hypothesis about the structural stability of such a *régulation* mode: it can be either stable or unstable and it is an issue for empirical assessment and not at all a constraint put upon the theory, at odds with the vision and the practice of neo-classical research. Long-run historical studies have actually shown that this succession of quite steady regimes and then of crisis periods is recurrently observed within the same capitalist economy, both for the US (Aglietta 1982), for France (Boyer 1979) and for most European countries (Boyer 1988).

Not a single but several configurations: the need for international comparisons

Thus, the opposition is no more between a pure market economy and a series of imperfect systems. Simultaneously the reference to a Pareto optimum is vanishing. Consequently, the very intricacy of the institutional architecture does play a role in the dynamics of the whole system, in the long run as well as the short run. *A priori*, there is more than one single best system, since Pareto optima are out of reach, and therefore each configuration has simultaneously strong features and detrimental weaknesses (Murakami 1996; Hollingsworth and Boyer 1997). Furthermore, there is no easy choice among alternative institutional architectures, since they result from a complex historical process combining social struggles, economic crises and political conflicts, that are largely idiosyncratic to each society. There may exist general classes of system, but a unique class is quite unlikely ... even as most economic theories tend to postulate that basically market economies define a unique system and should converge towards a single configuration, specially in the era of globalisation.

A second important methodological consequence has to be pointed out: the Japanese economy is not necessarily to be compared with the American one, supposed to be the key reference of any benchmarking. Any pair-wise comparison is misleading, since only a multilateral study may reveal both the common and the specific features of any single economy. The vision of the contemporary problems of the Japanese economy becomes quite different and in a sense much more accurate. After all, is not American capitalism the true exception (Lipset 1996)? From a theoretical standpoint, systematic international comparisons are some of the few available methods in order to turn any defined social theory, that by definition is local since it originates from a given society and is representative of a specific historical period, into a more general one (Bourdieu 1988). In this respect this book can be read as a generalisation of *régulation* theory in the light of the Japanese configuration and history.

Fresh interpretations of contemporary evolutions are generated by long-term historical retrospect

Most macroeconomic analyses of contemporary Japan focus upon short-term evolutions and economic policy in the very conventional sense: what should be the optimal monetary and budgetary policy in order to enjoy full employment with no inflation? The paradoxical evolutions of the 1990s suggest a quite different question: why such an atypical business cycle and growth slow-down? The dynamic pattern is much more important than the static analysis. Reconciling economic theory and history is specially important for Japan (Dopfer 1985; Murakami 1996) and this is a key objective for *régulation* theory (Boyer 1990a). It is why most of the chapters of this book provide a long-term historical background, starting at least from the end of the Second World War. Without such a time span, institutional change cannot be perceived, nor the transformation in the mode of *régulation*.

Simultaneously, the 1990s cannot be understood without a retrospective analysis of the trends observed during the 1980s: in a sense, the apparent success of the first period sets into motion the disequilibria that will show out during the second; over-capacity in some key sectors, introduction of new financial instruments into a quite traditional system of public supervision, surge of foreign investment and large movements in exchange rates. Thus, the related productivity slowdown is largely the consequence of the prevailing growth regime, at odds with real business cycle theories that perceive these evolutions as totally exogenous shocks. A long-term analysis therefore shifts the interpretation of the 1990s as well as the prospect for a renewed growth pattern.

From business cycle to structural crisis

A final requirement of any relevant analysis is to explicate a clear concept of crisis. *Per se*, a recession may be either the normal adjustment pattern, in order to level off the disequilibria generated during the boom period, or the typical reaction to an adverse external shock. The down-turn within a business cycle is not at all evidence for a crisis. Nevertheless, the use of *régulation* theory in order to capture the specificity of Japanese contemporary evolution suggests two possible forms of crisis.

On one side, an unprecedented exogenous shock, such as the propagation in the Japanese economy of financial innovations and an unprecedented exposure to speculation, may prove to be detrimental to the structural stability which used to be observed for perturbations coming mainly from international trade. Basically, the institutional forms that were tuned to respond to a precise set of endogenous and exogenous evolutions turn out to be unable to cope with this new perturbation.

On the other side, the inability of large firms, public authorities and the governments to design corrective measures leads to a second and more severe type of crisis. According to this second definition, the very functioning of the existing *régulation* mode triggers economic, financial and social evolutions that are destabilising the coherence of the institutional forms which are at the core of this *régulation* mode. Clearly, the 1990s confirm that the Japanese economy has entered into such a crisis: no clear recovery has taken place and quite all economic actors recognise the limits of the present institutional architecture but simultaneously are unable to propose and implement a more satisfactory one. Thus, even if the pattern of the Japanese contemporary economy is quite distinct from the deflationary depression that took place in the US in the inter-war period, in both cases the economies are experiencing a structural crisis . . . but they are different since they relate to contrasted *régulation* modes. This brings some clarity into contemporary debates (Okina 1999) and prevents major mistakes in analysing the present state of Japan. The purpose of this book is precisely to propose and develop such a general interpretation.

How *régulation* theory analyses Japanese capitalism and its crisis

This theory has been designed in order to comply with the five methodological principles previously elaborated. It might be useful for the reader to provide some guidelines that summarise the main concepts of the theory, a full presentation of which is available elsewhere (Boyer and Saillard 2000).

From two basic social relations to five institutional forms

Both a theoretical derivation and numerous empirical studies hint that any capitalist economy requires the existence, and ultimately the coherence, of five institutional forms.

1. The more pervasive one is without any doubt the market relation that is embedded into a *monetary regime* (Aglietta and Orléan 1998): it describes how financial deficits and surpluses are consolidated within the banking and financial systems. This is specially important for contemporary Japan as Chapters 4 and 6 suggest.
2. The capital labour relation, typical of capitalism, may take various forms that are captured by the motion of *wage labour nexus* (WLN). It describes the principles in division of labour, the methods for organising production, the wage system and the lifestyle of the wage-earners, possibly influenced by the existence of a welfare system. A precise assessment of this institutional form plays a major role in understanding the *régulation* mode operating in Japan, as put forward by Chapters 1, 2, 4, 5 and 7.
3. In this context, firms compete on product, credit and capital markets. The rules according to which they interact concern entry, bankruptcy, the acceptable degree of cooperation or collusion. They thus define alternative *forms of competition*. The ideal of pure and perfect competition is rarely observed and supposes highly sophisticated institutionalised rules, therefore many other forms tend to exist and are important for the dynamics of prices, profit and investment. This theme is dealt with by Chapters 2, 6 and 10.
4. Basically, the State is in charge of organising the compatibility of the rules governing the three previous institutional forms as well as providing the collective goods and the coordination necessary to production and capital accumulation, not to mention the more conventional roles of deciding budgetary and monetary policies. The *relations of the State with the economy* may take various configurations through time and across countries. The form of the State is the key, but not unique, ingredient of any 'régulation'

mode. Since the Second World War a major issue has been the nature of the welfare system and in this respect Japan displays a quite specific configuration as argued by Chapter 5.

5. Finally, the relations of a given economy with the international system as a matter of political and institutional organisation is not a question of pure market mechanisms. *The forms of insertion of the nation into the world economy* may be quite diverse for commodities, products, investments, labour, credit, intellectual property rights and may vary drastically from one country to another. Again Japan is a quite interesting case that is investigated by Chapters 3, 6, 8, 9 and 10.

Two methods for assessing the viability of a régulation mode

All these five institutional forms usually derive from institutionalised compromises (Delorme and André 1983). They channel individual and collective strategies according to the rules of the game, by nature partial, that are not necessarily compatible one with another. Only when the economic and social dynamics associated with such an architecture sustains an *accumulation regime* and organises the decentralisation of economic decisions in the context of a limited information and knowledge, does a coherent *régulation* mode exist. *Régulation* theory has deeply investigated the various factors able to deliver such coherent dynamic systems. Basically, two different mechanisms and approaches are available and put into practice by the contributors to this book.

- On the one hand, the relative strength of various groups and the related institutional forms may vary drastically. Therefore the hierarchy among institutional compromises can be an important factor in the cohesiveness of a *régulation* mode. If, for typical fordist configurations, the WLN is quite central and has an impact upon the monetary regime and the forms of competition, Japan exhibits a rather specific hierarchy in which the large company has a polar position in the institutional organisation of the whole system. Two chapters follow this avenue; Chapter 1 develops the hypothesis of the companyist compromise, whereas Chapter 2 and its macroeconomic counterpart Chapter 8 put forward the complex hierarchy governing the market-firm and wage-labour nexuses.
- On the other hand, a clear hierarchy is not a sufficient condition for a coherent *régulation* mode to exist: it is important to check that the corresponding macroeconomic regularities actually support a viable accumulation regime and the related form of the business cycle associated with each configuration. This method has been used with some success for the American and French cases. This book provides an extension to Japan, with quite fresh results, as shown by Chapters 3 and 8. Even if the contemporary Japanese economy belongs to the broad category of mass production and consumption growth regime, she does not exhibit the same pattern as American fordism for instance.

Market-led régulation *mode is not necessarily the rule*

Is this gap the main reason for the current financial and economic problems of Japan? Not at all according to this framework. *A priori*, there is no superior *régulation* mode that would impose its logic on all developed economies. First, it is not possible to import easily one institutionalised compromise from one society to another, since it is a quite idiosyncratic process and construct. Second, the fate of a given institutional architecture is not set by its reference and distance to an ideal one best way, but by its ability, or not, to organise the dynamic process according to which economic disequilibria are corrected by built-in mechanisms.

According to this vision, the adaptability and thus viability of the Japanese institutions have been quite impressive from the end of the Second World War to the early 1990s. At odds with the vision of a quite archaic and sclerotic Japan, various contributors give a lot of evidence about the flexibility provided by the companyist compromise or the hierarchical market-firm nexus. The accumulation regime has been transforming itself (Chapter 3) and the detail of the institutional forms revised, for instance, after the first oil shocks, giving birth to a quite efficient system indeed (Chapter 8). But of course, two objections may be addressed to this analysis. In the long run will not a given system impose its logic, due to superior results? If the answer is negative, then how do we explain the striking contrast, during the 1990s, between market-led regulation and other *régulation* modes?

Each institutional architecture exhibits strengths and weaknesses

An answer to the first question is that each *régulation* mode displays its own criteria for performance, far away from the reference to a Pareto optimum.

- Market-led capitalism, as observed in US and UK for instance, allows fast responses to short-run disturbances and displays a large capacity for radical innovations. But such a configuration is not without costs; few public investments and collective goods and large and even rising inequalities since the 1980s.
- By contrast, a large corporation-led capitalism, quite typical of Japan (Chapters 1 and 2), requires a large investment in the skills of blue- and white-collar workers and thus it limits social and economic inequalities. Nevertheless, such a system is quite slow in responding to unexpected shocks and experiences many difficulties in propitiating radical innovations, when facing for instance a shift in production paradigm or new financial instruments (Chapter 10).

Given the international trends, the prevailing technological paradigm, the initial domestic configuration, one or another brand of capitalism may deliver seemingly superior performances; at least for a given historical period. But this superiority can be eroded through time and it is precisely what happened to Japan. This theme is quite central to the present book.

The very success of a regime leads to its structural crisis

It is too easy to call for some irrationality, archaism, mismanagement of economic policy in order to interpret why the Japanese miracle turned into a quasi-nightmare and the fear that the financial crisis would unfold into a major deflation and cumulative depression. It is much more convincing to follow the basic hunch derived from regulationist researches. In many respects, the so-called exogenous perturbations reveal the underlying structural changes generated during the high-growth period. The success leads to a form of crisis and the related destabilisation calls for institutional redesign which may or may not take place given the structure of the political process and its interactions with the decaying *régulation* mode. The book provides many examples of such a paradoxical reversal of fortune.

- Thus the institutions that have proved to be quite efficient in *catching up* with the most efficient technologies and organisations at an early stage may become quite inefficient when the country has reached the technological frontier and needs to be competitive by other methods, linked for instance to radical innovations, more related to scientific advances (Chapter 10).
- *Learning by doing*, after importing from abroad technologies and knowledge, has been quite efficient for the rise of the Japanese manufacturing system from the 1950s until the 1980s. During this period, the banking and financial systems were only delivering the needed credit according to quite conventional and bureaucratised rules. But the emergence of a large surplus in the manufacturing sector calls for an opening of the Japanese financial system and the importation of some of the most sophisticated financial techniques. Unfortunately, the euphoria of the bubble years has prevented the bankers and financiers from learning how to manage these quite unstable financial tools (Chapters 6 and 10). Learning by doing should now concern finance, and not only manufacturing but the experience is not transferable.
- The *main bank system*, along with strong control by the Ministry of Finance, have been quite instrumental in channelling credit and investment into sunrise industries, by a full socialisation of the risk. What was previously a strength became, during the 1990s, a liability. A partial liberalisation of the financial system led to a huge amount of bad debts and revealed a quite shaky banking system. In reaction to this sudden discovery of the risk associated with finance in a liberalised context, the banks have engineered an unprecedented credit crunch, which propagates the crisis to the whole economic system (Chapters 6, 7 and

10). No irrationality or archaism but the very unfolding of the structural features of the Japanese companyist *régulation* mode.

- Similarly, the so-called *Japanese Employment System* (JES) used to combine job stability, on-the-job training, seniority wage and it was quite functional during the process of catching up and the high growth period. But when major uncertainties about the solution to be given to the financial crisis and the vagaries of the world economy trigger an unprecedented period of quasi-stagnation and large fluctuations, the JES is under severe strains. The absence of quick recovery makes difficult the restoration of profits and shows the limits of internal or organised labour mobility (Chapter 7). This is the other side of the coin of the companyist compromise, so admired during the 1980s. Again, the reversal is largely endogenous.
- Finally, the Japanese manufacturers had gained world market shares by *product differentiation* and a high quality, in the era of mass production of moderate differentiation and average or mediocre quality. But the competitive pressure exerted by Japan has been so intense that other manufacturers have struggled in order to get equivalent results, imitating the Japanese methods or innovating along new avenues. Finally, the excessive costs associated with product differentiation and fast renewal or design becomes apparent when, all around the world, industries have replied and adapted to the Japanese challenge. The Japanese system itself then enters into crisis (Chapter 10).

Institutions, growth regime, endometabolism and crisis: the content of the book in a nutshell

A feature common to all the chapters is to be noted: the same theoretical apparatus and empirical data are mobilised in order to analyse simultaneously the emergence, the maturation and ultimately the demise of the Japanese growth regime.

The first part diagnoses the core institutions governing the Japanese economy since the Second World War. Toshio Yamada stresses the role of what he calls a 'companyist' compromise according to which the commitment of workers is the counterpart of their long-term ties with the large company (Chapter 1). This compromise is complemented by managerial stability, itself linked to a rather patient financial system. There is strong evidence of institutional complementarity between the two major institutional forms: the WLN, the monetary and financial regime. Akinori Isogai, Akira Ebizuka and Hiroyasu Uemura put a strong emphasis upon the hierarchical organisation of the firms and its relations with subcontractors, that brings into the picture the very specific form of competition prevailing in the Japanese manufacturing system (Chapter 2). Furthermore, the authors point out the role of this structural complementarity in the design of an adequate incentive system, and how the hierarchical market-firm nexus is associated to a deep gender division of labour and role within the family and in the whole society. Hiroyuki Uni complements the previous institutional analysis by a macroeconomic analysis of the growth and accumulation regimes. Far from being balanced, productivity growth has been quite unequal between the export sector and the domestic sector. Furthermore since the 1960s, major changes have taken place in the sources of macroeconomic dynamism (Chapter 3). Thus, the Japanese economy is far from being static. Nowadays, a major challenge is about the search for a new WLN that would deliver a new and viable growth regime.

This is a transition towards the second part, devoted to the analysis of the major structural transformations that have taken place in Japanese institutional arrangements and architecture. Hironori Tohyama develops the idea that during the 'Golden Age' of rapid growth, wage coordination and forms of competition were complementary, but this property has been challenged by the structural changes taking place in the monetary regime after the mid-1980s. Afterwards manufacturing firms become more independent from the financing of the banking sector and simultaneously the banks have to compete harshly in order to enter into new segments of financial business. The author diagnoses a global regime change after 1986, when in spite of wage moderation, financial liberalisation triggers an unprecedented asset inflation (Chapter 4). Masanori Hanada and Yasuro Hirano investigate a usually rather neglected issue, i.e. the role of the industrial welfare provided by the large corporation in the viability of the companyist WLN. Therefore, the limited public welfare system and the labour management of firms appear quite complementary; for instance, the retirement pension system provided by each firm is significantly enhancing the incentive associated to the 'companyist' WLN (Chapter 5). Again the authors show that the progressive transformation of this complementarity, as well as the ageing of the Japanese population, call for the search for new solutions and compromises. Naoki Nabeshima analyses the progressive shift in the role of the financial system, from subordinate to the interests and dynamics of manufacturing to a leading role in the destabilisation of the corporate governance and more generally the *régulation* mode itself (Chapter 6). The old regulatory system becomes less and less efficient, but public authorities experience a lot of difficulties in designing a new one. Clearly the hierarchy of institutional forms has shifted in favour of finance since the mid-1980s and this move puts strong pressures upon the evolution of the past institutional architecture, a common conclusion with the previous chapter.

The third part then investigates the nature of the contemporary crisis and tries to diagnose some future restructuring of the institutions and *régulation* mode. Robert Boyer and Michel Juillard challenge the quite conventional idea that the rigidity of the Japanese employment system would be the main culprit and origin of the macroeconomic imbalances of the 1990s. Basically, the WLN displays a lot of flexibility but mechanisms are quite different from the pure external flexibility, typical of market-led economies. Furthermore, its destabilisation is more a consequence of the demise of the whole *régulation* mode than its origin (Chapter 7). In complement to Chapter 2, Hiroyasu Uemura tests the hypothesis of HMFN and provides an econometric analysis of the Japanese growth regime and its transformations. This regime appears to have drastically changed from the 1970s to the end of the 1990s; from profit-investment-led to export-led, with an underlying evolution of domestic demand towards a wage-led regime. Probably the large institutional and structural transformations of the 1990s are engineering a new regime shift (Chapter 8). Again, the empirical evidence strongly contradicts the vision of a quite static and archaic Japanese economy, even if the common conclusion of this third part is that contemporary Japan experiences a structural crisis of its *régulation* mode. Yasuo Inoue extends the analysis to the quite important issue of the role of Japan within East Asia and more generally, the international regime. He argues that the strategy of export-led growth has to be reconsidered and that the diversity of national trajectories within East Asia may help in designing adequate policies in order to overcome the crisis opened in 1997 (Chapter 9). Benjamin Coriat, Patrice Geoffron and Marianne Rubinstein provide a complete panorama of the evolution of Japanese structural competitiveness, with a strong emphasis upon the strengths and weaknesses of the national innovation system. An equivalent endogenous destabilisation is observed within the financial system, and these converging evidences show that contemporary Japan is facing a major crisis that calls for a significant redesign, specially in the area of science-led innovation and financial management (Chapter 10).

The conclusion draws some common themes and teachings to the whole book and argues that institutional redesign is probably still more important than the fine tuning of budgetary and monetary policies, that are so widely discussed by international organisations and scholars. Furthermore, Robert Boyer and Toshio Yamada show how *régulation* theory is extended and generalised by this long-term analysis of Japanese capitalism: more hierarchy than complementarity in institutional forms, confirmation of the diversity of *régulation* modes, strong specificity of the contemporary Japanese crisis with no historical equivalent, crucial role of the political process in the overcoming of structural crises. Nothing is more dangerous that the widely accepted belief that a pure economic determinism rules the way out of structural crises.

Part I

Institutional interpretations and theories

1 Japanese capitalism and the companyist compromise

Toshio Yamada

Introduction

During the long global recession of the 1970s and 1980s, Japan's high productivity growth rate enabled it to launch a huge export offensive and become an economic superpower. Yet after going from a period of high growth (1950s and 1960s) to a period of real economic power (1970s and 1980s), Japan underwent drastic change during the 'bubble recession' of the 1990s. The country now faces a prolonged period of very low growth. During the past quarter of a century, the Japanese economy has experienced a humiliating downturn from industrial winner to economic failure. At present, there is no end to theories reinterpreting the Japanese system, and it is no exaggeration to say that Japanese capitalism stands poised at one of the most important crossroads of the post-war era.

What has been the nature of Japanese capitalism of the 50 years of the post-war era, or the 25 years following the first oil shock, and how is it changing today? *Régulation* theory and its advocates seek to identify the Japanese system's mode of development, and then to explain the nature of the crises it is encountering and the transformations it is undergoing. To achieve this goal, it is necessary to identify the major institutional forms that regulate the mode of development, determine the nature of the overarching mode of *régulation* that they create, and, finally, identify the regimes of accumulation or growth that they generate. As a result it is possible to identify the nature of the crisis afflicting Japan, at the end of the 1990s, and determine the means by which it might be resolved.

Having posited this basic framework and methodology, the main purpose of this chapter is to present a hypothesis regarding the mode of *régulation* which has guided the post-war Japanese mode of development. The mode of *régulation* posited by *régulation* theory includes five major institutional forms; the wage-labour nexus, monetary and financial relations, interfirm relations, forms of the state, and the international regime. Here, the focus is the wage-labour nexus and monetary and financial relations (with some reference to interfirm relations). Labour and finance are key factors in the mode of *régulation*; furthermore, they lie at the heart of the Japanese economy and are thus crucial to achieving a full understanding of the present crisis.

In presenting this chapter's basic thesis, it would be possible to label as 'companyist *régulation*' or 'companyist compromise' the post-war Japanese mode of *régulation*. The two pillars of the companyist compromise are a labour-management compromise (or a labour-capital compromise) predicated on employment security and a financial compromise predicated on management security, and the complementarity between them. The impressive success and the subsequent failure of the Japanese economy from the 1970s to the 1990s can be explained in terms of the compatibility and the incompatibility of the two accords. The key to dissecting and examining the Japanese economy is companyism.

It is commonly stated that you cannot understand pre-war Japan without looking at farm villages, and you cannot understand post-war Japan without looking at companies. The poverty of the villages is often considered to have been an essential foundation for the imperialism and militarism of the pre-war era. Similarly, the prosperity of enterprises might be regarded as the secret of the rapid growth and rise to economic superpower status of post-war Japan, and of its peculiar company-centred social composition as well. So much so that the distinctive organisational groups of the 'enterprise' or the 'company' hold the key to understanding post-war and contemporary Japan. Whether its influence is judged through macroeconomy or through institutional forms, neither the market nor the state, civil society, unions, regions or even the family, exercise a more decisive influence than the enterprise. Companyism and the meanings embodied within this term must be considered at the outset (Baba 1997).

Labour-management compromise and job security

The companyist accord rests on two pillars, the labour-management compromise and the financial compromise, and builds on the isomorphic and complementary structural relationship which exists between the two. The two major resources of enterprises being human and financial, their most important functions are labour management and financial management. While the main aim of this chapter is to analyse the interactions and distinctive institutions of these two principal components, we will look first at labour and the formation of the post-war labour-management compromise, particularly at the regular male workers in large enterprises who typify the compromise (and who are often regarded as constituting the primary stratum of the labour market). In reality, of course, this stratum cannot be taken to represent the entire Japanese wage-labour nexus because it exists in a close and complementary relationship with the secondary labour market stratum. A discussion of this relationship is beyond the scope of this chapter (see Ebizuka, Uemura and Isogai 1997 and Chapter 2). Nevertheless, I will focus only on the regular, large-firm male workers, not merely because they constitute some 20 to 30 per cent of the total force, but because their accord with management has served as the dominant model of social values in post-war Japan.

What is the fundamental basis of the labour-management compromise? The usual answer to this question is 'jobs'. A large body of research has emphasised this point. For example, Nitta (1995) has stated, 'One of the most important issues of the post-war labour movement has been preventing dismissals'. Accordingly: 'Since dismissals were bad, an unspoken agreement that they should be avoided [was established] between labour and management'. As a result, the agreement became a sort of social principle. The protection and stabilisation of employment became the core principle of post-war industrial relations in Japan. This was in strong contrast to the United States, where, as Aoki observes, 'the American union is more concerned with wage issues than job security issues' (1988: 92). The Fordism-oriented American industrial relations compromise has emphasised wages rather than security. To further extend the point, the emphasis on wages means that it might indeed be categorised as a compromise:

**The acceptance of Taylorism ↔ The provision of productivity-
indexed wages**

In contrast, the major point of contention in Japan was the establishment of a compromise emphasising jobs and job security. In brief, managers extended strong employment guarantees to workers, while workers acceded to the 'unlimited duties' demanded by management (See Table 1.1).

According to Iwata (1977), unlimited duty means: 'It is strongly expected that the members of a given organisation will exercise responsibilities and duties whose limits are not specified, and whose natures are difficult to foresee.' The conditions and the hours of work to be performed by the members are not clearly specified in their contracts with the organisation.

Table 1.1 Comparison of the US and Japanese labour-management compromises

		Labour	*↔ Management*
US (Fordism)	Wages	Acceptance of Taylorism	Provision of wages indexed to productivity
	Employment	Limits on the nature and duration of duties	Flexible dismissal
Japan (Companyism)	Employment	Acceptance of unlimited duties	Provision of employment security
		Acceptance of	*↔ Gain of*
American workers		Subordination to management	Job control (= limited duties)
Japanese workers		Subordination to management	'Job-loss control' (= employment security)

Thus both the nature and degree of their everyday duties, and of their future tasks as well, are highly amorphous and subject to constant change. Major enterprises guarantee the jobs of their regular male workers in return for the acceptance of these unlimited duties. Since some dismissals and so-called involuntary early retirements do occur, it would be more precise to state that there is no absolute guarantee of job security, but rather an unspoken commitment by management to exert itself to avoid dismissals. Nevertheless, the following discussion uses the term 'job security' as a convenient characterisation of Japanese practice. As described above, we may characterise Japan's wage-labour nexus in the following formula schema:

The acceptance of unlimited duties ↔ The provision of job security

In the American Fordist system, labour demands wages indexed to productivity as compensation for its acceptance of Taylorism whereas workers in Japan gain job security to compensate for their concession to management in accepting unlimited duties. Moreover, this is not simply job security, but the continuous protection of employment carried out within the context of a unified enterprise structure. This means that it is a companyist form of job security. Thus the distinctive feature of the Japanese compromise is that it is fundamentally based on employment rather than wages.

If the main emphasis in the labour-management compromise is placed on employment, then we can see that it is not, of course, an element in the American Fordist system. Managers in the US are guaranteed the freedom to dismiss workers. Of course, contemporary economic systems have institutionalised legal protections for workers, so that even American managers no longer enjoy unlimited power to fire. Instead certain (seniority-based) rules have been enacted. In general, however, compared to Japan, there is a social consensus supporting the use of dismissals as an employment adjustment measure. It is within the limitations of this consensus that managers possess the 'freedom' to fire.

American workers commit themselves to their firms only partially or functionally; in short, they ensure that there are 'limited duties' (limits on the nature and duration of duties). In order to enforce these limits, unions exercise checks on management, or job control. Thus, if the American compromise is primarily about the nature of employment, then the trade-off of the acceptance of Taylorism for guarantees on the freedom to fire (the reverse side of the Fordist wage-centred compromise), may be turned into a set with the trade-off of guarantees of limited duty for guarantees for the freedom to fire. In employment terms, Japan's job security guarantee can be seen as a complete inversion of the American compromise, because it involves establishing a trade-off of the acceptance of unlimited duties against the provision of job security. The central foundation of the post-war Japanese labour-management compromise is this 'employment compromise'.[1]

Towards the formation of the employment compromise

Why does the Japanese labour-management compromise centre on employment rather than wages? Questions about how Japanese workers perceive industrial relations and how they try to resolve problems are easier to answer if we compare them with workers in the West.[2] The West is diverse, however, and this chapter focuses primarily on American Fordism. Europe is considered through this 'stylised fact' only to the extent that its institutions are congruent with those of the US.

The basic problem is that while contemporary society extols the freedom and equality of people in civil society on the one hand, it seeks on the other to establish the domination of authority in capitalist society. Inside an enterprise, this means that while workers demand equality in relations with management, in reality they must accept a subordinate position. In this regard the problem faced by workers in either Japan or the West is essentially the same. The difference is in the attempted means of resolving the problem. Here there is a conspicuous contrast.

In the West, workers acknowledged and accepted their subordinate status, then dealt with it by compartmentalising and limiting the internal tasks of the enterprise into functional roles. Workers limited the maximum scope of their own duties within enterprises, contractualised them, and then submitted only to orders pertaining to duties lying within the scope of the contracts. They seek to confirm themselves as nothing other than the subjects of contracts. In this manner, on the basis of concepts of freedom, equality, and possession, workers fully ensure their equal status with those (the managers) who purchase labour power as commodities of those (the workers) who are selling it. Labour power is organised as a commodity product and its purchasing conditions are established through contracts with management. After the purchase is completed workers prevent the arbitrary usage of this labour power through job control unionism. The resolution to the problem of internal enterprise submission is achieved through the equality of the market, and by the use of union restrictions. Differently stated, workers must accept a subordinate status, but by using contractual relationships or by 'clarifying' (limiting) contractual contents, submission is compensated, and limits are placed on the domination of capital.

Japanese workers also acknowledge their inferior status, but they conceive it on an individual-by-individual basis in limited terms as something that is temporary and transitory. Social and market relations are confirmed outside of the enterprise, so submission is not something spatially limited to the internal firm; rather in Japan's case it is a temporary process in one's individual history (or career path). The problem of submission is resolved, so to speak, through time.

There are essential conditions for the acceptance of this temporary submission. One's status as a worker is fully acknowledged (Saguchi 1991); further, both labour force and management maintain the consciousness that all workers in a single enterprise are 'producers' as well as 'workers', and are therefore homogeneous and equal. Japanese workers are not divided throughout enterprises but united on the basis of human character. They have not dealt with the reality of submission (authority relations) by checking them from the outside, but have attenuated them (where there are differences in rankings) by using parent-child, family, and peer relations to foster the perception of homogeneity. The abolition of status differentials between blue- and white-collar workers and the formation of enterprise unions after the war strengthened this perception. Whereas contractual relations in the West are premised on differences among workers and managers, Japanese workers have sought 'trust' relations based upon the homogeneity of all enterprise members.

But workers do not stop at obtaining equality in this fashion. The belief that subordinate status is temporary naturally gives rise to an eruption of energy from the worker that should in the future elevate him to a higher status: the competition for promotion. Ultimately, this is the pursuit of an equality of a type which enables workers to achieve (or get close to) managerial status. Stated the other way around, there is not the sort of class-based difference between workers and managers seen in the West; rather, we can conceive that in Japan there is a difference of viewpoints among the workers themselves (Hanada 1997). Labour-management relations can be regarded, not as a discontinuation of class, but as a continuous stairway on which individual status is indicated by differences across time. In comparison with the Western practices of ensuring equality through spatial limits to subordination (in workplaces) and market (class) restrictions, equality is promoted through time-based (subjective) limits to subordination and (individual) efforts to escape subordination.

Let us next consider the issue of employment. The major premise of the Japanese approach to managing subordination and equality is that workers will affiliate continuously with a single company, building long-term relations with it. Needless to say, this long-term affiliation to a firm constitutes job security itself. Only if employment is continued in the same enterprise does the hope of escaping a present status of subordination present itself. Of course, even if a person pursues his (or, occasionally, her) career in just one enterprise, for example, in reality the number that can successfully escape subordination through promotion is small. However, in a Japanese firm, all employees can, at least at the beginnings of their careers, see the superficial and exoteric openings of the possibilities of promotions. Whether lip service or illusion, it is the continuation of employment that is of greatest importance to workers.

The path to equality for Western workers lies in compartmentalising and limiting the reality of being employed. In contrast, the path chosen by Japanese workers is to maintain the maximum status of being employed; what they have striven to limit is the reality of losing one's job. The Japanese pursue equality within employment. This is the dominating vision of employment for Japanese workers. Differently stated, Western workers have bargained within the framework

Accepting subordination ↔ Job control

while Japanese workers have, figuratively speaking, bargained within the framework of

Accepting subordination ↔ Job-loss control

In other words, Japanese do not seek to restrict the contents of duties – of jobs – but rather to restrict the possibilities of job loss. In contrast to Western workers, who have refused the extension of labour contents beyond contracts but have in a sense accepted the risk of job loss, Japanese workers have refused job loss as a violation of their settlement with management, but have accepted the extension of labour content and changes within it.[3]

Needless to say, the employment transaction is not expressly stipulated in writing but exists in the form of unspoken agreements between labour and management. As a result, management is sometimes able to assert its power advantage, but even in these cases managers in large enterprises still see fit to establish the employment compromise, even if only in form. Such practices indicate that the employment compromise embedded in the structure of Japanese enterprises constitutes the fundamental compromise in Japan. It is because of this fundamental compromise that Japanese workers hurl themselves into meritocratic competition within firms, while on the outside they apply themselves with equal fervour to winning the battle for market shares for the firms to which they affiliate. The labour-management compromise in Japan is a structure of 'employment compromise-meritocratic compromise-enterprise growth compromise' centred within firms.

Financial compromise and management security

The above sections have examined companyist *régulation* through a focus on labour. As stated at the beginning of the chapter, human and financial resources are a company's most important assets, and this section will examine companyist *régulation* in terms of finance. Financial relations are not limited to the provision and procurement of capital, but include corporate governance and the control of enterprises. In short, finance and governance are different aspects of the same structure.

Unlike the US, the prevalent form of capital procurement in Japan has been indirect finance, notably bank loans. Although the importance of banks in Japan has declined, indirect finance continues to play a much more important role than in the US. Whereas the American and British forms of governance rely heavily on stock markets and markets for the control of companies, the bank loan-centred structure of finance in Japan has produced the 'contingent governance' of monitoring by main banks (Aoki 1994c). Further, the enterprise groups built around main banks have, through their shareholders, helped to support Japanese-style corporate governance. Corporate governance of major firms is implemented through both enterprise-bank relations and interfirm relations,[4] and this system corresponds to a main-bank-based corporate financial structure. This finance/governance structure can be regarded as the result of the particular transactions and compromises accompanying Japan's enterprise-bank relations and of mutual relations between firms within enterprise groups.

One aspect of enterprise-bank relations is that companies generally receive more financing from their main banks than is actually needed and therefore pay excess interest costs. This means that they extend special treatment to the banks in the conduct of financial transactions. In return, main banks not only provide information to company clients, but also extend emergency assistance to troubled firms. By bearing the burden of high interest costs, companies receive valuable information and financing from main banks, as well as special assistance in case of distress. In short, Japanese firms overpay interest to main banks, but what they demand – and receive – in the meantime is 'management security' in the form of 'continuous enterprise security' from the banks.[5] This give-and-take financial relationship can be termed the financial compromise. We can formulate this compromise between companies and banks as:

Preferential treatment for banks ↔ Security for company managers

High interest payments and other forms of preferential treatment extended to main banks can be regarded as premiums paid by companies to protect themselves from management risks. In general, it is well known that the capital procurement system performs simultaneously as a corporate governance system, but the most distinctive feature of the post-war Japanese financial structure is that it has also served as an insurance system to protect the long-term survival of companies. The enterprise-bank relationship of post-war Japan underlay not only finance and governance relations, but insurance relations as well.

This insurance relationship was not based upon company-bank relationships alone. Interfirm relations in the form of cross-shareholdings (within enterprise groups) performed management, security and insurance functions. Cross-shareholdings developed as a means of preventing hostile take-overs of companies and promoting stable shareholding, so we can conjecture that the close company relations which result serve as a means of strengthening management security. In reality, companies that are members of enterprise groups earn lower profit rates than those that are not, so it is proven that stability is more important to them (Nakatani 1984). Thus the formation of enterprise groups has the effect of serving as a type of insurance as well as risk sharing. We can depict the individual enterprise-enterprise group compromise in the following formula:

Preferential treatment for
members of enterprise groups ↔ Security for firm managers

Through this mutual company relationship as well as the company-bank relationship, or rather the main bank-centred enterprise group, post-war Japan's capital procurement/corporate governance system has simultaneously played the role of management security system. The unique nature of the Japanese financial system becomes more apparent if compared to the American financial system. In the United States, there is a division of labour among distinct institutions which exercise monitoring and rule-making functions before, during, and after investments. These institutions are investment banks and venture capital (before investments), credit rating agencies and the capital market (during the course of the investment), and hostile take-overs (afterwards). These institutions are, of course, engaged solely in financial or investment transactions, or in related monitoring, and not in taking charge of management security or risk insurance for companies.

As described above, the fact that the Japanese financial/corporate governance structure also provides a structure for ensuring the long-term survival of companies (management security) has three important implications. First, this financial compromise as a form of management insurance has a complementary relationship with the labour-management compromise underlying job security. Naturally, a crucial prerequisite for the realisation of the job security compromise is that there should be continuity – stable continuity – of management. It is through interfirm group relations and the company-main bank financial compromise that the guarantee of corporate continuity could be realised.[6] Stable shareholdings serve as the 'collateral' for stable employment, so the financial compromise underpins the employment compromise.

Second, the distinctive feature of the post-war Japanese system has been the strong, long-term relationships between labour and management, among companies, and between companies and their banks. This feature stands out against American practice. The strong, long-term relations of the principals can be ascertained from the institutionalisation of long-term employment in industrial relations, from *keiretsu* transactions and cross-shareholdings in enterprise groups, and from the long-term capital procurement, corporate governance, and management security supported by the MBS. In this sense, there is a homologous relationship between the sectors. It is because the three forms interact so closely that the Japanese system has functioned so well. Relations of trust and cooperation are formed among principals in the

Japanese system through their long-term relations, and these relations serve at the same time as insurance and security networks, enabling the economy as a whole to achieve high efficiency. Of course, a virtuous cycle does not always materialise, nor can all causation be purely positive. The problem with close relations is that they can generate exclusivity as well as distrust and disinterest toward outsiders, and they all too often give rise to non-transparent and unfair practices.

Third, the Japanese system is based on the foundations of the homologous and complementary relationships between labour and finance. The heart of the system is ultimately the security accorded to both employees and managers, and thus the priority given to the perpetuation and growth of the firm. Once again, we may call these compromises, which have guided post-war Japanese capitalism, 'the companyist compromise' and 'companyist *régulation*'. Companyist *régulation* derives its distinctiveness from the strong, long-term nature of the employment and financial (and transactional) relationships. Whereas the American model is a 'spot and contract model' stressing the pursuit of efficiency through short-term, fluid, and open relations, companyist *régulation* is a 'long-term trust model' emphasising the pursuit of efficiency through long-term, fixed, and closed relations.

Post-war Japanese capitalism and the 1990s crisis

How has companyist *régulation*, in the configuration outlined above, intervened in and piloted the post-war Japanese growth structure? If we do not clarify this point, neither the mode of *régulation* nor the growth regime can be fully explained. Did some feature of companyist *régulation* lead contemporary Japan into a growth system, just as the 'acceptance of Taylorism for productivity-indexed wages' in the post-war American labour-management compromise stimulated mass production and mass consumption, creating a Fordist mode of *régulation*? This is a crucial question, that Japanese '*régulationists*' have been tackling in their research. Figure 1.1 shows one view of the connection between the growth system and *régulation* mode in post-war Japan.

There is nearly full accord among researchers that there was a shift in the growth regime from profit- (investment-) led during the high growth era to export-led in the after-oil shock era (e.g., Uemura 1992, Chapter 8). Tohyama (1990) has described the profit-led growth pattern of the high-growth era as a distinctive macroeconomic cycle of 'productivity → profits → investment' while Uni (1998) characterises the export-led pattern of the after-oil shock era as 'productivity → exports → investment'. At the same time, Uni notes the 'export → production → employment' cycle. What was viewed as a typical export-led growth pattern in the early 1980s resulted in some of the productivity gains being lost to foreign competitors, but increasing exports still brought rises in productivity and in employment, and thereby proved effective in holding unemployment to low levels.

Further, as suggested by a large body of research, and in contrast to a typical Fordist case, post-war Japan's real wage formation does not seem to have been indexed to productivity. This was true of both the high growth era and the after-oil shock era. Thus, the high growth era, through the mechanism of a competitive wage formation of the 'production → employment' type, enacted an 'employment → real wage → individual consumption → production (= demand)' cycle (Boyer 1990b), but this demand regime declined from the 1970s.

There has been a productivity regime in operation throughout nearly the whole of the post-war era, featuring effects of investment ('investment → productivity'), Kaldorian effects on the economy of scale ('production (= demand) → productivity'), and innovation effects. Moreover, the productivity effect of employment security, or 'employment → productivity', was a unique Japanese characteristic (Isogai and Uemura 1996). Nevertheless, it has been repeatedly pointed out by Hirano (1996) that Japan cannot be analysed through the wage variable alone, and that employment must also be examined.

While considering the above points, the point to be reiterated here is that a circuit existed in which management security served as collateral for employment security, and employment security in turn was linked to a productivity-raising effect. Thus the causal chain: 'management security → employment security → productivity'. Figure 1.1 shows only the 'employment → productivity' link, but it should be seen that this distinctive circuit also existed in post-war Japan's growth system. Not only existed, but instilled several virtuous features into the Japanese economy until the 1980s.

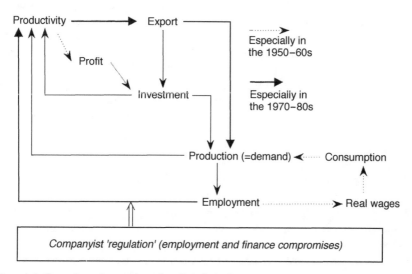

Figure 1.1 Growth regime and mode of *régulation* in post-war Japan with special reference to large firms.

However, in discussing the 'employment → productivity' circuit, a number of qualifications must be made. First, the circuit applied to core workers (regular male workers in large companies). Second, there is a general principle that productivity rises result in reductions in employment ('productivity → (−) → employment'). Third, employment security does not lead directly to higher productivity, rather the implicit employment security contract acts as an effective incentive mechanism in promoting practices such as meritocratic competition and skill formation that themselves bolster productivity. Fourth, while the 'employment → productivity' circuit was functioning during the high growth era, its importance was dramatically heightened following the oil shock.

The institutions of companyist *régulation* linked employment and productivity. All of the large firm-based institutions were constructed around fixed, long-term relationships. These institutions included the subcontracting system, *keiretsu* transactions, cross-shareholding, enterprise groups (a form of competition, to use the *régulationist* concepts), indirect financial institutions, MBS (monetary and financial relations), the convoy system of administration (a form of the state), and, finally, so-called long-term employment, seniority-based wages, enterprise unions, and meritocracy (the wage-labour nexus). It was through these relationships that collateralised management security and job security ultimately stimulated productivity rises. Thus the companyist *régulation* institutions implanted a superb productivity regime.[7]

As described above, companyist *régulation* and the investment-and-export-led growth regime clearly led Japanese capitalism from the high growth era through the stable growth era that followed the oil shock. Consequently, Japan ascended to the status of an economic superpower in the 1980s, and at the end of that decade through the beginning of the 1990s enjoyed a nearly unparalleled economic boom. As we know in hindsight, of course, the boom was caused by the distortions of the 'Bubble Economy'. As a result of the collapse of the bubble and subsequent policy-making failures, Japanese capitalism suffered severe financial instability and entered a long, and still continuing, recession or even depression. The 1990s may well be considered a period of crisis for Japanese capitalism, but what does the crisis mean for companyist *régulation*? Let me conclude by commenting on this point.

Conclusion

What is clear about the 1990s crisis is that the financial component of the previous mode of *régulation* has collapsed into paralysis (Nabeshima 1997). The share of bank loans in corporate capital procurement has declined substantially, as has the influence of main banks in corporate governance. On the other hand, however, the share of cross-shareholding remains high because the immaturity of the capital market means that it is not ready to exercise monitoring functions in place of main banks. Moreover, the banks themselves, threatened by the intensifying competition brought by financial liberalisation and globalisation, pursued risky investments, an unfortunate course which the convoy system of financial administration could no longer prevent. In the context of a new age, companies, banks, and the established system of corporate governance were all paralysed. From the end of the 1980s, corporate governance became a virtual empty shell, and the financial system consequently became unable to perform its 'insurance' functions in support of corporate management or enterprise continuity. The company-bank relationship collapsed. The term 'governance depression' applied by the Economic Planning Agency (1998) to the 1990s recession was well chosen. The companyist financial system presently finds itself in a deep crisis.

But what about labour? There is little chance that the labour-management compromise can survive in its previous form now that the financial compromise underpinning management security is in jeopardy, but it would also be premature to conclude that long-term employment and seniority-based wages are quickly collapsing. To be sure, there is increasing diversification and fluidity of employment (Miyamoto 1998), but while the sphere of long-term employment is contracting, regular male employees in large firms continue to be the core of the labour-management compromise. Whereas the financial compromise is vulnerable to globalisation, the labour-management compromise displays a much stronger path dependency. Thus, at present, its restructuring is proceeding at a positively leisurely pace.

What, then, is the condition of companyist *régulation* at present? Returning to the precepts of *régulation* theory, when even one of the core institutions becomes inappropriate, the established adjustment mechanisms prove unable to resolve an economic crisis, inevitably leading to a crisis of the system of *régulation*.[8] In the present domestic and international environment, and especially during the attempts to cope with the 'Bubble Economy' phenomenon, companyism actually strengthened the bubble, and certainly did nothing to prevent its development. After the bubble burst, moreover, companyism aggravated the recession and failed to reverse it. In short, companyism has lost its capacity to promote systemic adjustment. Companyism defined a Japanese mode of *régulation* which guided the nation through a cycle of 'companyism → exports → strong yen → companyism . . .' on a trajectory toward becoming an economic superpower; but in the end it has entered a vicious cycle of 'companyism → the bubble and its collapse → the collapse of the financial system → crisis of companyist *régulation*.

2 The hierarchical market-firm nexus as the Japanese mode of *régulation*

Akinori Isogai, Akira Ebizuka and Hiroyasu Uemura

Introduction

The institutional analysis of the Japanese economy has recently been the focus of many researchers who are engaged in the study of the economics of institutions. Japanese *régulationists* have made the most notable contribution to such analysis, emphasising that the mode of *régulation* of the post-war Japanese economy is that of 'Company-ism'. The core argument of the 'Companyism' hypothesis is that large firms are the centre of the mode of *régulation* and have strongly promoted social integration in Japanese society. So far, however, only the organisation of large firms has been discussed using this hypothesis.

In order to develop the 'Companyism' hypothesis in the larger framework of the Japanese socio-economic system, including the structures of the labour market and inter-firm relations, we propose the hypothesis of the 'hierarchical market-firm nexus' (HMFN) (Uemura, Isogai and Ebizuka 1996) which may be summarised as follows. First, it is necessary to understand the specific 'mode of *régulation*' of the Japanese economy in the post-war period as generated by the coordinated structural effects of an ensemble of various institutions, aiming as a whole to establish 'structural compatibility' in the socio-economic system. Second, the ensemble of institutions is hierarchically structured through firm organisation, the labour market and inter-firm relations. Therefore, we need a refined understanding of 'dualism' which can explain recent economic structures in Japan. Third, we argue that the HMFN as the mode of *régulation* of the Japanese economy has produced certain specific 'structural effects' in the Japanese socio-economic system, and has determined the dynamics of the economy since the 1970s.

This chapter presents a new approach to the institutional analysis of the post-war Japanese economy, taking into account recent developments in *régulation* and other theories. Then it develops the argument so as to explain recent structural shifts in the Japanese economy in the long-lasting recession of the 1990s.

The HMFN from the perspective of institutional analysis

'Régulation' approach and the institutional analysis of socio-economic systems

The concept of 'mode of *régulation*' is conducive to our discussion of the institutional arrangements of the Japanese economy. How can capitalist society perpetually reproduce itself, despite its many contradictions, conflicts, antagonisms, and violence? This is the fundamental *problématique* of the *régulation* theory. Capitalist society reproduces itself not only through the market mechanism but also various institutions which are 'embedded' in the socio-economic system. The 'mode of *régulation*' refers to a set of rules for the social game that are produced by the five institutional forms. Therefore, an important point for analysing the 'mode of *régulation*' is to investigate how major institutions articulate with one another and to make clear what structural effects this articulation produces socially and economically. In other words, an institution acquires its proper significance only in the context of the social arrangement of institutions in the socio-economic system.

When the ensemble of institutions causes the socio-economic system to reproduce itself continuously while maintaining structural stability, those institutions are regarded as 'structurally compatible' with one another (Hollingsworth and Boyer 1997). The way institutions work with each other may not only be complementary but also may promote a cumulative process of evolution and structural change through social conflicts. Therefore, in 'the institutional analysis of socio-economic systems', the mode of the articulation of institutions and coordinating mechanisms they produce must be investigated in a particular context in the socio-economic system as well as a particular stage of historical development.

'Wage-labour nexus' and 'market-firm nexus'

Régulation theory usually focuses upon the 'wage-labour nexus' ('*rapport salarial*') among other institutional forms. The wage-labour nexus is defined as 'the ensemble of conditions governing the use and reproduction of the work force' (Boyer 1981). Therefore, macro- as well as micro-economic factors should be considered in as far as they govern the use and reproduction of the work force; unfortunately, the analyses of the Japanese economy have focused primarily on the organisation of large firms. A firm organisation can be sustained only if it is supported by a network of institutions with which it is compatible. Therefore, the analysis of firm organisations must be complemented by the analysis of a set of articulated institutional forms. This is the only way to provide a bridge connecting the microeconomic analysis of institutions and individual behaviours with the macro-level analysis of economic dynamics. This circular causation is labelled the 'micro-macro loop' in the socio-economic system.

Contemporary Japanese economic structures will be examined in terms of (a) firm organisation, (b) the labour market, and (c) inter-firm relations. This framework of analysis is based on our view that the labour market is one important component of the wage-labour nexus, but that particular arrangements in the labour market are reproduced together with institutional arrangements based on firms' strategies and the firms' socio-economic context. For example, hierarchical segmentation in the labour market results in the creation of hierarchical inter-firm relations corresponding to the kind of workers a firm employs, and in turn, inter-firm relations reinforce segmentation in the labour market.

When these three components are structurally compatible, a particular wage-labour nexus also seems to be stable. We call this framework of analysis the 'market-firm nexus' (MFN). This helps to analyse the relationship between micro-economic level of firm organisation and macro-economic dynamics. Analytically, the important point is how the three components become structurally compatible and what kind of 'structural effect' they produce through a set of coordinating mechanisms.

The hypothesis of the HMFN

The post-war Japanese economy may be analysed from the viewpoint of the MFN. However, even if the complementary relationships between firm organisation, the labour market and inter-firm relations are recognised, it is impossible concretely to specify institutional components without investigating institutional arrangements in a relevant country. The capital-labour relationship in the post-war Japanese economy is often characterised as 'micro-corporatism'. This usually means a regime in which there is a capital-labour accord at the firm level. The core ingredient in the capital-labour accord is said to be the exchange of job security for the active commitment of workers to their company. However, the following conditions are necessary for job security to produce efficiency rather than inefficiency, idleness, and inflexibility in the framework of the MFN.

Firm organisation

There must be incentive mechanisms to stimulate the work effort of employees, so that the firm remains productive, such as the promotion system, the seniority wage system, the retirement-pay system, and company-based welfare in 'the competence-based grade system' all of which are deeply embedded in Japanese firms. To provide a sufficient number of employee positions, firms engage in fierce competition to gain larger market shares. In these circumstances, firms are quite likely to reduce the number of core workers eligible for lifetime employment so as to lower overhead costs, and also to promote multi-skilling in order to enhance the productivity of workers, as they cannot be easily laid off.

Labour market

A penalty for leaving a company prematurely is needed to encourage the integration of workers into companies with lifetime employment. In other words, the potential threat of being fired must be reinforced by a financial penalty. In the Japanese economy, this is brought about by the costs of job change and downward mobility in a hierarchically segmented labour market with pronounced differentials in the conditions of employment.

As for wages formation, such factors as education and experience are controlled for, there still exist definite wage differentials closely related to firm size in the Japanese labour market. In addition, company-based welfare is very different in large firms and small and medium-size firms. Therefore, the differential in terms of lifetime incomes is quite large, and this makes for an increased financial penalty for a mid-career job change and downward mobility in the segmented labour market. For instance, a male white-collar employee in the manufacturing sector changing firms at the age of 40 loses around 10 per cent of his lifetime income in 1996, but around 13 per cent in 1985 (Ministry of Labour 1998a: 228).

In this way, seniority wages in combination with firm size differentials and the downwardly-mobile, hierarchically-segmented labour market make it enormously expensive to change jobs in mid-career. As is well known, the difference between workers' current incomes and a weighted average of income prospects at the time of separation is called 'job loss costs' in the Social Structures of Accumulation (SSA) Theory in the United States (Bowles 1985; Bowles and Boyer 1990). These theorists argue that the larger the costs of job loss, the greater the work effort. In this argument, they assume that job loss costs are strongly influenced by conditions in the external labour market. In the case of the Japanese economy, however, the risk of unemployment is quite low, and workers are unlikely to actually be laid off. Therefore, this framework of analysis must be modified in order to be able to explain the hierarchically structured socio-economic system in Japan. In this chapter, the costs of mid-career job change in terms of lifetime incomes are labelled 'institutionalised job-loss costs'. This phenomenon is highly institutionalised, but, in a sense, it seems to be a 'functional equivalent' of job-loss costs in the competitive labour market.

Inter-firm relations

Three conditions must be satisfied to maintain lifetime employment in a capitalist market economy, in which uncertainty dominates and unexpected fluctuations occur constantly. First, wages must be adjusted flexibly to follow economic fluctuations. Second, a buffer must exist to protect the employment of core workers during economic fluctuations. Third, there must be no drastic change to destroy the structures which function as a core and as a buffer. What attracts attention in Japanese inter-firm relations is the prevalence of subcontractor systems.

The subcontractor systems are hierarchically structured according to the scale of capital and the number of employees, and they act as buffers in the following ways. First, there is pressure to reduce the number of employees with lifetime employment in large firms, causing further pressure to externalise labour-intensive production processes and to purchase products externally from small and medium-size firms. These factors promote the formation of the subcontracting system. In this regard, the subcontractor system acts as a buffer for the core structures of a large firm. In addition, the smaller the firm size, the higher the proportion of part-time workers: 17.6 per cent for a firm with fewer than 30 employees, 9.9 per cent for firms with over 1,000 employees (Ministry of Labour 1996: 39–41). Second, there is asymmetry between a parent company and its subcontractors in their terms of trade; the pressure of competition among a large number of subcontractors worsens their terms of trade, and makes the productivity of a parent firm, measured by value-added, increase substantially by lowering its costs. As a result, it contributes to the increase in profits of the parent company. Furthermore, competition among subcontractors and the network of inter-firm relations also improve the quality of their products. Third, in addition, the subcontractor system has, interestingly, been functioning as a social buffer, in other words, an apparatus for stabilising society. In fact, even in the period of recession, small and medium-size firms absorb workers, and this minimises the unemployment rate in the Japanese economy (Muramatsu 1995, and below).

Thus, it is possible to conclude that the 'micro-corporatism' organised on the basis of job security in large firms is quite limited in scope in the national economy as a whole, and it is necessarily complemented by a specific MFN consisting of firm organisation built on 'the competence-based grade system', the downwardly-mobile hierarchically-segmented labour market, and hierarchical inter-firm relations containing the different types of flexibility. This HMFN seen in the post-war Japanese socio-economic system is illustrated in Figure 2.1.

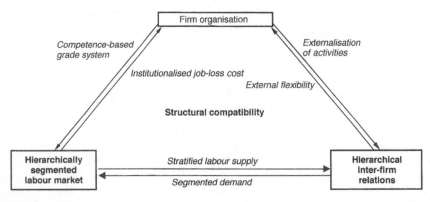

Figure 2.1 The hierarchical market-firm nexus hypothesis.

The HMFN as a set of complex coordinating nechanisms

This section analyses the functional role of the HMFN as a set of complex coordinating mechanisms in the Japanese economy, focusing attention on the three dynamic structural effects: the incentive mechanism, the flexibility of wages and employment, and the productivity-enhancing effect.

Trends and cyclical fluctuations of differential structures

The HMFN consists of firm organisation, the hierarchically segmented labour market and hierarchical inter-firm relations, and it plays a role as a dynamic coordinating mechanism in the process of capital accumulation. The characteristic dynamics of the hierarchical structures are determined by firm-size profitability differentials, firm-size wage differentials and male-female wage differentials. These hierarchical differentials in the Japanese economy fluctuate cyclically in a very dynamic way (Figure 2.2).

First, firm-size differentials in terms of value-added productivity and average wages decreased dramatically as a trend until the late 1960s, and this corresponded to 'the weakening of dualism' in the high-growth period. Following the full establishment of the HMFN in the 1970s, however, firm-size wage differentials have been fairly stable, contracting during the boom in the late 1980s and expanding again in the recession in the 1990s. As for capital-labour ratio, differentials in terms of the capital-labour ratio between large firms and small and medium-size firms have decreased steadily. However, value-added productivity differentials have not decreased at all. This is because small and medium-size firms cannot utilise high-tech facilities

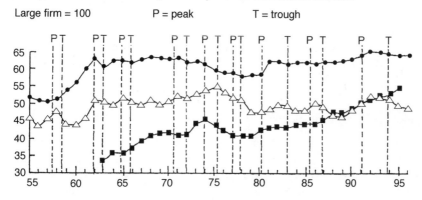

Figure 2.2 Fluctuations and trends of differential structures (manufacturing).
Source: Small and Medium-size Firm Agency, *The White Paper on Small and Medium-size Firms*, 1998.

efficiently, and because parent companies purchase parts from their sub-contractors at low prices.

Second, cyclical fluctuations in the firm-size differentials: differentials in value-added productivity reveal an interesting pattern, increasing in expansions and decreasing in contractions. This seems to be caused by the fact that the level of capacity utilisation and the level of innovative activities rises much more in large firms than in small and medium-size firms during expansions. In Japan, a large firm typically 'hoards' labour due to the job security of regular workers and fears of shortages of skilled workers. Therefore, labour productivity increases sharply in expansions and exhibits pro-cyclical fluctuations, especially in large firms. In contrast, firm-size wage differentials increase during contractions and decrease during expansions. This phenomenon has been seen since the period of high economic growth (Odaka 1984).

On closer examination, the effect of economic fluctuations on firm-size wage differentials is more complicated, when medium-size firms (100–999 employees) and small firms (10–99 employees) are compared with large firms (over 1,000 employees). The wage differentials of male workers increased gradually until the middle of the 1980s, and then decreased in the late 1980s. Faced with a long recession and a rising unemployment rate after the mid-1990s, Japan experienced once again an increase in the firm-size wage differentials of male workers. Therefore, the firm-size wage differentials of male workers have been fluctuating cyclically, responding to conditions in the labour market. However, this can only be seen in the differentials of male workers between large and small firms which are in fact quite sensitive to the unemployment rate. This can be explained by the fact that male workers' wages in large firms are not very sensitive to demand conditions in the spot labour market, while those in small firms are (see Table 2.1 *infra*). As for the wage differentials of female workers, they are not sensitive to the unemployment rate at all, and they have gradually decreased. This seems to be caused by the fact that the category of 'female worker' involves an increasing number of part-time workers who are the object of the numerical flexibility of employment even in large firms. In fact, the percentage of part-time workers has increased in the 1990s.

The HMFN as an incentive mechanism

How does the Japanese company persuade its employees to behave in harmony with the goals of the company? The post-war Japanese economy uses a very specific incentive mechanism based on the HMFN. The idea of 'involvement by the incentive system' (*implication incitée**) (Coriat 1991) helps to extend and develop this model of Japanese firm organisation.

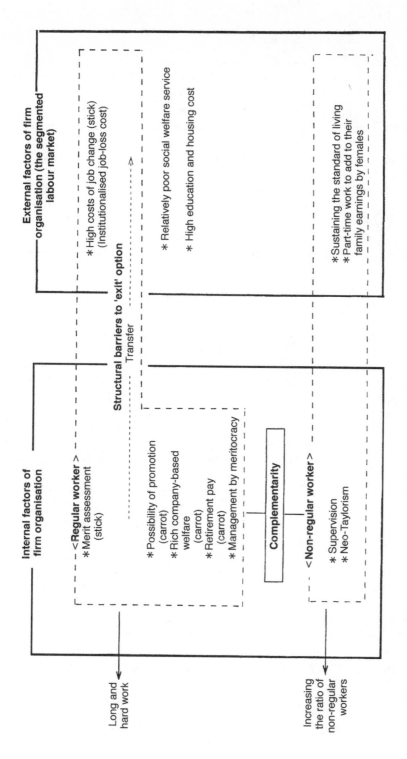

Figure 2.3 How incentive mechanism works in the hierarchical market–firm nexus.

Structures of the incentive mechanism

The active commitment of manufacturing workers to their companies is regarded as a quite specific 'structural effect' of the HMFN as a whole in Japan (Figure 2.3).

Two aspects of the system must be analysed. One is the difference between internal factors acting within firm organisations and external factors, i.e. the socio-economic environment of firm organisations; and the other is the difference between regular and non-regular workers. The system uses both stick and carrot approaches.

To begin with, there is the 'ranking hierarchy' (Aoki 1988) of a firm organisation. In the Japanese firm this is called 'the competence-based grade system'. The competence-based grade is defined as 'the task-performing competence' (*shokuno**). However, such competence is not defined as the ability matched to a particular job, but rather as a company-wide work activity, and assigned a company-wide ranking. What needs to be emphasised here is that wages are separated from jobs by means of this firm-specific task-performing competence. Therefore, it should be noted that the wage system in Japanese firms is quite different from the payment-by-job schemes in the West. Ranks (*shokuno-shikaku**) in the competence-based grade system are only loosely associated with specific job classifications. In this sense, the 'competence-based grade' is better understood as a level of status rather than a qualification for a particular job. Regular workers are categorised as holders of a certain status and paid in accordance with age and status.

While their wages rise at regular intervals, and also in accordance with promotion to higher ranks on the basis of age and tenure, large portions of wages are paid depending on the competence-based grade assigned to workers rather than the grade attached to their particular jobs. The most crucial factor in deciding their wages and promotion is the assessment by a direct supervisor (*satei**). What is important in an employee's integration into a company is that it is the assessment not only of his performance but also that of his potential ability based on such factors as adaptability to technical changes, loyalty to his company, cooperation with fellow workers, eagerness to work, and so on. In these circumstances, employees are forced to take an interest in mastering other skills, even those that do not concern their present jobs. Furthermore, merit assessments result in different rates of promotion in the long term. Thus, it causes the differentials in lifetime incomes. The differentials created by the promotion system based on merit assessments and the wage determination system in accordance with rankings have incentive effects on employees and make them compete with one another within their companies. For this reason, employees focus on improving their status and advancing in status rank.

For non-regular workers, the picture is quite different. They are isolated from the career course in the internal labour market, and have no chance to be promoted after taking on-the-job training like regular workers. Therefore, the incentive to continue to work for those workers is mainly their need to sustain a decent standard of living, because they face not only large differentials in wages, retirement pay, and company-based welfare but also relatively poor social welfare and high education costs. They usually work under direct monitoring, and often in a neo-Taylorist production process.

Costs of job change and 'institutionalised job-loss costs'

In the HMFN, an employee who has quit his company in mid-career must expect a large financial and social penalty. The costs of job change for regular male workers in large companies are quite large. Their former wage level cannot be maintained after their job changes, and their wage growth will decelerate. From the estimation of wage functions in both Japan and the United States, Higuchi (1991) draws the conclusion that the effect of the length of service years on wages is larger in Japan than in the United States. Hashimoto and Raisian (1985) also find that tenure has a greater effect than total years of work experience in Japan, while the reverse is true in the United States. Furthermore, an employee who has quit his company in mid-career usually has to be re-employed in a firm of lower rank in the hierarchy of firms in the Japanese socio-economic system. He must also expect a considerable decrease in his retirement pay. With these high costs of job change, workers are encouraged to remain with their companies and to work hard.

Noticeably, the incentive effect of the costs of job change cannot be explained only by the upward sloping wage profile. This is due to the hierarchical structures. The costs of job change increase sharply due to the complementarity between two kinds of factors, that is, one concerning internal firm factors such as retirement pay, mandatory retirement, company-based welfare and the exclusive recruitment of new graduates, the other concerning external factors such as hierarchical inter-firm structures, relatively poor social welfare services, high education costs, and high housing expenses. In the segmented labour market in the context of hierarchical inter-firm relations, it is commonly accepted that a mid-career job change will bring about downward mobility.

The HMFN and its subsystems give rise to the structural effect of 'institutionalised job-loss costs', which play a crucial role in stimulating the work efforts of male employees in large companies, and is effective even during economic fluctuations, as it is highly institutionalised. In other words, the incentive effect of institutionalised job-loss costs keeps regulating workers' efforts even in quasi-full-employment situations.

Flexibility of wages and employment

The HMFN includes complex coordinating mechanisms to maintain the flexibility of wages and employment in the Japanese economy. These mechanisms are highly institutionalised, and they are also quite complementary to the incentive mechanisms based on 'the competence-based grade system' in large firms.

The complex coordinating mechanisms of wages

In the Japanese economy, wages are sufficiently flexible to cope with various economic conditions. This does not, however, mean that the labour market is arranged like a perfectly competitive market. It is quite segmented and highly institutionalised according to the HMFN

The annual growth rates of nominal wages in the different sizes of firm (Ministry of Labour 1998b) exhibit several patterns. First, the growth rates of nominal wages were widely dispersed at the beginning of the high growth period in the early 1960s. This suggests that firms of different sizes dealt with different segments of the heterogeneous labour market. In the mid-1960s, however, nominal wages rose sharply in small and medium-size firms due to the shortage of young workers, so firm-size wage differentials decreased dramatically. Nominal wages increased almost at the same rate in all sizes of firm in the late 1960s, and this tendency was strengthened in the 1970s. These changes seem to have been caused by the fact that there came to exist a kind of institutional coordinating mechanism to keep the growth rates of nominal wages in differently sized firms in line with one another after the full establishment of the HMFN. Second, quite different patterns of nominal wages are observed between the 'Izanagi Boom*' in the late 1960s and 'the 'Heisei Boom*' in the late 1980s. Namely, nominal wages, especially those of small and medium-size firms, rose sharply in the late 1960s, but the increase then became much more moderate, even in a boom in the late 1980s. This seems to have been brought about by complex coordinating mechanisms embedded in the HMFN.

Next, we have to investigate the complex coordinating mechanisms of wages in the HMFN, especially focusing on those in the 1980s. Various econometric estimates for nominal wage determination for different categories of worker (firm-size, male/female) deliver the conclusions of Table 2.1.

For male workers in a large firm (with over 1,000 employees), nominal wages are sensitive to the total ordinary profits of corporations, the unemployment rate at the end of the previous year (rather than the current ratio of job offers to applicants), and the consumer price index in the previous year. This suggests that nominal wages are determined by a kind of profit-sharing mechanism (Hirano 1994) as well as a formal wage-bargaining procedure that considers the unemployment rate and inflation, which seems to be partly ensured by the spring offensive system (*shunto**) in spite of its diminishing influence and changed orientation in the 1980s (Tsuru 1992a, 1992b). On the other hand, for male workers in small firms, nominal wages are not sensitive to the total ordinary profits of corporations, while they are very sensitive to the ratio of job offers to applicants in the same year and the consumer price index in the previous year. Therefore, the wage determination

Table 2.1 Dualistic wage determination according to firm-sizes, male/female

	$P\hat{R}OF_t$	U_{mt-1}	$\hat{P}_{t-1}$	d	$\bar{R}^2$	DW
$\hat{W}_m(L)t$	0.014*	−3.304**	0.497**	12.06**	0.9131	2.380
	(2.40)	(−4.26)	(6.33)	(5.32)		
$\hat{W}_m(S)t$	0.000	−3.069**	0.444**	11.38**	0.9037	0.967
	(0.1)	(−3.99)	(5.70)	(5.07)		

	$P\hat{R}OF_t$	U_{ft-1}	$\hat{P}_{t-1}$	d	$\bar{R}^2$	DW
$\bar{W}_f(L)t$	0.006	0.752	0.713**	0.6057	0.8752	2.545
	(0.51)	(0.51)	(3.88)	(0.13)		
$\bar{W}_f(S)t$	0.006	−3.414*	0.296*	12.37*	0.8218	2.434
	(0.73)	(−3.01)	(2.27)	(3.87)		

	$P\hat{R}OF_t$	$RJOA_t$	$\hat{P}_{t-1}$	d	$\bar{R}^2$	DW
$\hat{W}_m(L)t$	0.016	2.802	0.816**	−0.1534	0.8242	3.032
	(1.58)	(1.98)	(7.52)	(−0.11)		
$\hat{W}_m(S)t$	0.009	4.052**	0.803**	1.322	0.9123	2.376
	(1.27)	(4.30)	(11.12)	(−1.43)		
$\hat{W}_f(L)t$	0.011	0.133	0.646**	2.676	0.6669	2.249
	(0.78)	(0.07)	(4.48)	(1.49)		
$\hat{W}_f(S)t$	0.004	2.705	0.713**	0.2699	0.7351	2.774
	(0.36)	(1.67)	(5.77)	(0.17)		

Source: Ministry of Labour (1998b), *The Basic Survey on Wage Structures*, Statistics Bureau, *The Labour Force Survey*, and Ministry of Finance, *Corporation Statistics*

Notes:
Numbers in parentheses are t-statistics. **(*) denotes significance at the 1%(5%) level on a t-test. $\hat{W}_m(L)$: the growth rate of male workers' nominal wages in firms with over 1000 employees. $\hat{W}_m(S)$: the growth rate of male workers' nominal wages in firms with 10–99 employees. $\bar{W}_f(L)$: the growth rate of female workers' nominal wages in firms with over 1000 employees. $\hat{W}_f(S)$: the growth rate of female workers' nominal wages in firms with 10–99 employees. $P\hat{R}OF$: the growth rate of total ordinary profits of corporations. U_m: the unemployment rate of male workers at the end of the year. U_f: the unemployment rate of female workers at the end of the year. $RJOA$: the ratio of job offers to applicants. $\hat{P}$: the growth rate consumer price index (1985 = 100)

of male workers in small firms is influenced very strongly by conditions in the spot labour market. As for female workers, only wages in small firms are sensitive to the unemployment rate and inflation, while wages in large firms do not fit into the equation. Different wage determination mechanisms may coexist for female workers in a single large firm.

With the complex wage-determination mechanisms, firm-size wage differentials are brought about on the basis of value-added productivity differentials and the segmentation of workers into regular workers and non-regular workers in large firms. Wage setting for male workers in large firms is highly institutionalised, and for male workers in small firms it is rather competitive. Therefore, wage differentials between workers in these two categories fluctuate counter-cyclically. In the HMFN, two mechanisms guarantee wage moderation. On the one hand, the increase in wages is moderated by the profit-sharing mechanism and the spring offensive system (*shunto*) in large firms; on the other hand, the increase in wages is also limited by low value-added productivity in small firms. This set of complex coordinating mechanisms may account for the striking fact that the Japanese economy did not experience a wage explosion even in the situation of quasi-full employment in the late 1980s.

Complex coordinating mechanisms of employment

In the Japanese economy until the mid-1990s, the unemployment rate has been very low compared with those in other advanced countries. This does not, however, mean that there is an explicit rule to maintain job security in the economy as a whole. Employment is rather flexible at the micro level. This is brought about by complex coordinating mechanisms in the HMFN to maintain the unemployment rate at a very low level as well as making employment flexibility. To fully comprehend the complex coordinating mechanisms of employment in the Japanese economy, it is necessary to take account of the hierarchical inter-firm relations and the existence of various types of non-regular workers whose employment is very sensitive to economic conditions.

The employment of non-regular workers fluctuates according to economic conditions, and it plays a very important role in ensuring the flexibility of employment. Over the period 1969–93, the standard deviation of regular workers employment is 1.20, that of temporary workers 5.31 (EPA 1994). Furthermore, the flexibility of non-regular workers in various forms makes possible the long-term employment relationship of regular workers by reducing wage costs in a large firm. Therefore, in a sense, the external flexibility of non-regular workers is complementary to that of the internal flexibility of regular workers.

Second, from the macro-economic point of view, the transfer of workers from a parent company to its subcontractors and the absorption of employment by small and medium-size firms act as coordinating mechanisms to maintain the overall level of employment during recessions. This coordinating mechanism of employment through inter-firm relations is often called the 'quasi-internal labour market'. Therefore, the stability of employment, especially that of regular workers, is ensured not only by the implicit compromise in large firms, but also by the inter-firm coordinating mechanism and the segmented labour market in the HMFN.

In this way, the coordinating mechanism of wages and employment determines the fluctuations of wages and wage shares at the aggregate level. The growth rates of nominal wages among different sized firms converged closely in the late 1970s, and moderated even in a boom in the late 1980s. This effect of wage moderation played a crucial role in sustaining stable trends in wage shares during the 1980s. The growth rates of nominal wages by industry have been dispersed according to earnings conditions in each industry since the late 1970s (Okina, Takeuchi and Yoshikawa 1989). In other words, since the late 1970s, when the HMFN was fully established, the growth rates of nominal wages have been equalising with one another within each industry, but the equalisation of wages between industries has been deteriorating.

Structural compatibility in the HMFN: flexibility and productivity-enhancing mechanisms

This issue should be discussed with reference to different time horizons: short-term, medium-term, and long-term. For the short-term coordinating mechanism, flexibility is especially important. In fact, one of the remarkable features of the Japanese economic system is its flexibility in coping with economic fluctuations and structural changes. In *régulation* literature, emphasis is placed on internal flexibility in large firms, and the flexibility in the Japanese economy is regarded as a kind of 'offensive flexibility' (Boyer 1988b; 1992). However, Japanese economic flexibility is derived from very complex structures; another way of looking at the issue is to examine the 'structural compatibility of internal and external flexibility'.

Different types of flexibility are imposed on each type of workers. The internal flexibility of regular workers in large firms, i.e., flexibly extended working hours, the active commitment of workers to their companies, the high level of skill formation in on-the-job training, and the promotion of innovation, is closely complemented by the external flexibility of wages and employment of non-regular workers in large firms and both regular and non-regular workers in small (and medium-size) firms. Therefore, it is necessary to investigate the structural characteristics of flexibility, especially from the viewpoint of the structural compatibility of internal and external flexibility based on the HMFN.

Of course, such internal flexibility is indeed of a dynamic, 'offensive' character; the result of organisational innovation based on a long-term time horizon, organisational planning to respond effectively to fluctuations in demand (like the just-in-time system), long-term skill formation promoted by on-the-job training, and the flexible reallocation of workers within firms (Boyer 1995a). These factors are the source of Japanese firms' dynamic efficiency. Moreover, productivity is enhanced in the long run not only by the effect of the division of labour within the subcontractor system but also by the competitive pressure on subcontractors that forces them to introduce new technologies into their production processes. However, this dynamic efficiency is brought about on the basis of both the job security of core workers in large firms and the existence of non-regular workers and the hierarchical inter-firm relations in the HMFN. Japanese firms adopt growth-oriented strategies in order to maintain job security and make promotion schemes work, and employees naturally share the commitment to growth since it enhances the likelihood of promotion. Consequently, firms are likely to invest vigorously and promote organisational growth and innovation. This, in turn, makes it possible to establish internal mobility and to strengthen employees' active commitment to firms, both necessary for flexible coordination and innovation in firm organisations. Here there is circular causation, namely the 'micro-macro loop', between the active commitment of workers and the growth of the firm.

The long-term coordinating mechanism needs further consideration, however, the following line of discussion seems reasonable. Longer-term structural changes such as developing a new business area by moving along a new 'technological paradigm' are encouraged by the structural effects of the HMFN. First, competitive pressure among subcontractors to innovate and to introduce new technology into their production processes plays an important role in promoting those structural changes. In fact, there is particularly fierce competition among subcontractors of the same rank, so it is easy to implement the innovative reorganisation of production processes in a parent firm (including both the externalisation and internalisation of activities) and, consequently, similar reorganisation in subcontractors. This effect, together with the effect of the division of labour in the subcontracting network, enables a parent firm to reduce its costs and cope with a difficult economic situation. Second, in the process of restructuring, which inevitably involves some degree of uncertainty, it is much easier for a parent firm to coordinate employment and wages with subcontractors which utilise non-regular workers effectively. In fact, the number of female non-regular workers increased in the 1980s, as information technology was introduced into businesses.

In this way, the structural compatibility produced by the HMFN means that internal and external flexibility complement each other. Therefore, the strength of the Japanese economy lies in its ability to produce structural compatibility on the basis of the HMFN, and its structural effect enhances productivity and encourages structural changes in the long run.

Socio-economic reproduction of the HMFN

Given the view presented here of the institutional analysis of the socio-economic systems, complementarity between different institutions should be discussed not only in terms of the economic system but also for the reproduction process of the socioeconomic system as a whole. The reproduction of the HMFN is illustrated from the viewpoint of 'circular and cumulative causation' (Figure 2.4). It reveals that the specific division of domestic labour between men and women in families and women's part-time jobs in companies are indispensable parts of the social reproduction of the HMFN.

First, the structural compatibility that the HMFN produces can be maintained in the reproduction process of a socio-economic system as a whole. Second, the reproduction process of the HMFN involves not only economic agents such as workers belonging to a firm organisation but also

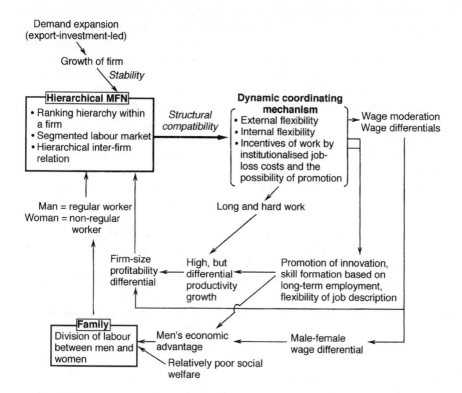

Figure 2.4 The social reproduction of the hierarchical market-firm nexus.

their family members. This framework for analysing the interaction between the conditions of economic growth and the environmental factors of social reproduction is useful for understanding how social changes, such as the increasing number of working women and the ageing society, affect economic performance.

Structural shifts in the HMFN in the 1990s

The purpose of this section is to discuss changes in the HMFN in the long recession which started with the collapse of the Bubble Boom in 1991. The question here is 'Is the HMFN reaching its limit, or newly evolving in the 1990s?'.

'Restructuring' of the HMFN

The HMFN has changed during the 1990s. On one side the growth rate slowed down from 4.2 per cent in the 1980s to 1.4 in the 1990s, whereas it was around 9.9 before 1973. But, on the other side, we have had the increase in the standard error/average rate of the growth ratio (from 0.20 before 1973 to 0.43 in the 1980s and 1.0 after 1991 (EPA 1998a)). This means that the risk of economic fluctuation is increasing relative to earlier periods, and this makes business managers feel uneasy about the future course of corporate management. In fact, Japanese firms have started a rather drastic adjustment of employment levels, which exceeds that of 'the belt-tightening management' after the first oil shock. The first characteristic is a fall in aggregate employment observed in the manufacturing sector. Second, employment adjustment is pursued not only in manufacturing industries but also in all other industries. Third, adjustment has focused primarily on managerial and white-collar workers, following the restructuring of large-size firms. In this way, the present adjustment of employment is much larger than any previous one in terms of scale and duration, and the number of workers whose employment is secure is surely decreasing. Therefore, not a few people predict that the Japanese labour market will soon be much more mobile, that is, that there will be 'increasing fluidity of employment'. At same time, Japanese firms have begun to re-examine the seniority wage system.

Moving on to inter-firm relations, (the indispensable basis of structural compatibility of the HMFN), the subcontractor system is also experiencing major structural changes, under the impact of the long recession. Recent changes in the subcontractor system have been brought about by restructuring parent companies, an increase in foreign direct investment by parent companies, and such long-term environmental changes as the ageing both of managers and employees in subcontractors. Even in this recession, the number of subcontractors and the percentage of parent companies' transactions with subcontractors have not shown much change as a whole, though subcontractors' transactions with parent companies and the volume of orders have decreased. This decrease in orders is caused by the selection of subcontractors by parent companies which make efforts to reduce the number of parts used in manufactured products, while the decrease in the subcontractors' transactions with parent companies also shows that a process of 'de-subcontracting' has been initiated by subcontractors. This is called the 'increasing fluidity' in subcontractor structures. The selection of subcontractors itself has been pursued, but it is unusual for parent companies to establish strict requirements for their subcontractors, which are facing increased competition with imported goods because of the rapid appreciation of the yen. Parent companies require subcontractors not only to work to high quality at low costs but also to adapt to small-scale and batch production, to shorten times for delivery and to invest in new products and technologies. On the one hand, there are naturally some subcontractors who cannot keep up with such strict requirements, while on the other hand, there are subcontractors who maintain strong ties with their parent companies. In this way, we can see the 'increasing fluidity' of the subcontractor system as well as the 'polarisation' of subcontractors in this recession.

Status quo and future of the HMFN

The third change has occurred in Japanese firm organisation. Since the collapse of the Bubble Boom, there have been negative factors such as the huge amount of bad debts credits, and instability in the financial system due to the sharp fall of stock prices and land prices. These factors inevitably force Japanese firms to transform the structure of corporate governance. Two problems deserve attention. The first is whether the incentive mechanism is changing, both within firm organisation and in the HMFN, under the pressure of the changes occurring in the wage and employment systems. The second is whether this recession will bring about changes in the structural compatibility of internal and external flexibility in the HMFN. To achieve a clear understanding of the present state of the HMFN, it is useful to discuss the possibility of structural changes within it, making a distinction between, first, changes at the aggregate level and, second, those at the level of each individual firm.

A comparison between the wage profile in 1975 and that in 1985 shows that the curve became steeper for white-collar workers (Figure 2.5a) and for blue-collar workers as well (Figure 2.5b), and that the wage differentials by age and tenure widened. As for the change in the shapes of wage profile from 1985 to 1995, a different figure can be observed. The curve for white-collar workers has flattened somewhat, and the wage differentials by age and job tenure have slowly decreased. The peak of the curve for blue-collar workers moved from the late forties to the late fifties. This seems to be brought about by the rising educational level of workers and the lengthening of tenure for middle-aged workers.

In fact, Chuma (1997) finds that there exists a substantial lengthening of tenure of middle-aged male workers in the 1980s and early 1990s, and that this tendency holds true in all industries and firm sizes. Therefore, as far as middle-aged male workers are concerned, it is reasonable to suppose that long-term employment is not weakening, but rather is spreading to wider spheres. As a result, we cannot see any remarkable change in the separation rate in different sized firms (Ministry of Labour various years).

In this recession, judging from trends in accession rates, employment adjustment has been realised mainly through cutbacks in hiring and accession. There is an especially remarkable decrease in the accession rate in large firms in the manufacturing sector. This restraint in accession is partly due to the effect of the rapid increase in employment at the period of the Bubble Boom. Even in this recession, however, companies have used the same methods of employment adjustment, such as cutting back the hiring of both new graduates and mid-career workers. No drastic change can be seen in the adjustment of employment up to the present. As a result, companies continue substantial 'labour hoarding' in the manufacturing sector. Therefore, there has been no change in the attitude to job security and the patterns of employment adjustment in large firms.

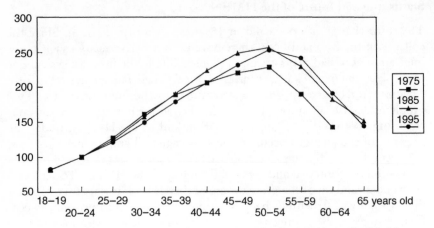

Figure 2.5a Changes in the wage profile (manufacturing/male white-collar/20–24 years old = 100). Source: Ministry of Labour, *Basic Survey on Wage Structure*, each year.

However, the pattern of adjustment is quite unequal across firms of different size (Figure 2.6). The decrease in employment has been very sharp in large firms with over 500 employees, while employment has been maintained in small and medium-size firms. Thus, small and medium-size firms still play a role as the 'sponge' of employment, even in this recession. Trends of employment between the manufacturing and non-manufacturing sectors, reveal an interesting structural shift in employment in this recession. Workers who have been dismissed in the manufacturing sector are partly absorbed in the non-manufacturing sector. In 1998, however, there was a

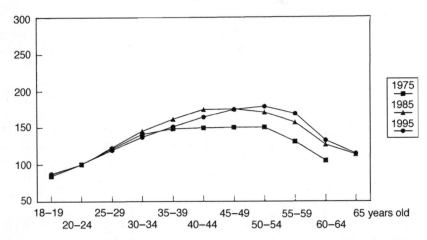

Figure 2.5b Changes in the wage profile (manufacturing/male blue-collar/20–24 years old = 100). Source: Ministry of Labour, *Basic Survey on Wage Structure*, each year.

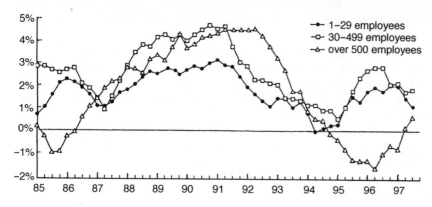

Figure 2.6 Changes in employment in the different sizes of firms (annual growth rate).
Source: Small and Medium-size Firm Agency, *White Paper of Small and Medium-size Firm*, 1998: Fig. 1-1-65.

sharp decrease in employment in small and medium-size firms and in the non-manufacturing sector. This may be due to the fact that employment decreased in the construction sector, and that one of the after-effects of the collapse of the Bubble Boom was a decline in the wholesale and retail trade, financing and insurance, and real-estate sectors. By contrast, employment in the service sector is still increasing, due to the growth of the worker dispatching business and outsourcing business. Therefore, employment is being maintained at the aggregate level in this recession, because small and medium-size firms in the manufacturing sector as well as the service sector in general are absorbing employees in spite of the decrease in employment in large firms in the manufacturing sector.

As already discussed, the only notable change in the HMFN is the 'increasing fluidity' and 'polarisation' in the subcontractor system. In addition to this change, the most urgent problem at present is that small and medium-size firms are having more and more trouble obtaining loans to maintain investment. It is likely that this credit crunch is forcing small and medium-size firms to reduce the number of employees. It is not clear at this moment whether the financing situation in small and medium-size firms will improve, because it largely depends on how fast the huge amount of bad loans accumulated during the Bubble period will be disposed of. However, we think that the more important factor is long-term environmental changes such as the restructuring of parent companies, the increase in their direct investment in Asian countries, and the ageing of employees. These changes, if they continue, might destroy the coordinating mechanisms promoting the flexibility and dynamism of the economy which the subcontractor system has been realising through its hierarchical structures to cope with industrial transformation. Of course, at the level of each firm, there is no doubt that such long-term changes as rapid ageing and the rising educational level of the work force generate rising labour costs which bear heavily on the corporate management. For that reason, each firm has started re-examining its organisation concerning wages and employment.

A question to be asked here is whether the 'increasing fluidity' of employment will undermine the norm of job security, which has been shared by both corporate managers and employees. At least so far, it is reasonable to answer this question as follows. The attempt to re-examine institutions within firms does not invalidate the methods of personnel management based on the competence-based grade system, but rather modifies them. A concrete example is the attempt to introduce the new competence-based grade called a 'professional job' which aims at remodelling the schemes of pay and promotion based on merit assessment. On the one hand, the existing competence-based grade system is maintained as a whole, and, on the other hand, the principle of 'meritocracy' is applied more strictly to the new 'professional job' grade. In this sense, the norm of job security has not been discarded in large firms. Equally important, the number of non-regular workers such as part-timers continues to increase. Therefore, we can see that, even in this recession, the coordinating mechanism of employment, where the employment of non-regular workers is very sensitive to economic fluctuations, has not lost its ability to render the external and internal flexibility complementary and to make possible the long-term employment of regular workers.

Moreover, Japanese firms, reconsidering the structure of corporate governance, have attempted to introduce the 'holding company system' as an institutional change within firm organisations. How will the introduction of the holding company system influence the structures of the HMFN? First, the holding company plays the role of monitoring the corporate management in place of the monitoring by main banks, and it is expected that this will make it possible to detect the deterioration of financial conditions in subsidiaries at earlier stages. This will, in turn, make it possible to promote long-term structural changes, including the exploitation of new business areas, the business restructuring accompanied by the scrapping of unprofitable business sectors and the transformation of industrial structures. In these processes, naturally, the subcontractor system of the division of labour faces some complicated changes. It is likely that transaction relations in the subcontractor system will become more rigid, and also that the selection of subcontractors will become more exacting. In addition, it is likely that the number of subcontractors aiming at 'de-subcontracting' will increase greatly. This will mean further development of the 'increasing fluidity' in the subcontractor system. Second, in the holding company system, if a holding company hires employees for 'professional jobs', new schemes of pay and promotion could be incorporated into firm organisations without discarding the existing personnel management systems. However, the institutional framework, that is, the tax, commercial law, and accounting systems which will underpin the holding company system, remain still incomplete. Therefore, it is still uncertain at present what effects the introduction of the holding company system will have on the set of complex coordinating mechanisms in the HMFN.

Concluding remarks

Until now, there has been no drastic structural change in the incentive mechanism and the 'structural compatibility' of the HMFN, apart from 'increasing fluidity' and 'polarisation' in the subcontractor system. Of course, there exist such long-term environmental changes as rapid ageing and the rising educational level of the work force, and there is no denying the fact that these changes are forcing each firm to re-examine its existing organisation. Nevertheless, these attempts to re-examine the institutions, which are concerned with compensation, promotion, recruitment, working hours, and so on, do not necessarily amount to a discarding of the existing institutional structures. These attempts aim at a partial and gradual reshaping of the existing structures and are expected to maintain them as a whole.

However, some research topics remain. One of the points concerning the attempts to re-examine organisation at the level of each firm is that if the principle of 'meritocracy' is applied to the determination of wages and promotion for most employees, it will make the shape of the wage profile flatter. Furthermore, the attempt to reform the company pension system in order to raise the portability of each employee's pension to other companies will lower the costs of job changes. These changes at the level of each firm could have a considerable effect on the structure of incentive mechanisms based on the 'institutionalised job-loss costs'. However, two important matters remain for discussion. First, the hypothesis of 'institutionalised job-loss costs' should be refined to explain its historical evolution, and various statistical time-series quantitative data to confirm it should be compiled. Second, a model should be constructed to clarify the relationships between the change in 'institutionalised job-loss costs' and employees' job change behaviours. At any rate, these are research topics to be considered in our future study.

3 Disproportionate productivity growth and accumulation regimes

Hiroyuki Uni

Introduction

The purpose of this chapter is to explain the dynamics of capital accumulation in post-war Japan, with attention to the structural change which accompanies economic growth. Final demand is divided into three elements: consumption, investment, and exports. The percentages of these three elements in the total final demand changes in response to the rise of national income or the development of international trade, but so does the commodity composition of each element. Various structural changes occurred successively in post-war Japan and deeply influenced the dynamics of capital accumulation.

Although economies affected by structural change follow unique macro-economic laws, it must be noted that institutions also play an important role. The relationship between structural change and capital accumulation is mediated by institutions through 'modes of *régulation*'. Japanese institutions regarding wages and employment differ significantly from those of other countries. This chapter examines how the institutions regarding employment guarantees affected capital accumulation. The first section breaks down changes of the profit rate into changes in its component variables, using macro-economic data and shows that changes in the price of capital goods in relation to other commodities contribute to changes in the profit rate. The second section explains that this relative price change is derived from a disproportional increase in labour productivity, and that the primary cause of this disproportional increase is a structural change in the total final demand. The third section examines the specific structural change that occurred in post-war Japan. The next section verifies the strength of the dynamic increasing returns which are the second cause of the disproportional increase in labour productivity. Clearly, the institutions regarding employment guarantees amplified dynamic increasing returns in Japan. Finally, there is a brief description of a scenario explaining the crisis in the Japanese economy in the 1990s, and reflections on the possibilities for structural change and the mode of *régulation* in the future.

Acceleration and deceleration of capital accumulation

Profit rate has set the tempo of capital accumulation in post-war Japan. The profit rate changed more dramatically in Japan than in the United States (Figure 3.1), the amount of capital stock in Japanese corporate enterprises rising at an annual average rate of 12 per cent from 1956 to 1970 – a 'period of rapid economic growth'. This high rate of capital accumulation was made possible by a high average profit rate of 24 per cent. If fluctuations in the business cycles are ignored, there is a rising trend in the profit rate and an acceleration of capital accumulation in the period of rapid economic growth. Although the profit rate was 16 per cent in 1957, the first business cycle peak in this period, it reached 32 per cent at the last peak, in 1970. In the mid-1970s, the Japanese economy entered a 'period of stable growth', the profit rate falling to 15 per cent in 1976. From 1976 to 1990, the average profit rate was 17 per cent, and the average rate of capital accumulation 7 per cent. In the 1990s, after the 'bubble economy' collapsed, the profit rate began to decrease, and capital accumulation slowed down.

Why did capital accumulation in post-war Japan pass through stages of acceleration, stabilisation, and deceleration? The first step is to break down the changes in the profit rate into changes in its component variables. The profit rate is expressed as follows:

$$
\begin{aligned}
\text{Profit rate} &= \text{Profit income} \,/\, \text{Nominal fixed capital stock} \\
&= \frac{\text{Profit income} \times \text{Nominal GDP}}{\text{Nominal GDP} \times \text{Nominal fixed capital stock}} \\
&= \frac{\text{Profit income} \times \text{Real GDP} \times \text{GDP deflator}}{\text{Nominal GDP} \times \text{Real fixed capital stock} \times \text{Fixed capital stock deflator}} \\
&= \text{Profit share} \times \frac{1}{\text{Capital coefficient}} \times \frac{\text{GDP deflator}}{\text{Fixed capital stock deflator}}
\end{aligned}
$$

Therefore, the rate of growth in the profit rate can be represented as follows:

$$
\begin{aligned}
\text{Rate of growth in profit rate} = {} & \text{Rate of growth in profit share} + \text{Rate of decrease in} \\
& \text{capital coefficient} + \text{Rate of decrease in relative price}
\end{aligned}
$$

The first term of the above equation represents the effect of changes in income distribution. The second term represents the effect of changes in the capital coefficient. The third term represents the effect of changes in the relative price, i.e., the price of fixed capital stock as measured by output flow. The main reason for changes in the relative price is the differential in productivity growth between goods that are used as fixed capital, and other commodities. One cause of this differential is purely technological – the tempo of innovation varies by sector, according to structural change in production technology. The effect of 'dynamic increasing returns' in a high-growth

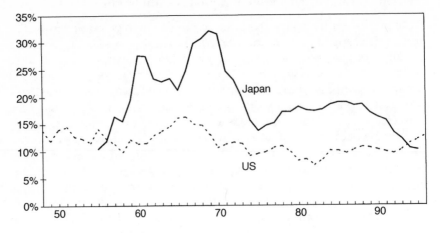

Figure 3.1 Profit rate in corporate enterprises.

economy (see next section) is another important factor: the growth in labour productivity for a certain commodity is affected by the growth in demand for this commodity. A disproportional growth in demand, i.e., a structural change in the final demand causes disproportional growth in labour productivity. Therefore, the third term in the above equation expresses the effect of structural changes in production technology and the final demand.

There are four rough trends in the profit rate of Japan and the US in the post-war period (Table 3.1). For Japan there is a 'period of rapid growth'

Table 3.1 Rates of growth of the profit rate and its components
(average annual percentage rates in corporate enterprises)

(1) Japan

	1957–70	1970–76	1976–90	1990–95
a) Rate of growth of the profit rate	5.0	−12.7	0.7	−9.4
b) Rate of growth of the profit share	0.5	−7.7	0.1	−6.3
c) Rate of decrease of the capital coefficient	1.9	−4.4	−1.3	−5.7
d) Rate of decrease of the relative price	2.6	−0.5	1.8	2.6

(2) The United States

	1959–66	1966–81	1981–90	1990–96
a) Rate of growth of the profit rate	4.3	−4.3	2.0	3.8
b) Rate of growth of the profit share	1.1	−2.3	0.8	2.8
c) Rate of decrease of the capital coefficient	2.9	−0.6	1.2	1.3
d) Rate of decrease of the relative price	0.2	−1.4	0.0	−0.3

when the profit rate rose at an average annual rate of 5 per cent, then a period of sharp decline in the first half of the 1970s. This is followed by a 'period of stable growth,' when the profit rate remained almost steady. Finally, in the 1990s, it declined gradually. So why did the profit rate change so dramatically? Table 3.1 clearly indicates that the profit rate rise during the period of rapid growth was mostly attributable to declines in the capital coefficient and the relative price. The average annual rate of decline in the relative price of capital goods was 2.6 per cent, which accounts for about half of the rise of the profit rate. This means that structural changes in the production technology and the final demand greatly contributed to the rise of the profit rate. Because income distribution was stable in the 1960s (Figure 3.2), it can be assumed that it had little influence on the profit rate. After public service workers participated in '*shunto**' in 1960, the wage determination system was established in almost all sectors in Japan, so the wage share remained stable throughout the decade.

The fall of the profit rate in the first half of the 1970s was mostly attributable to the decline in profit share and rise in the capital coefficient. In this period the profit rate was greatly affected by a jump in the wage share which occurred first because, the bargaining power of labour unions grew stronger as a result of labour shortage and, second, because this increased power remained by inertia for some years after the collapse of high economic growth (Yoshikawa 1995: 189). This jump in the wage share translates into a partial rearrangement in the *régulation* of income distribution.

During the period from 1976 to 1990, the profit rate was very stable. Firstly, income distribution was stable (Figure 3.2). Secondly, the decline in the relative price of capital goods had a positive effect, which cancelled out the negative effect of the rise in the capital coefficient (Figure 3.3). However, the profit rate declined in the 1990s, because both the capital coefficient and the

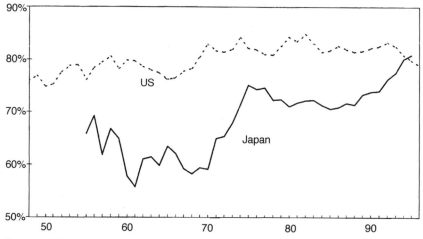

Figure 3.2 Wage share in corporate enterprises.

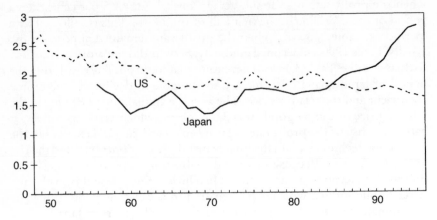

Figure 3.3 Capital coefficient in corporate enterprises.

wage share began to escalate rapidly, and the relative price of capital goods was not declining enough to cancel out their effect.

Thus, structural changes in production technologies and in final demand greatly affected the profit rate in Japan. Structural change was the main cause of profit rate increases during the period of rapid growth, and of stability in the period of stable growth. Structural changes had important effects on capital accumulation in post-war Japan; this is particularly clear in comparison to events in the US, where the profit rate also changed in the post-war period, although the changes were smaller in magnitude than those in Japan. It rose at an annual rate of 4.3 per cent from 1959 to 1966, declined from the mid-1960s to the early 1980s, and rose again in the 1980s and 1990s. The relative price of capital goods remained almost steady when the profit rate rose – in other words, structural changes (here, relative price) did not significantly affect capital accumulation in the post-war US.

Disproportional productivity growth

The main reason for the decline in the relative price of capital goods may be that their labour productivity grew more rapidly than that for other commodities, except in the period 1970–75. The rate of growth in labour productivity for each commodity is determined using the following method. The amount of direct and indirect labour required to produce one unit of the commodity is calculated using 'vertical integration' (Pasinetti 1973) based on input-output tables. The rate of decrease in this value is equivalent to the rate of growth in total labour productivity. Next, the rates of growth in labour productivity are aggregated with regard to durable goods (which consist of capital goods and consumer durables) and other commodities (Table 3.2).

Did such disproportional productivity growth also occur in other countries? It is difficult to apply the method used for Japan to other countries,

Table 3.2 Rates of growth in labour productivity and final demand in Japan (average annual percentage rates of growth)

	Labour productivity			Final demand		
	Durable goods	Other commod- ities	Difference	Durable goods	Other commod- ities	Difference
1960–65	8.5	5.9	2.6	12.1	7.7	4.4
1965–70	11.4	7.5	3.9	16.6	8.7	7.9
1970–75	3.0	3.1	−0.1	3.4	4.4	−1.0
1975–80	3.2	2.5	0.7	5.0	3.7	1.3
1980–85	3.6	2.4	1.2	4.1	3.4	0.7

so instead the changes in the relative price of investment goods are examined. The relative prices of investment goods are measured by the consumption goods using those deflators in the national accounts (Figure 3.4).

The relative price declined more remarkably in Japan than in any of the 25 countries examined; the differential in productivity growth was extraordinary in post-war Japan. Kaldor's concept of 'dynamic increasing returns' helps to explain why this was. As the rate of growth in output gets larger, so does the rate of growth in labour productivity (Kaldor 1966). This is called Verdoorn's law or Kaldor's second law. The result of Kaldor's study of the manufacturing industry based on the annual data of 12 countries from 1953–64 was as follows.

$$\rho = 1.035 + 0.484g \qquad R^2 = 0.826$$
$$(6.91)$$

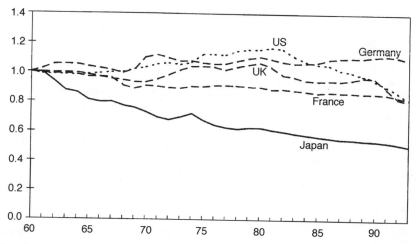

Figure 3.4 Relative price (investment goods/consumption goods).

ρ denotes the rate of growth in labour productivity, and g denotes the rate of growth in output. The figures in parentheses are t-values.

Assuming that 'dynamic increasing returns' occurred in Japan, then the large differential in output growth between capital goods and other commodities, and the exceptionally large coefficient of g, (which represents the strength of dynamic increasing returns, 0.484 in Kaldor's estimation), were both conditions for the large differential in productivity growth. The following sections examine the existence of these two conditions in postwar Japan.

Successive structural changes

In fact, the demand for durable goods grew more rapidly than that for other commodities throughout most of the periods (Table 3.2). When such a differential in demand growth persists, the percentage of durable goods in the total final demand will rise. Therefore, in Japan, the structural change in final demand satisfied the first condition mentioned above.

The final demand can be divided roughly into three elements and two commodities. The structural change in post-war Japan occurred in each of these three elements. Table 3.3 shows the percentage of each element in the total final demand in 1955 and in 1990, as aggregated from data in the final demand section of the input-output tables. The percentage of durable goods rose from 17.7 per cent in 1955 to 33.9 per cent in 1990 at the aggregate level, and it increased for each component: investment, consumption, and exports.

Three parameters describe structural change. s, represents 'capitalists' propensity to save', i.e., the percentage of investment expenditure in the profit income. When capitalists' appetite for investment is high, this parameter is large, and affects capital accumulation positively; an increase in s leads to structural change involving an increase in the percentage of durable goods. β, represents the percentage of durable goods in the total consumption expenditure. This includes purchases of automobiles and household electric appliances, and also the residential construction that is usually included in

Table 3.3 Composition of the final demand (percentages)

(1) 1955	Consumption	Investment	Exports	Total
Durable goods	6.7	9.8	1.2	17.7
Other commodities	71.5	1.1	9.7	82.3
Total	**78.2**	**10.9**	**10.9**	**100.0**

(2) 1990	Consumption	Investment	Exports	Total
Durable goods	12.3	15.5	6.1	33.9
Other commodities	58.9	3.6	3.6	66.1
Total	**71.2**	**19.1**	**9.7**	**100.0**

Table 3.4 The demand structure parameter and its components

(1) Japan

	s	β	γ	k
1955	0.26	0.09	0.12	0.48
1960	0.47	0.13	0.12	0.76
1965	0.42	0.15	0.18	0.79
1970	0.50	0.18	0.19	0.89
1975	0.46	0.17	0.37	1.06
1980	0.46	0.17	0.46	1.12
1985	0.46	0.14	0.58	1.09
1990	0.55	0.17	0.39	1.20

(2) The United States

	s	β	γ	k
1958	0.37	0.17	0.17	1.27
1963	0.35	0.19	0.19	1.26
1967	0.45	0.16	0.17	1.29
1972	0.47	0.17	0.21	1.41
1977	0.46	0.16	0.29	1.31
1982	0.63	0.12	0.25	1.42
1987	0.51	0.15	0.28	1.43
1992	0.42	0.12	0.46	1.26

investment. When a 'Fordist mode of consumption' is popular, this parameter increases, and leads to structural change involving an increase in the percentage of durable goods. The third parameter, γ, represents the ratio of the exports of durable goods to domestic investment. If the trade balance is fairly even, a country with net exports of durable goods is a country with net imports of other commodities. When this trade pattern expands, domestic production will specialise in durable goods.

None of the changes in s, β, and γ in post-war Japan (Table 3.4) show a long-term trend. Their combined effect can determine the demand structure parameter, or k – the ratio of the total durable goods demand to profit income (Uni 1998: 56–67). We can express k as follows, where λ denotes a ratio of wage income to profit income.

$$k = (\gamma + 1)s + \beta(\lambda + 1 - s)$$

So, if other variables are constant, an increase in s, β, γ, or λ leads to a rise in k. As Table 3.4 shows, the value of k increased dramatically during the period of rapid growth in Japan and has continued to increase gradually since 1975. Such a continuous increase in k was not seen in the United States. Then why has the demand structure parameter increased continuously in post-war Japan?

First, the increase in s represents capitalists' growing appetite for investment. The value of s jumped from 0.26 in 1955 to 0.47 in 1960 because of 'capital accumulation promotion policies' and the financial institutions that were established in the first half of the 1950s. The following policies had an invigorating effect on plant and equipment investment. The Japan Development Bank was founded in 1951, and supplied key industries with low-interest funds. High rates of depreciation, the tax exemption system on key products, and other such measures for the broadly favourable tax treatment of business were implemented. The foreign exchange allocation system instituted in 1949 played a large role in protecting and fostering domestic industry (Nakamura 1981: 43–5). Supported by these institutions, the steel industry promoted the Second Rationalisation Plan, the electric power industry implemented a five-year investment plan, and the petrochemical industry constructed new plants. Thus, the heavy and chemical industries implemented large investment plans in the second half of the 1950s. However, the value of s has remained almost steady, with only small fluctuations since 1960 and the contribution of s to the long-term increase of the demand structure parameter has been small. Therefore, there must have been changes in β and γ that greatly contributed to the increase in k.

The increase in β represents an increase of durable goods within the total consumption expenditure. The value of β rose continuously from 0.09 in 1955 to 0.18 in 1970. As the above equation shows, β must be multiplied by $(\lambda + 1 - s)$, giving a value of approximately 2.5. Therefore an increase in β can raise k greatly.

The increase in β during the period of rapid economic growth was fairly certainly based on the diffusion of 'the Fordist mode of consumption'. This transformation of consumption was made possible by the fact that the wage share stabilised and income differentials between various social strata contracted. As shown in Figure 3.2, although the wage share declined in the 1950s, it stabilised in the 1960s. This means that the rate of increase in wages was almost equal to the rate of increase in labour productivity. And, in the 1960s, wage differentials according to the size of the firm, and income differentials between city and rural areas both contracted. As a consequence of the comparatively equal purchasing power among households, the diffusion of consumer durables rose.

However, if the diffusion of consumer durables is close to saturation, the growth of demand becomes small. For example, the diffusion index of electrical appliances, such as washing machines, refrigerators, and colour televisions, approached almost 100 per cent in the mid-1970s. Residential construction grew at the annual rate of 15 per cent from 1955 to 1973, but stagnated from 1974 to 1985 because of soaring land prices. Moreover, the percentage of overall household expenditures made for education and medical care has continued to increase since the 1970s. As a result of these changes, the value of β fell from 0.18 in 1970 to 0.14 in 1985.

Finally, the change in γ, shows the ratio of exports of durable goods to domestic investment. This value rose gradually during the 1960s, sharply from

Table 3.5 The changing pattern of Japanese growth

1950-60	'investment-led' structural change: rise of s
1960–70	'consumption-led' structural change: rise of β
1970–75	change in income distribution: rise of λ
1975–85	'export-led' structural change: rise of γ
1985–90	'bubble-led' structural change: rise of s and β

0.19 in 1970 to 0.58 in 1985. The decrease in β in this period had a negative effect on γ, but the rise of γ cancelled this out, causing k to increase overall.

The sharp rise of γ indicates the success of 'export-led growth' in Japan. There are three reasons for this success. The first reason is that the Reagan Administration maintained a 'strong dollar', the second is the 'export-biased' increase in labour productivity in Japan, and the third is that after the first oil shock, wage increases were curbed in Japan earlier than in the United States. Under these conditions, the dollar was overvalued, and dollar-based export prices of Japanese goods dropped causing a rapid increase in the amount of Japan's exports. However, the US dollar began to depreciate through the coordinated intervention in the exchange markets by all of the G5 nations after the Plaza Agreement in 1985.

With the rapid appreciation of the yen, it became difficult to continue the export-led growth, and γ has declined greatly since 1985. The values of s, β, and γ vary according to changes in social, institutional, and technological conditions. Therefore, the long-term increase of the demand structure parameter, k, is not guaranteed. However, k did in fact rise continuously in post-war Japan, owing to the successive occurrence of the following various structural changes.

To sum up, all these structural changes define various periods for Japanese growth (Table 3.5). They largely converge with previous institutional and econometric analyses (Boyer 1992; Uemura 1992; Yamada 1992) as well as with the conclusions of Chapter 8.

Dynamic effects of employment guarantees

Except for the period 1970–75, the above structural changes caused the output of durable goods to grow more rapidly than that of other commodities. According to Verdoorn's law, this leads to a higher rate of growth in the labour productivity of durable goods. The size of the differential of productivity growth also depends on the strength of dynamic increasing returns (the coefficient of g in the equations below).

The following equation is the result of estimation using the 1976–96 annual data of the manufacturing industry. Figures in parentheses are t-values.

Japan:
$$\rho = 1.15 + 0.588g \qquad R^2 = 0.803$$
$$(3.14) \quad (8.81)$$

The United States: $\rho = 2.47 + 0.176g$ $R^2 = 0.335$
                    (8.26) (3.10)

Figure 3.5 shows these two estimated equations in a line graph. Compared with the United States, the case of Japan is characterised by a larger coefficient of g and a smaller constant. Although we show here only the estimation for the manufacturing industry, many other industries yield similar results. In Figure 3.5, the line representing the United States' figures has a gentle slope showing that output growth has less effect on the productivity growth. On the other hand, the line representing the Japanese figures has a steep slope, indicating that output growth greatly affects productivity growth. In this case, if the rate of output growth is higher than approximately 3 per cent, productivity growth in Japan is higher than in the United States, and vice versa.

Why do the two countries differ in terms of the relationship between output growth and productivity growth? The main reason is the difference in the institutions for employment adjustment. Because the degree of employment security is higher in Japan, the coefficient of g is larger, and the constant is smaller than in the United States (see Figure 3.5). During the period from 1976 to 1996, the fluctuation of the rate of output growth was large in both countries – standard deviation at 4.3 in Japan and 4.1 in the US. The two countries differed considerably in the fluctuation of employment growth and productivity growth. Employment growth fluctuated less in Japan than in the US (standard deviations were 1.7 and 2.9 respectively), but productivity growth fluctuated more in Japan than in the US (with standard deviations of 2.8 and 1.3). If the amount of employment is elastic

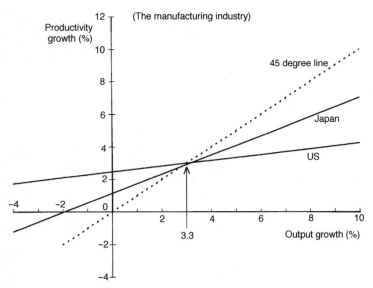

Figure 3.5 Comparison of Verdoorn's laws for Japan and the US.

to the amount of output, as in the United States, fluctuation in productivity growth is small. However, the value of this fluctuation was large in Japan because the amount of employment is not elastic to the amount of output.

It is well known that there are various ways to adjust employment in response to the business cycle. In the United States, the main method is the lay-off system. A manager can determine the number of workers laid off without negotiating with the labour union, although the manager must designate workers laid off according to their seniority. This makes it possible to flexibly adjust the amount of employment. In Japan, in contrast to the United States, there are many institutions that guarantee employment even during a recession (see Chapter 7). Employers and employees recognise the norm of 'lifetime employment' and, although this norm in fact applies only to core workers, dismissals of even peripheral workers take a long time because of institutional constraints. When the economy goes into recession, firms do not implement personnel reductions immediately, but reduce operations and reshuffle or loan employees, thus keeping them employed. The Employment Insurance Law enacted in 1975 obliges the government to give financial assistance to firms implementing such adjustments during recession in order to maintain the level of total employment. Generally speaking, large Japanese firms implement personnel reductions only after operating at a loss for two years. Thus, in Japan, productivity growth slows down during a recession because of labour hoarding. The difference between the US and Japan shown in Figure 3.5 results from different institutional ways of adjusting employment.

It is often said that rigidity of employment has negative effects on economic growth. It also has positive effects, however: the Japanese type of employment security promotes productivity growth in sectors where output is growing rapidly. This happens because if stagnating sectors hoard their workers, the mobility of workers becomes small. Consequently, it is difficult for growing sectors to recruit new workers in the labour market. Furthermore, sectors that are growing now may stagnate in the future. If the manager forecasts that a dismissal would be difficult in the future, he becomes prudent in increasing employment at present. These restrictions on the supply and demand of labour promote labour-saving efforts. A second reason is that the employment guarantee makes it possible for workers to accumulate more skill and knowledge making labour productivity potentially higher. Actually, productivity growth in Japan is higher than in the United States when the rate of output growth is above 3 per cent (Figure 3.5). Dynamic increasing returns in Japan are strong as a result of both the negative and positive effects of the institutions securing employment.

The previous section showed that various drastic structural changes occurred successively in post-war Japan. Thus it was necessary to mitigate changes in employment structure, at least regarding core workers – it takes several years to derive a new skill from existing skills and, in such a period, immediate dismissals based on the decline of output may result in social instability. Therefore, the institutions securing employment were very necessary.

Possibilities of structural change in the future

Origins of the 1990s crisis

The fall of the profit rate in the 1990s was caused by increases in the wage share and the capital coefficient (Table 3.1, *supra*). The increase in the wage share may just be a fluctuation caused by the business cycle. But the increase in the capital coefficient may be a long-term trend, given that it began in the mid-1980s (Figure 3.3, *supra*). One immediate cause of the increase in the capital coefficient was the fiscal and monetary relaxation in the 'high-yen recession' after the Plaza Agreement in 1985. Excessive speculation in real-estate raised land prices, taking advantage of the urban redevelopment boom at that time, and also caused soaring stock prices. As these rises in asset prices created potential profit, firms pushed to invest in equipment and plant. Another reason for this active investment was that firms could easily get funds by equity finance from the deregulated capital market, under rising stock prices. Capitalists' propensity to save rose from 1985, after a long stagnation (Table 3.4, *supra*). The capital coefficient is equal to the product of two variables: 'the amount of capital stock per unit of productive capacity' and 'the operating ratios'. The increase of the capital coefficient beginning in 1985 stemmed mainly from the increase in the former variable.

The fall in stock prices and land prices beginning in 1990 changed business conditions. The decrease of potential profit or the actual potential loss suppressed capitalists' appetite for investment. The stagnation in investment and consumption caused an increase in the capital coefficients by pushing down operating ratios. It is important to note that 'the amount of capital stock per unit of productive capacity' continues to increase in the 1990s, a fact often attributed to the rise in investment in research and development. However, the drastic increase shown in Figure 3.3 cannot be explained just by a change in technological conditions, and probably also stemmed from bubble-like over-investment owing to the governance structure of Japanese firms. Stockholders and labour unions are so weak that they have little influence on predictions of profitability, the selection of fields in which to invest, and the administration of a business plan.

The profit rate fall in the 1990s is comparable to the fall in the first half of the 1970s, in terms of scale and length. Capital accumulation clearly went into a crisis. In these phases, each economic unit searches for a way to escape the crisis, and each fights the other over which method should be adopted. New modes of *régulation* constitute an escape route. In the 1990s, the institutions securing employment are actually under debate in Japan. Some people insist that employment security should be weakened to lower labour costs and make the production process more flexible, in correspondence with intense international competition.

As the previous section illustrates, the acceleration of capital accumulation in post-war Japan was supported by structural changes in the final demand. If similar structural change occurs in the future, the Japanese economy may be able to avoid a crisis similar to the one it presently faces.

What are the emerging régulation *modes?*

Will 'investment-led' structural change be possible in Japan? It is difficult to increase capitalists' appetite for investment, because a great deal of equipment and plant are not presently operating due to over-investment during the economic bubble period. There remains the possibility of increased investment in information technology, which is advancing rapidly.

Next, will 'export-led' structural change be possible? Since the Plaza Agreement in 1985, the yen-dollar exchange rate has been adjusted as follows: a rise in the amount of Japan's exports causes the appreciation of the yen, which in turn decelerates Japan's exports. As long as such an adjustment of the exchange rate lasts, a continuous rise in exports is difficult. Furthermore, regarding products with mature technology, because the international competitiveness of developing countries is rising, Japan's exports will decline, unless it innovates new export products.

Finally, will 'consumption-led' structural change be possible? Consumption expenditure for durable goods is divided into three elements: 'machinery as consumption goods', such as automobiles and household electric appliances; 'residential construction'; and so-called 'social capital construction'. The amount of durable goods per person may increase, as new 'machinery as consumption goods' such as personal computers continue to appear, and, also because in Japan, basic needs have not yet been satisfied regarding housing and 'social capital'. However, because the expenditure for information services is also increasing side by side with that for information equipment, it is not possible to say that the percentage of durable goods in the total consumption expenditure will increase by virtue of the diffusion of information technology. Furthermore, people begin to reconsider the ways in which durable goods are used and whether to possess them at all, as the crisis in the ecological system and the environment becomes clearer. For example, the possession of personal cars has reached its physical limit in urban areas, and public transport is therefore re-evaluated.

Some suppliers have begun to reconsider the method of promoting sales by continually introducing minor model changes. Some consumers have begun to reconsider throwing away goods after using them for a short time. Thus, if both suppliers and consumers recognise ecological constraints, and develop recycling and co-ownership of durable goods, the annual production of durable goods will be depressed.

To sum up, it will be difficult to achieve structural change in investment, consumption, or exports that leads to a higher rate of growth in the output of durable goods. When this kind of structural change is realised, capital accumulation can accelerate under the constraint that the wage share and the capital coefficient remain constant. When this kind of structural change is not realised, it becomes necessary to reduce the wage share or the capital coefficient if an acceleration of capital accumulation is to occur. In such circumstances, labour-management relations become antagonistic, and the mode of *régulation* created during a period of structural change will be modified.

Conclusion: the search for a new wage labour nexus

The Japanese employment system must be reformed. If this kind of structural change does not occur, the rate of growth in output may end up less than 3 per cent even in the machinery manufacturing industries that have grown so rapidly until now. When this happens with the present Japanese employment system, productivity growth is smaller than in the United States. Since the machinery manufacturing industries are exposed to international competition, low productivity growth leads to these industries' long-term decline.

An important task for management in this situation is to create a new mechanism that raises productivity under low output growth. The US layoff system is an extreme example of such a mechanism. If a similar method were applied in Japan, either through the reduction of working hours or the dismissal of workers, the amount of labour demand would decrease. If working hours are reduced, it is necessary to determine exactly how much wage income is lost. If workers are dismissed, one has to decide who gets dismissed, how to pay for the costs of occupational change and unemployment, and how to compensate for the deterioration of workers' skills and knowledge due to the shortening of their length of service.

These circumstances make it necessary to reconsider how we define and realise 'affluence' in the realms of labour and life, taking into account slow economic growth and ecological constraints. The increase in free time and the 'de-commodification' of leisure activities are the two important keys.

The reduction of working hours is necessary if we are to maintain full employment where there is a decreasing demand for labour. The principle of income distribution during the period of rapid growth was the 'indexation of wage increases to productivity growth', through which the wage rate rose at the same rate of growth in labour productivity. A principle for the future must be the 'indexation of the increase in free time to productivity growth'. In other words, to maintain full employment when the supply of labour power cannot increase, working hours must be reduced at the same rate of growth as labour productivity. Then, just as the former indexation was realised through institutions like the *shunto** and the social security system, the new indexation must be realized through new institutions, which spread the reduction of working hours throughout the whole society.

There must be new modes of *régulation* in realms other than labour. There are two types of human needs: for commodities and non-commodities. It may become more important in the future to satisfy needs for non-commodities, such as communication with friends, self-cultivation through creative hobbies, and participation in associations. The affluence arising from the fulfilment of these needs is qualitatively different from the affluence resulting from the increase in the consumption of commodities. In order to achieve this new qualitative affluence, it is necessary to 'de-commodify' leisure activities and increase free time. Our current lifestyle could be transformed by controlling our increasing dependence on commodities.

APPENDIX: SOURCES OF DATA

Figures 3.1, 3.2, 3.3, and Table 3.1.

Annual data was obtained from the following sources, using the following methods.

Japan

Source: Table 1.IV.2, and 2.II.1 of Economic Planning Agency, *Annual Report on National Accounts 1997*.
Profit income = 'entrepreneurial income (private incorporated enterprises)' + 'Interest and dividends (household's property income)'.
Wage income = 'compensation of employees' − 'Ratio' * 'entrepreneurial income (private unincorporated enterprises)' − 'compensation of employees in the public sector'.
See Yoshikawa (1995, p.184) for a full account of this method.
Nominal fixed capital stock = Net fixed assets (incorporated enterprises).
Source: Economic Planning Agency, *Annual Report on Capital Stock of Private Enterprises 1997*.
Real fixed capital stock = 'Real capital stock (incorporated enterprises)'.

The United States

Source: Table 1.16 of US Department of Commerce, *US National Income and Product Accounts 1959–96*.
Profit income = 'corporate profits with inventory valuation and capital consumption adjustments' + 'net interest'.
Wage income = 'compensation of employees'.
Source: Tables 7 and 8 of US Department of Commerce, *Fixed Reproducible Tangible Wealth, 1929–96*.
Nominal fixed capital stock = 'current-cost net stock of fixed non-residential private capital (corporate business)'.
To compute real fixed capital stock, 'chain-type' quantity indexes were used. Each pair of adjacent values was averaged to estimate mid-year values.

Figure 3.4

Regarding 'private final consumption expenditure' and 'gross fixed capital formation (excluding 'residential buildings')', annual deflators were computed from current values and constant values in OECD, *National Accounts*. Relative prices were computed as follows.

Relative price = deflator of gross fixed capital formation/deflator of private final consumption expenditure.

Tables 3.2, 3.3, 3.4

Source: Management and Coordination Agency, *Linked Input-Output Tables*, US Department of Commerce, *The Benchmark Input-Output Accounts for the U.S. Economy*.

First, the final demand sections of input-output tables were aggregated into the following form.

	Consumption	*Investment*	*Exports*
Durable goods	a	b	c
Other commodities	d	e	f

Durable goods include output in sectors such as 'general machinery', 'electrical machinery', 'transportation equipment', 'precision instruments', and 'construction'. Consumption includes 'private consumption expenditure', 'consumption expenditure of government', and 'residential construction and social capital formation (derived from *National Accounts*)'. Investment includes 'gross domestic fixed capital formation (excluding "residential construction and social capital formation")' and 'increase in stocks'.

Next, we computed each parameter as follows.

$s = (b + e)/\text{profit income}, \quad \beta = a/(a + d), \quad \gamma = c/b,$
$k = (a + b + c)/\text{profit income}$

See Uni (1998, pp.127–30) for full account of this method.

Figure 3.5

Source: OECD, *Main Economic Indicators*.

Rates of change were computed in the following index regarding the manufacturing industry.

Output; Industrial Production.

Employment; Employment.

Hours of work (Japan); Monthly Hours of Work.

(The United States); Weekly Hours of Work.

Productivity = Output / (Employment * Hours of work).

Part II

The wage labour nexus, forms of competition, financial regime

Major structural transformations

4 The capital-labour compromise and the financial system

A changing hierarchy

Hironori Tohyama

Introduction

At present, the Japanese economy is facing a series of reforms designed to overcome the current financial crisis by moving the Japanese financial structure from a bank-based to a market-based system. In assessing the financial crisis and reforms, it is essential to focus on asset inflation since the rapid drop of over inflated asset values such as real-estate and equities led to the present financial turmoil. At the same time, it can be demonstrated how the relationship between the financial sector and employment policy was associated with the asset inflation of the 1980s.

The first part of this chapter focuses on how wage bargaining units have been transformed and examines the evolution of capital-labour compromises. Based on this analysis it can be shown that wage and price setting has become consistent with international competition since the mid-1970s. The next part of the chapter considers the political-economic implications arising from the changes in capital and labour relations and the increasing competitiveness of Japanese exporting industries. Next, the impact of the stagnating domestic markets will be linked to larger enterprises accumulating money capital. Thus the intermediary role of the banking sector in linking money capital to productivity resources in firms changed, which in turn led to problems with the behaviour of banks and firm management. Finally, the results of an easy monetary policy in the institutional context developed are shown to enhance the problems of financial speculation and over-inflated values.[1]

Changing patterns in wage bargaining

In the mid-1970s capital and labour reached a compromise concerning wage determination which influenced subsequent wages and prices. This section focuses on the historical emergence and the long-term significance of the compromise.

There are nation-wide organisations on both sides of labour and capital in the post-war Japanese wage bargaining system. However, they are not able directly to intervene in individual unions and firms when dealing with wage negotiations. Their authorities are decentralised, and employer or union organisations are fragmented. Neither capital nor labour can be recognised as unitary actors.

Nation-wide organisations are not concerned with speaking for the interests of individual firms or industries but rather with presenting the interests of the group as a whole. Given the decentralisation of unions and firms, the task nation-wide organisations have to cope with is to aggregate the interests of members and mobilise them when trying to reach their goals for the benefit of the group as a whole (Pontusson 1992). Although authority in both labour-force and business is decentralised in terms of an organisational structure, they can be coordinated across the economy (Soskice 1990; Riel 1995).

In this mobilising process nation-wide organisations explicitly have to put forward strategic targets and coordinate diverse interests within their groups. Cleavage within their own groups must be addressed (Iversen 1996). Capital and labour will set up certain strategic targets. The interaction between capital and labour is likely to create or change an institutionalised compromise.

From labour-led coordination . . .

From the 1960s to the early 1970s, a virtuous circle between productivity increases and the growth of markets and employment was created in the Japanese economy. Increasing productivity growth in the manufacturing sector reduced relative prices of manufactured goods, leading to expanding markets as well as increasing real wages. At the same time, expanding markets were linked with productivity increases through economies of scale. On the basis of this virtuous circle, there was likely to be more room for capital to accept labour's demand for wage hikes. Economies of scale and productivity growth accordingly amplified the permitted range of wage increases (see Chapter 3). This mitigated conflicts between labour and employers over how to share productivity gains. The nation-wide organisation of employers, Nikkeiren (Japan Federation of Employers' Association), was not urged to coordinate the interests of individual employers for the benefit of employers as a whole when coping with labour's demand.

Economic literature has firmly established employers' preference for enterprise-based bargaining (Koshiro 1983; Kurita 1994). Nation-wide labour organisations had to decide how to mobilise and aggregate their dispersed resources so as to reach their strategic targets of wage increases and the standardisation of wage increases. It is the '*shunto*'[2] that formulates this demand for the labour side.

Labour was successful in coordinating decentralised wage negotiations under *shunto* which led to wage increases and their homogenisation. *Shunto* coordinates unions in major companies. Other individual unions are supposed to make use of coordination when negotiating with their own employers. The *shunto* system thus presupposes that unions in larger companies take the initiatives in their own industries and are extremely influential in wage negotiations in smaller firms' unions. Unions in larger firms offer an integrated demand for wage hikes. Subsequently other individual unions launch their own wage negotiations with reference to the demands of the larger unions. This system allows enterprise-based unions to negotiate wage hikes on a nation-wide basis without interference in enterprise-based collective bargaining. The *shunto* system is thus designed to mobilise labour's dispersed power only in the Spring by means of cooperative relationships among unions in larger firms. Once a year this system enables labour to enhance their influence on enterprise-wide collective bargaining.

From the 1960s to the early 1970s, wages increased steadily and job opportunities continued to widen against the background of tight labour markets (see Chapter 2). There were no obvious conflicts among unions. Clear cleavage could not be found within labour movements. Labour emerged as a unified and coherent actor under *shunto*. This resulted in nation-wide coordination of decentralised bargaining units. The institutionalised compromises in this period constituted a labour-led and decentralised wage bargaining, resulting in steadily increasing real wages (Table 4.1).

In the mid 1970s both labour and employers changed their strategic targets, which had a knock-on effect on the previously decentralised system of wage bargaining. Taking soaring inflation and slow growth into consideration, labour changed its strategic focus from wage increases to maintaining employment. Private-sector unions contributed greatly to changing their strategy. Leaders in the private-sector unions shared with employers the view that higher wage hikes bring about inflation and have a negative effect on economy as a whole, that wage increases damage firms' international competitiveness and are harmful to maintaining employment.[3]

Table 4.1 Strategic targets and changes in bargaining units

	1960s to the early 1970s	*1975 to the late 1990s*
Strategic target of capital	Reaping increasing returns to scale	Curbing wage inflation
Strategic target of labour	Wage hikes and homogenisation of wage increases	Maintaining employment
Bargaining units	Coordination of decentralised bargaining units under the lead of labour	Coordination of decentralised bargaining units led by capital

... To firm-led coordination

Under the leadership of private-sector unions the labour force's strategy was transformed, reflecting divisions within the movements. Tekko Roren (Japan Federation of Iron and Steel Workers Unions) belonging to Sohyo (General Council of Trade Unions of Japan)[4] was the private sector union with the most clout. In 1966 it officially joined IMF–JC[5] and as a result Sohyo lost support from the influential private-sector labour unions and gradually lost its position as the leading labour association. Conflicts between the private-sector unions under the lead of IMF–JC and the public-sector unions led by Sohyo emerged (IMF–JC, 1984). Since then labour movements under the lead of Sohyo have become isolated from the private-sector unions.

In the mid-1970s labour force divisions came into the open and the initiative in wage struggles shifted from the public-sector unions to the private-sector ones. Labour started to pursue maintaining employment in exchange for moderate wage hikes (Garon and Mochizuki 1993; Ohmi 1994). The transformation of strategy does not immediately lead to changes of institutionalised compromise regarding how to share productivity gains.

So far, little is known about how the strategy of capital is developed. As some empirical studies on capital–labour relations in advanced capitalist economies pointed out, employers have the initiative in institutional changes (Pontusson and Swenson 1996; Sako 1997). Employer coordination has been more significant in securing wage moderation than union coordination (Soskice 1990; Riel 1995; Glyn 1995). It is therefore important to analyse employers' strategies and how diverse interests among employers are coordinated, when addressing the evolution of institutionalised compromises in Japan.

Before 1969 Nikkeiren laid emphasis on wage determination. Individual employers should offer wage increases based on their own abilities to pay. The result of *shunto* in the 1974 bargaining round was an enormous wage increase of 32.9 per cent bringing an atmosphere of crisis among employers and inducing Nikkeiren to give priority to curbing wage increases for the benefit of capital as a whole. Nikkeiren began to advocate the productivity standard principle, i.e. to keep the rate of nominal wage increases at or below the equivalent of the real GNP growth rate minus the rate of employment growth. The employer's strategy of curbing wage increases in the 1975 *shunto* was based on this principle.

Nikkeiren used three methods to coordinate the diverse interests of employers and mobilise their power resources for the purpose of achieving its strategic target (Takagi 1976; Shinkawa 1984; Mori 1992; Hancock and Shimada 1993). First, the concerted action by the presidents in major companies: before the 1975 spring offensive, Nikkeiren called 'Conference for 11 Presidents in Major Companies' which involved, amongst others steel, shipbuilding, automobile and electrical industries. Nikkeiren sought to confine wage increases to 15 per cent and the presidents agreed to comply with this guideline.

Secondly, for the purpose of making its wage guideline more effective, Nikkeiren focused on the leading industries. Nikkeiren insisted that large companies should restrain themselves from large wage increases even if they had the ability to pay, taking into consideration the depression and the problems that smaller firms were facing. The steel industry was a particular target because it led the spring wage offensive and was a thriving industry in those days. In the previous presidents' conference, industries damaged by the depression – automobile, shipbuilding – had urged the steel industry to offer more moderate wage increases. Therefore the steel industry committed itself to preventing wages from increasing more than 15 per cent.

Third, although it was impossible for Nikkeiren to intervene in the enterprise-based bargaining by addressing the formal organisational structure of the employer side, they could put pressure on individual companies to comply with the wage guideline through monitoring. Nikkeiren got employers nation-wide to act together to accomplish its strategic targets. Thus, it could coordinate individual enterprise-based wage negotiations without changing the institutional framework of enterprise-based wage bargaining.

Conflicts between private-sector and public-sector unions came into the open and the initiative in *shunto* shifted to the private-sector unions. Since then, under the lead of the private-sector unions and in cooperation with their employers, workers started to pursue maintaining employment via the survival of their own companies. The strategy of capital to curb wage inflation was high on its list of priorities. Nikkeiren successfully coordinated the interests of individual industries and firms to attain its strategic target and coordination of decentralised bargaining units emerged once again. However, it was the employers that took the initiative in changing an institutionalised compromise (Table 4.1).

Political and economic implications: competitiveness surge, but trade frictions

Changes in wage bargaining units in the mid 1970s had political economic implications. Wage compromises between capital and labour strengthened Japan's international competitiveness which led to intensified conflict with the US. Power over wage negotiations had shifted from the labour side to employers. Since then, wages have been determined at the initiative of employers. In addition, it was the export-related manufacturing sector, and not domestic market industries, that led in mutating wage and price settings: firms sensitive to their international competitiveness were playing a major role in setting wages across the economy. Furthermore, private-sector unions took the dominant position in wage negotiations. Thus labour force leaders began to share their employers' economic outlook and see their firms' international competitiveness as a priority in wage negotiations.

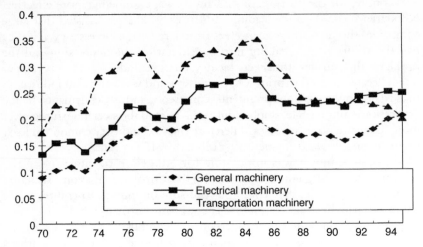

Figure 4.1 Export-output ratio, Japan 1970–1995. Source: *Keizai Kikakucho*, 1997.

In the mid 1970s bargaining units in larger enterprises adapted to international competition. This contributed to increased export levels from the mid-1970s to the mid-1980s; exports in the selected industries increased after the first oil shock in 1973 through the mid-1980s except during the second oil shock in the late 1970s (Figure 4.1). Exports to the US have accelerated since 1983 as a result of US monetary policy keeping the exchange rate of the dollar high.

Trade conflicts cropped up between two countries which were of critical significance in changing the Japanese financial system. In post-war Japan, the mobility of capital was controlled and less than perfectly mobile capital turned into productive resources in firms through the banking sector. Trade conflicts undermined domestic controls that linked capital to productive resources in firms. The US government started exerting economic and political pressure on Japan to deregulate domestic financial markets and internationalise Japanese currency with a view to reducing the trade imbalance.[6]

Changing financial patterns

In post-war Japanese industry, banks controlled the mobility of capital and linked money capital to firms' productive resources. Long-term loans offered through the MBS[7] discouraged firms from speculating in stocks or real-estate. The banking sector served as a kind of socio-economic infrastructure for firms to grow.

In the 1970s larger firms began to turn to financial intermediation, accumulating money capital, reducing the need to obtain external finance. They became less dependent on the banking sector even when they needed to obtain external financing. This led to dismantling the existing system by which it was the banking sector that injected capital into industry. This section considers how the relationship between them changed and how banks responded to the change.

Industry becomes more independent from the banking sector

Larger firms sought to reduce not only labour expenses but also financial costs and thus they reduced the size of external financing and searched for funds at lower costs. At the same time, domestic Japanese markets began to decelerate because of the economic stagnation since the mid-1970s. The annual average growth rate of sales in major firms dropped from about 16 per cent in 1965–73 to around 12 per cent in 1974–80. Consequently the growth rate of financing in larger firms drastically declined (Nihon Ginko).

As a result of the money capital accumulated in the 1970s and 1980s, it was less important for larger firms to raise capital from external sources. Internal financing accounted for 31.9 per cent of total fund raising (see Table 4.2), while external financing accounted for 47.4 per cent up to 1973. Since then the percentage of external financing declined and internal financing increased. The latter exceeded the former in 1981–93. Thus internal reserves and the ratio of internal reserves to net profits for the period both increased sharply in the latter half of the 1970s, declined in the early 1980s and increased drastically again until the 1990s (Figure 4.2).

In addition to reducing external funding, larger firms altered external fund-raising methods. Bank borrowing drastically declined from 38.9 per cent in the 1960s to 8.9 per cent of external financing in the 1980s. Financing via the stock market became more popular. Larger firms began to issue shares in foreign markets, taking advantage of deregulation since the 1980s. Consequently, firms in the industry sector were less dependent on the banking sector. The relative independence of larger firms from banks meant there was no longer a disincentive to speculate on the stock market. The percentage of financial assets as a part of total operating assets increased from 25.7 per cent in 1981–86 to 35.6 per cent in 1986–87 (Table 4.3). Basically, firms obtained financing at low interest and invested it to increase financial earnings.

Table 4.2 Fund raising in major enterprises (percentage)

	1965–1973		*1974–1980*		*1981–1993*	
Internal financing	31.9		39.3		56.9	
Internal reserves		7.9		8.0		11.5
Depreciation		24.0		31.3		45.4
Outside financing	47.4		45.0		34.8	
Banking borrowing		38.9		29.5		8.9
Corporate bond		5.3		8.4		14.5
Capital increases		3.2		7.1		11.4
Other	20.7		15.7		8.3	

Source: Nihon Ginko (various years).

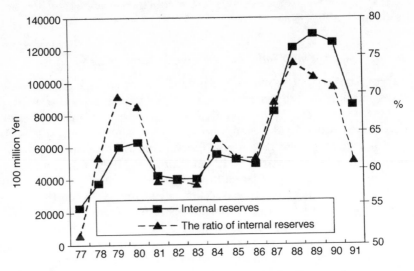

Figure 4.2 Internal reserves, 1977–1991. Source: Okurasho (various years).
Notes: The ratio of internal reserves = internal reserves/net profits for the period.
Net profits for the period = (current profits + special profits) – (special loss-corporate tax and tax).

The accumulation of money capital inside larger firms triggered changes in the relationship between banks and firms and bargaining units also became independent not only from the banking sector but also from the financial sector. Hence, the changing financial sector was unlikely to lead to immediate changes in the wage-labour nexus under the existing institutional framework.

Banks go into new business

These changes left banks with contracting lending markets and the nature of their competition changed. Banks lost major business customers and had to

Table 4.3 Operating assets in major enterprises (percentage)

	1965–1973	1974–1980	1981–1986	1987–1990
Operation funds	22.2	17.5	0.6	9.5
Inventory funds		14.8	14.3	−1.8	8.7
Mutual trading credits		7.4	3.2	2.4	0.8
Equipment funds	41.5	49.8	65.1	40.8
Financial assets operation	23.8	21.6	25.7	35.6
Cash and deposit		9.4	5.9	8.2	14.5
Short-term securities		2.5	6.2	4.1	2.9
Loans and investments		11.9	9.5	13.4	18.2
Other	12.5	11.1	8.6	14.1

Source: Nihon Ginko (various years).

develop a new customer base to replace larger firms by increasing loans to small and medium-size firms in the 1980s, from 51.8 per cent of total loans in 1985 to 70.3 per cent in 1994 (Nihon Ginko Kin'yu Kenkyujo 1995). In addition, city banks accelerated loans to real-estate agents in the latter half of the 1980s.

Equally important, major Japanese banks established local subsidiaries in foreign markets and entered the securities business in the 1980s. Securities firms simultaneously entered banking, meaning that banks were exposed not only to competitive pressure for loans from other banks, but also to competition from other financial institutions such as securities firms.

After 1986: a global regime change

The Japanese economy experienced soaring stocks and real-estate prices in the latter half of the 1980s. The Bank of Japan's policy of excessive monetary ease, along with the results of the moral hazard of commercial banks under government protection, caused rapid fluctuations in prices of stocks and land. However, economic actors were constrained by a particular set of institutional structures. Monetary policy does not always induce economic actors to behave in the same manner since policies are transmitted through institutional configurations. Institutional configuration, especially capital–labour compromises in bargaining units and the connection between bargaining units and the banking sector in the latter half of the 1980s, is an essential element in the analysis of inflated stock and real-estate prices. As seen above, it was actually the larger firms that took the initiative in institutional changes, establishing bargaining units consistent with international competition on one hand, while becoming less dependent on the banking sector through accumulating money capital inside on the other. Institutional changes had three main impacts on various economic actors. First, labour unions accepted wage settings consistent with their firms' international competitiveness. Second, there no longer existed a disincentive for management to speculate in stocks and real-estate. Third, commercial banks faced shrinking lending markets and a new form of competition.

How do these institutional changes relate to one another and what are the implications for monetary policy and asset inflation? The evolution of monetary policy with respect to land prices in the latter half of the 1980s can be grouped into three phases.

- Increased land prices since 1985 were triggered by the business concentration of urban functions in Tokyo. Land prices in the business areas increased by 28.8 per cent because Tokyo was expected to become a centre for international financial markets in response to the period of deregulation of financial markets. By contrast, the increase in land prices of residential and industrial areas remained single-digit until 1986.

- Faced with an economic recession due to the appreciating yen after the Plaza agreement, Japanese monetary policy reduced call rates to help ease the deflationary forces. This measure virtually assured a soaring number of loans by banks to real-estate investors in 1985–86. While the growth rate of all lending was previously around 10 per cent, lending for real-estate increased by more than 20 per cent in the same period.
- The Bank of Japan cut the discount rate to an unprecedented low at 2.5 per cent, immediately after the G7 Louvre agreement was announced. The feeling was that a further declining dollar was undesirable. This led not only to rising land prices in business areas but in residential and industrial areas as well since 1987.

The above picture could easily lead to the view that the Bank of Japan's policy of monetary ease, and the moral hazard of banks under government protection, caused soaring prices of land and stocks. However, asset-inflation must be coupled with the specific institutional context of monetary authorities and banks.

Wage moderation but asset inflation

Prices are indexes relevant to a financial policy and have an effect on the behaviour of monetary authority. Let us compare the evolution of consumer prices, wages, and prices of stock and land during two periods (Figure 4.3). In 1972–73, the Bank of Japan adopted an easy-money policy to prevent the

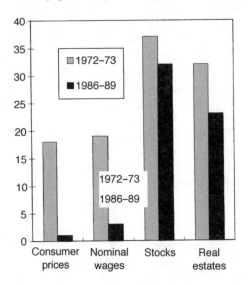

Figure 4.3 Growth rate of consumer prices, wages, stocks and real estates (per cent): 1986–1989 versus 1972–1973. Source: Okurasho Zaisei Kin'yu Kenkyujo (1993).

exchange rate of the yen from rising. Subsequently prices of stocks and land soared similarly to the latter half of the 1980s. In 1972–73, wages and consumer prices as well as prices of stocks and land increased dramatically, however from 1986 to 1989, the rate of increase in wages and consumer prices were moderate although prices of stocks and land rose. Apparently, bargaining units behaved differently and sent different signals to monetary authority in 1986–89 from those of 1972–73.

Another factor in the relationship between bargaining units and monetary authorities is the effect that the signal of a low interest rate policy has on the behaviour of management. As already seen, the disincentive for larger companies to speculate in stocks or land lessened as they became less dependent on the banking sector. In this institutional context the signal of low interest rate policy is likely to induce companies to speculate in stocks and real-estates.

Major funding sources for larger firms in capital markets in the latter half of the 1980s were capital increases, convertible bonds, and warrant bonds. Against the backdrop of soaring stock prices, the ratio of capital increases to external financing reached 34.3 per cent. Corporate bonds accounted for about 40 per cent of external financing, of which roughly 80 per cent was used for equity financing (Nihon Ginko). Firms speculated a considerable amount of the funds in equities and real-estate. The ratio of financial assets to total assets remained around 25 per cent until the first half of the 1980s although it fluctuated slightly, but it increased rapidly in the latter half of the 1980s and reached a little over 35 per cent (Table 4.3). Short-term securities increased largely due to booming investments in stocks. Major firms aggressively increased loans and investments in associated companies which deepened the interlocking shareholdings. Firms speculated in real-estate, leading to increasing land prices which in turn facilitated firms' borrowing from banks because of the increased collateral value of land. This spurred further speculation.

Easy monetary policy now means real-estate speculation

The signal of low interest rate policy, given contracting lending markets and intensified competition explained above, induced banks to increase loans to real-estate agents. There are two markedly different periods of evolution in the contribution of outstanding loans by major industries to money supply. Comparing the early 1970s and 1986–89, there is a striking contrast between the manufacturing industry and the real-estate sector. Lending to the manufacturing industry in the 1970s remained high although it was falling in the early 1970s. Therefore, money capital was still linked with productive resources in firms via the banking sector in the 1970s (Figure 4.4(a)). However, percentages contributed by the manufacturing industry turned negative in 1986 and remain negative afterward, implying that the banking sector did not serve as the medium that linked money capital to productive resources in firms (Figure 4.4(b)).

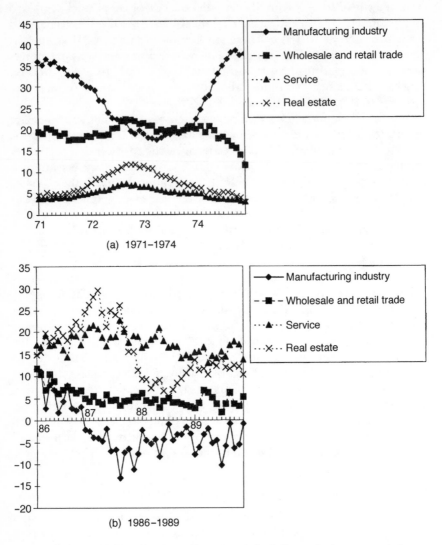

Figure 4.4 Contribution of loans to money supply by industry during two periods (percentage). Source: Yoshikawa, 1996.

In 1987, the highest percentage contribution can be found in real-estate. Prices of land soared in the early 1970s as they did in the latter half of the 1980s. However, the contribution of real-estate was roughly 10 per cent, in contrast to nearly 30 per cent in 1987, implying that the signal of low interest rate policy induced banks to increase loans to real-estate agents in the latter half of the 1980s unlike in the early 1970s. Apparently, the same signal (low interest rate) was received differently by the banking sector in the different periods. Institutions had changed, so had industrial structures. In this way, soaring stock and real-estate prices were the result of the Bank of Japan's policy of monetary ease coupled with the new institutional context. Different bargaining units for wage negotiation, a different banking sector strategy and transformed sectoral structures deliver an unprecedented financial economic pattern.

Conclusion

From the evolution of capital-labour compromises in bargaining units and changes in the financial system, some theoretical and institutional implications can be derived. A basic concern is the interrelated changes in the financial system and Japanese employment system, through compromises reached between capital and labour. Both internal and external factors acted as a trigger for changing the financial system.

A new institutional regime

Bargaining units responded to the international competitiveness in the mid-1970s. This contributed to increasing exports to the US and subsequently brought about trade conflicts between two countries which gave rise to external pressure on the Japanese financial system, as the US government pressed Japan to deregulate domestic financial markets. Second, since the 1970s when larger firms began to face a slowdown in domestic markets, they have made all-out efforts to cut financial costs as well as labour costs. This led larger firms to accumulate money capital internally and become less dependent on the banking sector. This brought an internal pressure for the banking system that was faced with intensified competition among financial institutions.

In conclusion, changes in the financial system were due to the fact that Japanese bargaining units became consistent with international competitiveness and less dependent on the banking sector. Thus, the interlocking relationship between bargaining units and the banking sector in the Japanese economy was attenuated; consequently, it may be inferred that compromises or agreements reached inside larger firms are likely to be maintained even under a changing financial system.

The current financial reforms are not necessarily a cure

The Japanese financial system is undergoing drastic institutional reforms that are designed to change it from a bank-based system to a market-based system. The question is whether problems concerning asset inflation can be removed by this financial reform. The basic idea behind this reform is that soaring prices of stocks and land in the 1980s were generated by the moral hazard of banks under government protection. However, as has been pointed out, asset inflation was brought about by a particular institutional context of bargaining units and the banking sector. The disincentive for larger firms to speculate in stocks or land is weakened. Contracting lending markets and intensified competition among financial institutions urged banks to increase loans to real-estate agents. As a consequence, the linkage between money capital and productive resources in the industry sector and the mediating role of the banking sector was attenuated. Accordingly money capital was poured into stock markets or real-estate. Hence, the central issue for the Japanese economy seems to be how money capital can be re-connected to firms' productive resources in the manufacturing sector. It is dubious whether the current reform will succeed in doing this, as it makes the financial system more vulnerable to speculation.

5 'Industrial welfare' and 'company-ist' régulation

An eroding complementarity

Masanori Hanada and Yasuro Hirano

Introduction

Fordist growth in most developed countries, including Japan, has been based on the consumption of goods and services by wage and salary earners. For proponents of *régulation* theory, the reproduction of social labour-power is a factor which lies at the heart of their analysis of modes of *régulation* and, in particular, of industrial relations. Patterns of consumption and forms of social organisation are two fundamental components of our subject. Indeed, the level of consumption is one of the key determinants of capital accumulation at the macro-economic level. This study hopes to provide the basis for further theoretical and empirical research, although it is limited to an examination of 'company-ist' *régulation* in Japan and of the situation and role of the Japanese company in this process.

The chapter first discusses theoretical issues about welfare and presents the resulting hypotheses. It then examines the specificity of 'industrial welfare' in Japan by means of an analysis of the composition of labour costs in the international context. In order to study the links between state social policies and company industrial welfare, it is necessary to examine the characteristics of industrial welfare in Japan and its inherent problems, the most serious of which are linked to company administered payments of retirement allowances at mandatory retirement age. Finally, there is an analysis of the problems resulting from the need to care for the elderly, a key factor which places constraints on company-administered industrial welfare in Japan.

Welfare in theoretical perspective

From an economic point of view, the successful reproduction of social labour-power depends on the workers obtaining and spending adequate revenue. Wages make up the bulk of revenue for wage earners and most expenditure is devoted to the household. However, as capitalism has evolved, indirect income has played an increasingly important role in providing social protection. At present, the reproduction of social labour-power is ensured not only by the distribution of revenue between capital and labour, but also by indirect income, deriving from the state, from companies and from the non-profit sector. Historically, state policies have played a crucial role in determining social policies, which have covered three principal areas of concern: work and employment, social welfare (including health, income support in the face of various risks, and social services), and finally, housing, education and leisure. These policies will be referred to as 'state welfare'. Complementing such governmental policies are other employment benefits, collectively agreed or determined by convention, paid for or subsidised by companies. Here these benefits are called 'industrial welfare'.

If one considers Japan in isolation, the expression 'company welfare' might seem more appropriate than 'industrial welfare' because in Japan, as will be demonstrated below, industrial welfare is provided essentially within the confines of the enterprise. However, in other industrial countries too, one can find various forms of income 'supplement' (or fringe benefits) often determined by convention or collective agreements within particular economic or industrial sectors. For this reason, both company and sector-wide policies (and the incomes they generate) are considered to be industrial welfare.[1]

The increasingly important role of indirect incomes in Japan can be easily demonstrated (Figure 5.1): social expenditure in relation to national income increased during an initial period because of health spending and later due to spending on pensions (old-age, widows', etc.). In considering the role of industrial welfare in the reproduction of social labour-power, it is important to clarify not only the way in which enterprises treat their employees (with regard to wages and employment), but also how it helps them individually and as members of a family. Moreover, while considering the beginning and end of an employee's working life, one needs to be aware of the links between each company and its social milieu.

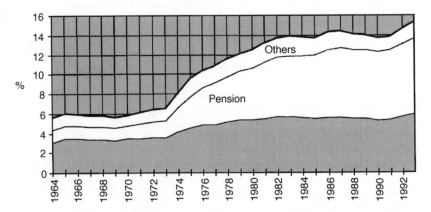

Figure 5.1 The evolution of welfare in Japan: 1964–1993 (spending on social protection shown as a percentage of Japan's national income).

'Life-course' is a concept often used in the analysis of social mobility of employees by sociologists such as Blossfeld (1986). A 'life-course' is determined by the character of individual people and by the circumstances (especially the job market). Here, the concept of the individual career is expanded to allow for the analysis of each stage of an individual's life. Thus, this expansion facilitates the understanding of the reproduction of individual labour-power and of industrial relations within the framework of the links between the state, the company and individuals (as well as their families).

The hypothesis of company-ist *régulation* is another key issue. The institutionalised capital/labour compromise represented by Fordism can be observed in the formation of the system of social protection and its development (Aglietta 1979; Delorme and André 1983). The provision of a guaranteed income for those who do not work, such as the unemployed and the retired, has been one of the essential elements of the mass consumption system since the Second World War and, along with mass production, has allowed for extraordinary economic growth. The social compromise in Japan has followed a course which has been quite distinct from Fordism (Hanada 1997; Yamada 1994): 1961 was a milepost in that the retirement system, a prominent feature of contemporary Japanese society, was extended to the entire population. Not until 1970, however, did the level of loans reach that of European countries. These simple facts make it impossible to make an analogy between the Japanese mode of *régulation* and canonical Fordism.

How specific is industrial welfare in Japan?

In order to analyse the Japanese configuration, it is necessary to make an international comparison of the relation between industrial welfare and direct income. Industrial welfare is not a phenomenon peculiar to Japan. However, if the company-ist *régulation* hypothesis is pertinent, one would expect industrial welfare to be more developed in Japan than in other countries.

Actually direct wages make up the bulk of the cost of labour in Japan (Table 5.1). Indirect salaries (including social security benefits and industrial welfare) are lower than in European countries except for the UK.[2] In fact, Japanese employees have relied on direct income to live, at least until the recent past. Direct wages have been the main factor providing them with security.

In 1984, industrial welfare constituted a bigger component of labour costs in Japan than in the UK, West Germany and Italy, but less than for France. Moreover, after the UK, Japan has the closest connection between industrial welfare and mandatory social security. The reason for the high linkage in the UK is the low level of social security contributions there, a fact which is explained by the peculiar system of social welfare in that country. Its resources are based more on fiscal solidarity[3] than on the insurance concept which is dominant in continental Europe,[4] as much for retirement as for health. This study is limited to those countries that have

Table 5.1 Comparison of the structure of labour costs in Japan and European countries

1975	West Germany	France	Italy	UK	Japan
Direct earnings	79.89	70.87	69.89	85.61	80.79
including payments of days not worked	12.8	9.34	11.77	8.9	
Statutory expenditure for social security	15.97	18.26	27.4	6.81	6.03
Industrial welfare	4.18	10.82	2.71	8.44	13.18
Total	100	100	100	100	100

1984	West Germany	France	Italy	UK	Japan
Direct earnings	76.5	66.9	72.3	82.8	79.75
including payments of days not worked	11.4	9.4	10.9	10.4	
Statutory expenditure for social security	16.4	19.4	32.2	7.6	7.58
Industrial welfare	7.1	13.8	3.1	9.9	12.67
Total	100	100		100	100

Sources: for Japan, Ministry of Labour; for European countries, *Labour Costs* (Eurostat).

adopted the social insurance system. This comparison is hampered by the fact that the statistics available for Europe and Japan do not permit a direct comparison between different countries. It will be necessary then to define industrial welfare from the statistical perspective and to modify the classification of available statistics in order to compare industrial welfare systems.

At least until 1979, the relative weight of industrial welfare was greater in Japan than in the other countries studied such as France, the Federal Republic of Germany, and Italy (Table 5.2). The total amount of industrial welfare in Japan is considerable and constitutes a particularly large portion of indirect income. It is true that the relative importance of industrial welfare has been decreasing steadily because of the increase in mandatory social security contributions. However, industrial welfare still constitutes a greater proportion of labour costs than mandatory social security contributions.

Relative weakness of social security and its replacement by company-level industrial welfare are characteristics often attributed to Japan, whence it is argued that industrial welfare is a substitute for public social security. This is not our hypothesis. Firstly, we shall compare industrial welfare as

Table 5.2 International comparison of industrial welfare (proportion of labour costs in per cent)

	Year	Manual workers	Non-manual workers
France	1975	10.0	11.8
West Germany	1975	3.9	4.5
	1992	6.0	8.3
Italy	1975	3.1	1.9
	1992	5.7	4.3

Source: Labour Costs, Eurostat.

part of the ensemble of state social policies (covering education, housing, health, old age, etc.). Then industrial welfare differs across companies and plays a role in the social integration of employees into their companies.

The company-ist system in search of interpretations

There are two raisons d'être for industrial welfare: one is the scale-effect of industrial welfare contributions, and the other is the reduction in company taxes derived from welfare schemes. That does not mean that industrial welfare is always systematically constituted inside companies. Industrial welfare can also be organised by profession, industry or region. In the US for example, the professional dimension is important, while in Europe it is the professional category (management or worker) which is of greater significance (Koike 1988; Inoki 1995). How is industrial welfare constituted at company level and how does it facilitate the integration of employees into their companies?

Two analyses may be taken as representative: the first is by Koike (1988) who seeks to examine the inculcation of skills from the perspective of the theory of human capital, and the second is by Lazear (1979) who attempts a theoretical analysis of the situation in the United States using economic rationality.

Industrial welfare as the consequence of skill formation: Koike's analysis

Koike explains the particular characteristics of lump-sum retirement allowances and compulsory retirement in terms of the practice of long-term employment and the extent of professional training. According to Koike, on-the-job training is more efficient than recruiting people who already have the required skills. Long-term employment is a necessary condition for in-house employee training. If this practice is entrenched in a company, there shall be no difficulty in offering industrial welfare (especially benefits in kind) to improve working conditions. Koike considers that in-house training and skill acquisition constitute investments which benefit both company and employees. While Koike's analysis is to some extent valid for Japan, he over-extends it by applying it to Western countries as well. Koike holds that industrial welfare for white-collar workers in other developed countries should be provided by companies. He argues in favour of a 'white-collarisation' of Japanese workers, since the employment system applies to all Japanese workers whatever their status (worker, clerk, etc.), while in the West the equivalent system is limited to white-collar workers.

Turning to Europe one finds that while it is not only white-collar workers who benefit from industrial welfare, available statistics show that white-collar workers receive relatively more from the system than do other employees. In Italy, the opposite is the case (Table 5.2 *supra*). In European countries, a portion of industrial welfare is provided by sector-wide collective conventions. Thus, industrial welfare cannot be seen as something provided exclusively by companies.

In France, as far as social security payments resulting from conventions, contracts or charities are concerned, collective conventions provide the basis for retirement pensions which complement the basic governmental pension (CERC 1986; 1987). Certain industrial pension schemes are federated nationally. Complementary pensions schemes have been made mandatory by law. There may also be 'super-complementary' pensions which may correspond to Japanese company pensions. This is often the case in big French industrial groups. For health expenditure, mutual benefit societies offer complementary coverage against risks not covered by the social security system (e.g. for hospitalisation, dental and ophthalmological care, etc.).

Moreover, there are two categories of benefits in kind, social services managed by enterprise committees and those managed directly by employers. Enterprise Committees are run by employers and employee representatives. They finance cultural, sporting and tourist activities as well as sporting and holiday facilities. Employers are obliged by law to contribute 0.2 per cent of their total wage bill. Any employer contributions above that amount are completely optional and left to the discretion of the company. The contributions vary enormously from sector to sector and also from company to company. The employees may benefit from enterprise committee payments which are above the legally required amount, from discounts when purchasing company products, from company housing for managers, company cars and other forms of transport, as well as from the payment of telephone accounts, etc. Since these benefits are classified as professional expenses, it is difficult to evaluate them. Thus, there are no reliable statistics.

Industrial welfare plays an important role in France (see Table 5.2). However, its role is significantly different from that of industrial welfare in Japan. First, the collective agreements for each sector, beyond the level of the individual company, play an important role in industrial welfare. Second, most forms of company level industrial welfare in each company are based on the participation of the employees in enterprise committees or on contractual arrangements.

If one follows Koike's reasoning, one reason for industrial welfare not being provided at company level would be the lack of in-house training in the absence of long-term employment. However, this analysis fails to explain the provision of industrial welfare at sector level. In short, the industrial welfare system cannot be explained in terms of in-house training alone. From the theoretical point of view, this means that the theory of human capital is not adequate for this topic. It is also necessary to take into account the 'path dependency' of the historic formation of institutions and rules. In France, collective agreements play an important role in the provision of industrial welfare and this is related with the type of labour unions and their historical evolution. Thus a historical perspective is necessary successfully to analyse industrial welfare.

Compulsory retirement age as a rational device for firms: Lazear's analysis

Retirement allowances and forced redundancies are often considered to be in the economic interests both of companies and employees. The latter will remain for long periods with their company if the retirement system is stable. Lazear (1979) analyses forced redundancies from the theoretical perspective based on the economic rationality of firms. Young employees usually receive salaries inferior to the results of their work (marginal labour productivity), while older employees will receive salaries superior to the results of their work. Consequently, once they have reached a certain age, they will begin to make up for the salary lost when they were young, and at a particular moment they will have made up for their losses. From that moment, their salary will be superior to their marginal productivity. At this point it would be beneficial for employees if they were to continue working, but not beneficial for the company. As a result, one can expect employees to be forced to leave companies at the very moment when there is an equilibrium between their accumulated earnings and the accumulated results of their working life in the company. Then, neither party will lose.

The retirement pension in American companies is the equivalent of retirement allowances in Japan and can be considered to be that portion of lost earnings which employees recover when they leave the company. In both cases, employment is seen as a long-term relationship, and behaviour is judged accordingly. This perspective discourages 'shirking'. Employees are encouraged to commit themselves to their work and to improve productivity. Accordingly, their wages are increased. On the other hand, the company will have an interest in laying off its employees the moment their salary overtakes their marginal productivity. However, it will probably not do so since such a practice could damage its reputation. In the labour market it would lose the trust of its employees and it would have difficulty in replacing them with new employees. Lazear's argument has two advantages: he has pointed out the economic rationale underlying involuntary redundancy, and the importance of productivity incentives. However, there are two weaknesses in his argument.

In the first place, with regard to the system of compulsory retirement, Lazear presupposes the existence of long-term employment, but does not justify this presupposition. He writes of the advantages to both company and employees of long-term employment. In fact, these advantages should be seen as the cause rather than the effect of long-term employment. He evaluates the length of service by using simple econometric equations based on factors such as sex, race, education and place of residence. To the extent that he neglects the issue of work organisation, which is of fundamental importance, this analysis is clearly inadequate. Moreover, the history and specificity of institutions has to be taken into account. For example, while in the US employees can be laid off in time of recession, the same people may later be re-employed according to the American seniority system. In this case the total length of service may be increased.

In the second place, Lazear considers that the system of compulsory retirement always has a rational basis. However the economic justification is not necessarily valid for all periods. In Japan, the retirement system appeared in the 1930s. Its appearance was determined by the process of industrial rationalisation and by worker resistance during that period. Economic logic was not the basis for the system, nor did the different parties justify their actions in accordance with that logic.

For all that, Lazear does not reduce everything to market mechanisms. He accepts the importance of the role of social and political conditions in establishing the economic system. He states clearly that the retirement age is not determined solely by market equilibrium, but by social protection, or to be more precise, the age at which benefit payments commence. He merely suggests the need for an analysis of institutional forms, but fails to address this need.

Retirement pension system: complementarity between corporate and public policies

The provision of a guaranteed income has been the principal element of policies designed to enhance the well-being of elderly people. Income for this section of the population derives from State retirement pensions and revenue from work, with some additional income from personal savings and help from family members. Elderly people have a choice between receiving retirement pensions upon stopping work, or continuing to work and receiving a partial pension. This choice should be made, insofar as social conditions allow,[5] according to their philosophy of life, the state of their health, their experience of life and acquired skills. In reality, this choice depends on the one hand on the level of the retirement allowance and on the other, on working conditions such as wages and working hours. With regard to Japan, one must take into consideration the system of involuntary redundancy at a fixed age. This system became very widespread after the war and it has been adopted by 90.5 per cent of companies employing more than thirty people. It must be noted that the retirement age in a company does not correspond to the age when one begins to receive the full retirement pension. The discrepancy between the two ages has a particular impact in Japan.

There was no legislation regarding the fixing of the retirement age until 1998, from which time companies could no longer make their employees retire before the age of sixty,[6] as they had been able to under earlier legislation. In 1994, 77.1 per cent of Japanese companies fixed their retirement age at sixty, while 7.1 per cent fixed it at more than sixty. On the other hand, 15.9 per cent fixed it at less than sixty. This last figure had been 36.1 per cent in 1990. This means that until recently there were a considerable number of employees who left their companies before the age of sixty. The retired employees cannot however receive their full pension until they are sixty-five. A transitory measure is in force which allows employees covered by the old system to receive full pensions at the age of sixty by means of a special allowance. In general, however there is a five-year gap between retirement and receipt of a full pension.

Financing retirement enhances companyist régulation

Historically, the system of mandatory retirement, combined with a retirement allowance, was introduced with the goal of strengthening the bonds between workers and their companies. Companies were faced with the task of having to train the skilled workers they were unable to recruit in the external labour market. This situation defines one of the special characteristics of Japanese capitalism which, in its so-called 'late-comer' phase, had only recently introduced advanced technology from overseas. At the same time, the retirement system played and continues to play a dual role, encouraging employees to work hard and at the same time discouraging them from leaving their company in mid-career (see Chapter 2). In this way, the system serves to integrate employees into their companies.

The amount of the retirement allowance is calculated by multiplying the basic wage by a pre-determined coefficient,[7] which is progressive as a function of seniority. Consequently, the longer an employee has worked for a company, the larger the retirement allowance will be. The mandatory retirement system does much to ensure that employees remain in the same company.[8] In other words, if employees change companies in the course of their professional lives, they lose part of the retirement allowance that they would have received, had they remained in the same company. Some calculations of the amount an employee would lose as a result of changing companies[9] are built upon two possible scenarios for a white-collar worker with a university degree. In the first scenario, the worker remains with the same company. In the second, s/he changes companies at the age of thirty-seven and works until the age of fifty-seven. In this latter scenario, the two companies involved are presumed to be in the same sector to avoid salary discrepancies between sectors.[10] The cost of retirement allowances includes company pensions, contributions to mutual benefit associations, and indemnity aid for small and medium-sized companies (Table 5.3).

What would occur when an employee of company Y1 moves to company Y2, where both companies are large-scale enterprises in the electrical machine industry? The retirement allowance for employees of Y1 after 37 years of service is 22,529,000 yen, and for Y2 employees after the same period of service, the allowance is 23,482,000 yen. There is not much discernible difference between these two large firms.

When an employee who has worked for fifteen years at company Y1 resigns to move to company Y2 at the age of thirty-seven, s/he receives a 2,855,000 yen retirement allowance. After twenty years service in Y2, s/he receives 11,405,000 yen. The sum total of the two allowances is 14,240,000 yen. This is only 63 per cent of the sum s/he would have received had s/he remained in Y1 without changing jobs.

A second example concerns a worker in the transport machine industry who moves from a large-scale company Z to a medium-sized company T. The retirement allowance for Z employees after thirty-seven years service is 23,600,000 yen, while for Y employees it is 20,748,000 yen. There is not much discernible difference between these two large firms.

When an employee who has worked for fifteen years at company Z resigns to move to company T at the age of thirty-seven, s/he receives 2,207,000 yen retirement allowance. Then s/he remains with T until the age of fifty-seven. After twenty years service in T, s/he would receive 8,263,000 yen. The sum total of the two allowances is 10,470,000 yen. This is only 44 per cent of the sum s/he would have received had s/he remained in Z without changing jobs.

Table 5.3 Difference in retirement allowance for various situations (in yen)

Electric machine company	Y1 (7000 employees)	Y2 (4500 employees)	Total of Y1 and Y2
The allowance of Y1	22 529 000		
The allowance of Y2		23 482 000	
Allowance when employee changes from Y1 to Y2	2 835 000	11 405 000	14 240 000

Transport machine company	T (550 employees)	Z (6000 employees)	Total of T and Z
The allowance of T	23 600 000		
The allowance of Z		20 748 000	
Allowance when employee changes from T to Z	2 207 000	8 263 000	10 470 000

On the basis of these two simplified examples, it would appear that changing companies dramatically diminishes the amount of the retirement allowance. Clearly the way of calculating the retirement allowance plays a decisive role in keeping employees in the same company, and thus serves to integrate them socially into their company. This is a compliment to the 'companyist compromise'.

Lump-sum retirement payments and public pensions

In Japan the lump-sum retirement payment (*taishokukin*) is the amount which employees receive at the moment when they leave their company. This sum is calculated on the basis of the length of service in the company. It is much larger than the retirement payments in European countries. Japanese employees who have worked for thirty-five years in the same company may receive between thirty-six and forty times their last basic monthly salary. The size of this payment compensates for the inadequacy of the public pension system. Surveys by the Labour Ministry show the costs incurred by companies in providing lump sum allowances and company pensions. Table 5.4 shows the cost of retirement allowances, pensions, contributions to mutual benefit associations, and indemnity aid for small and medium-sized companies; these costs were higher than the mandatory employers' contributions until 1988, and were at the same level in 1991. However, that does not necessarily mean that the amount employees receive in their retirement allowance is greater than the mandatory old-age pension. This is because employees too contribute an amount equal to employers and the scheme also receives government subsidies. For all that, company expenditure on the allowances and other related matters is still the largest component of industrial welfare spending (Table 5.5) – it is even fair to say that companies

Table 5.4 Employer contributions to the retirement pension and lump sum retirement allowance (in yen)

Size of firm	Employer contribution pension		Cost of retirement allowance	
	In yen	Relative to the large firm (more than 5000)	In yen	Relative to the large firm (more than 5000)
Overall	18795		18453	
More than 5000	22378	100	34257	100
Between 1000 and 4999	20249	90.5	20818	60.8
Between 300 and 999	18355	82.0	15204	44.4
Between 100 and 299	16229	72.5	10246	29.9
Between 30 and 99	16008	71.5	7735	22.6

Source: Ministry of Labour; *Survey of Social Work Establishments.*

Note
Distribution by size of firms.

Table 5.5 Comparison of family benefits, housing allowances, health costs and retirement allowance for 1983 (in yen)

	Family benefits	Housing allowances	Health costs	Retirement allowance
Overall	6,354	2,965	616	12,333
More than 5000			1,761	21,076
	9,136	3,280		
Between 1000 and 4999			714	15,483
Between 300 and 999			363	15,312
	5,200	3,200		
Between 100 and 299			182	8,830
Between 30 and 99	3,198	2,258	128	5,792

Source: Ministry of Labour *Survey of Social Work Establishments, Survey of wages and work hours.*

Note

Distribution by size of firms.

partly replace the state in guaranteeing an income for retired employees, at least in the interval between retirement and the time they begin drawing the public pension. Note that this system brings large inequality between large companies and small and medium size firms

Even though the public pension is in principle no more than proportional to the amount of basic contributions, it does play an important role in providing a basic income. It allows low-income people, the handicapped and widows, who have not made contributions for the stipulated length of time, nonetheless to receive a basic public pension. Company pension schemes never take such considerations into account.

Nevertheless, that part of industrial welfare concerned with providing a guaranteed income after retirement can hardly be considered to be completely independent of state social policies. To enhance the system of state social protection, legislation has partially integrated company pensions into the state system. This has been achieved in two ways:

- By means of the 'qualified pension',[11] which involves reducing taxes on company pension funds. There are a certain number of conditions that must be met before a company can benefit from this system.
- Through employee pension funds that are paid for by contributions from both employers and employees.[12] From the moment this latter system is introduced in a country, it replaces the public pension and at the same time adds a complementary pension. This system provides a substitute for that provided by state social policies and improves on the state system in a similar way to the national health insurance association.

In 1993, 35.6 per cent of those employees covered by the Japanese employee pension scheme (*kousei nenkin*) were also members of the employee pension fund (*kousei nenkin kikin*). Many of the employees making up that 35.6 per cent worked for large companies. Thus industrial welfare, particularly in the case of large companies, tends to play a complementary role to those state policies aimed at the provision of a guaranteed income for retired people.

The early retirement system

The ageing of employees in a company would result in an increase in labour costs if salary scales based on seniority were to be maintained. Introducing early retirement schemes provides one way of avoiding these increased costs. Company early retirement schemes involve offering employees a supplement to their retirement allowance if they agree to take early retirement (at the age of fifty in many cases). According to Labour Ministry surveys in 1994, 42.5 per cent of companies employing more than 5,000 workers have early retirement schemes in operation. The situation is similar for large British and German companies; employees are given early access to company pensions if they retire before the mandatory limit. However, for all the similarities the significance of early retirement is not the same in Japan as in Western countries, because in Japan the age when one becomes eligible for the public pension does not coincide with the mandatory retirement age.

In the US, company pension schemes define the age of both normal retirement and mandatory retirement. Reaching the former gives one the right to receive a full pension and it is forbidden to fix mandatory retirement at an earlier age than normal retirement. Professional pensions in the UK are linked to the public pension. The same can be said for complementary retirement schemes in France. The early retirement system guarantees income after an employee stops working. In these countries it is taken for granted that retirement will coincide with access to the pension. To be more precise, retirement from work is a necessary condition if an employee is to receive a pension. In the face of a high unemployment rate, early retirement often serves as an instrument of social policy (OECD 1995). The early retirement system allows companies to reduce labour costs. This is as true for other countries as it is for Japan. However, the social implications are quite different.

In Japan, industrial welfare is organised and defined principally at the company level. In as far as guaranteeing life after retirement is concerned, industrial welfare is not linked directly to State welfare. This fact explains the degree of integration of employees into their companies. However, this very integration results in careers being excessively dependent on companies and large inequalities among workers, according to the firm they work for (Tables 5.4 and 5.5, *supra*). Therefore, the practices and rules which determine industrial welfare in Japan should be seen within the context of the entire company-ist industrial relations system: industrial welfare and industrial relations are two coherent elements which together constitute the company-ist *régulation* mode.

Reform of the pension system and the raising of the retirement age

Since the inauguration of the universal pension in 1961, the public pension system has continued to improve with time. Elderly people can rely increasingly on the old-age pension as the amount of the allowance increases. Nevertheless, it must be noted that the initial amount of the pension is minimal: until 1965 it stood at 10,000 yen, more or less $28 per month. In 1973, the amount was increased to an average of 60 per cent of the average revenue during one's career. In 1986 a radical reform of the pension system came into force with the unification of seven pension schemes covering various professional categories into a two-tiered system. For all residents of Japan aged between twenty and fifty-nine, the reform created a national, mandatory basic pension with fixed contributions to which was added a pension for employees which was, and still remains, proportional to the amount of past contributions. This second pension is divided into two schemes: a general scheme for employees in the private sector (*kousei nenkin*), and a mutual aid association for public servants (*koumuin kyousai*). The amount of contributions is relative to wages and the amount of the pension is in principle proportional to the length of time one has contributed.[13]

There were two reasons for this reform: first, the need to eliminate the differences between the schemes and second, the desire to avoid a future financial crisis. Under the old system, the retirement pension is paid from the age of sixty, and under the new system from the age of sixty-five. Since the public retirement pension is insufficient, the lump-sum retirement payment is an important source of funds for elderly people, and is paid to those who reach the retirement age fixed by their company. At present, pension costs for companies have overtaken those of the lump-sum payments. In any case, the gap between retirement and receipt of full pension will oblige a certain number of people to work after the retirement age of their company. Because of this, companies have put into operation a means of prolonging contracts and of re-contracting people. However, in most cases re-employment involves a considerable drop in salary. Only 20 per cent of companies maintain the same wage level after proposing a new contract. Those who do not benefit from these measures may continue working for another company.

Conclusion: major challenges ahead

It has become clear that successful social reproduction is primarily, but not exclusively, company business, even though complemented by State policy. This is precisely the ' "company-ist" *régulation* mode'. This system has been effective and efficient until recently in increasing productivity and promoting mass consumption. But the rapid ageing of the population raises a problem which is difficult to solve. At present, life expectancy in Japan is almost eighty for men and is more than eighty-two for women. If men work until the age of sixty-five, they face the prospect of fifteen more years without work. There are three specific facets to the problem posed by an ageing society.

First, the provision of a guaranteed income after retirement is a question of redistributing money to elderly people within a capitalist economy. Second, it is necessary to offer health services to elderly people. Social insurance provides these services in Japan, and medical charges are reduced for people above the age of seventy. Third, even when medical treatment is ensured, provision of care and after-care for those who have been incapacitated by illness is needed. This conclusion considers the first and third facets of the problem in order to examine the possible transformation of 'company-ist *régulation*'.

Financing retirement: a challenge to industrial welfare?

The main issue involving the provision of a guaranteed income is the fact that on the one hand the right to a subsistence living is ensured by the public pension system, while the maintenance of a decent standard of living and the satisfaction of personal needs are ensured by individual savings and private pension schemes. The two-tier pension system, with a basic pension and complementary pension is in accord with this concept. However, this system is at present facing financial difficulties because of both the slowing down of economic growth and the ageing of the population. Consequently, public authorities are proposing to reduce benefits and to raise the age when benefit payments begin.

The principal role of the public pension system in the provision of a guaranteed income lies in the implementing of a system of inter-generational mutual aid. While most people in a market-led society who do not have an income, such as the disabled, the elderly, the retired and the unemployed, depend on individual savings or family aid, there are some who do not have these resources. In order to ensure that the right of all elderly people to a living is respected, it would be preferable to put in place a system which offered a minimum income without the elderly having to depend either on the family or on their past efforts. The social security system which is public and backed by the State is such a system.

In Japan, company pensions are being continually affected by changes in the industrial structure. In a declining industry, the fact that beneficiaries are numerous in relation to the total added value for a company will result in financial difficulties for company pension funds. If the present 'pay as you go' scheme is maintained, it is clear that there will be enormous difficulties in funding company pension schemes. If financial stability is to be given priority, a public pension will be preferable to company schemes. If the system is to a provide a guaranteed income for retired people, some reforms will be necessary to give stability to the system and to protect pension rights for all.

The present Japanese company pension system is based on the principle of shared contributions which are fixed through calculations taking into consideration factors such as the death rate, the level of resignations, the interest rate in the financial markets, and wage increases. These factors enable the fund to cover allowances which have been fixed in advance. When it is difficult to calculate the real results, there may be profits or losses for the fund. In the event of losses, it is the company which must cover the deficit.

When company pension funds use an alternative system, the fixed contribution system, the amount of the allowance will be the sum of contributions and the return on fund investments. In this case, there is no need for the company to cover losses even when there is a deficit. The risks are borne by the beneficiaries. Consequently, while this system is unstable from the perspective of the beneficiaries, to the extent that the amount of pension payments will be uncertain, it gives financial stability to the system. In any case, company pension funds are invested in the financial markets, where the security of financial products is traded off against their profitability. Investors put together portfolios with a view to achieving a compromise between risk and profitability. Intelligent fund managers should avoid speculative investments to minimise enforceable risks. But, if there is a large deficit which must be covered by the company, there may be considerable pressure to cover this deficit through further investment. High-risk investments may result in large deficits. These high deficits in turn increasingly lead investors to seek investments with higher rates of return but with a higher level of risk. Deregulation of pension fund investments may induce the managers of fixed benefit pension funds to follow this highly dangerous course of action. In a worst-case scenario, not only the financial equilibrium of the pension fund will be endangered but also macro-economic stability, since the total volume of pension fund transactions is sufficiently large to destabilise the financial markets. In order to protect the right to pension allowances, regulation of the reserve funds can be intensified and increased reliance can be placed on the payment certification system. Such measures would be of less significance for fixed contribution schemes.

Another factor to be considered is the transferability of pension rights within the fixed contribution company pension system. It will become crucial to the extent to which, in the context of the present crisis, restructuring of the Japanese economy leads to more job mobility. If emphasis is placed on the desirability of a pension fund being independent and transferable, then private pensions would appear to be preferable to company pensions. Company pensions do, however, have the advantage of being a tool for the management of labour. This is one reason for maintaining the system of company pensions.

As far as company pensions which are a type of private pension are concerned, it would be better if they were managed using the system of fixed contributions which would continue throughout the employees' working lives. However, the transferability of fixed contribution pension systems may serve to weaken the links between an employee and the company.

Consequently, the social integration resulting from company *régulation* may well be neutralised.

Care for elderly people: a clear limit to companyist régulation

As far as the two forms of social services provided for elderly people are concerned, home care is provided mainly by the public sector but the care offered far from matches the demand and retirement homes are more efficient than home care. However, in some Japanese urban areas, poverty is visibly present among the elderly. The problem of quality of care is ever-present with regard to retirement homes. The conditions for admission are stringent with regard to health and financial status. The decision to allow entry is not made by the institution itself, but by the Welfare Bureau. Consequently, relations between pensioners and institutions are often problematic. In short, the social services, which are the mainstay of social policy regarding the elderly, do not adequately meet the considerable and varied demands placed on them.

In this context, one can question whether companies can substitute for the state. While it is true that there are companies which do provide home care, they are very rare. While it is possible for companies to implement some measures such as introducing a system of leave enabling employees to care for needy family members, this would help only those elderly people who have family members who could help. However, at the present time when the nuclear family has become the dominant form, it is difficult to believe that such families alone can care for elderly people, and above all those with special needs. Consequently, it is left to the social services to provide relief for the families of the elderly.

What are the possible solutions? The market does not at present provide a convincing or viable solution since it does not furnish the necessary or appropriate information either to care providers or to recipients of care (Hirano 1996). Nor does it seem likely that companies have much to contribute in this area, since the need is for the provision of appropriate services rather than for the payment of monetary allowances. Companies cannot be expected to provide these services which are in fact rarely found anywhere and which demand skills unavailable in the business world.

It can be concluded then that it is necessary to implement effective care provision for elderly people along with some system of collective payment.[14] Company-ist *régulation* cannot cope with such a task. In the face of the present crisis in Japan, it is both desirable and necessary to integrate the welfare system into the demand regime.

6 The financial mode of *régulation* in Japan and its demise

Naoki Nabeshima

Introduction

Recently many *régulationist* studies on the post-war Japanese economy have been made following the usual viewpoint that places the wage-labour nexus in a key position (see, for example, Uemura, Isogai and Ebizuka 1996), so the financial analysis of the Japanese economy from the *régulationist* perspective remains undeveloped. Because modern capitalist economies are 'monetary production economies' with highly developed financial systems, monetary and financial factors play an essential part in their dynamics. Above all, it is difficult to portray economic conditions since the late 1980s without referring to the role played by the financial system. Therefore, in using *régulation* theory to further the study of Japanese capitalism, it is necessary to explain the role played by the financial system in the historical evolution of the post-war Japanese economic system. In addition, it is necessary to clarify the nature of the structural compatibility which existed among the various institutions such as the wage-labour nexus, the financial system, and inter-firm relations, which made up the Japanese economic system, and why this compatibility has recently declined.

A distinctive feature of *régulation* theory and other paradigms in the political economy tradition is that they try to explain not only the working of the market mechanism but the long-term dynamics of capitalist economy from a broad social and political perspective. One such factor is social conflict. According to *régulation* theory, there must be an 'institutionalised compromise' to mitigate conflict between social classes and groups, to ensure economic stability and to promote capital accumulation. When there is an agreement that reflects the relative power relations among competing classes and groups, social cohesion is realised for the first time. In the historical process of formation of a financial system, as well, conflicts between capital and labour, finance and industry, and among financial institutions also play an important role. Conflicts among classes and groups have affected the generation, development, and general transformation of the Japanese financial system. *Régulation* theory deepens our understanding of the contemporary Japanese economic crisis, providing some new insights into the effects of the malfunctions of the financial system on macroeconomic performance.

This chapter describes the financial system which supported the accumulation regime in the post-war Japanese economy, and explains the role of the financial system in the transformation of the accumulation regime after the 1970s. The primary analytical method used is *régulation* theory, supported by recent results of mainstream economic approaches such as Comparative Institutional Analysis.[1] The Japanese financial system is examined in terms of 'institutional complementarity', focusing on the relationship among certain elements of the financial system. From this perspective, the post-war Japanese financial system consists of: (a) intervention and regulation by the financial authorities; (b) the structure of corporate finance; and (c) the structure of corporate governance. The ensemble of these three elements is provisionally labelled a *financial mode of régulation*.[2] Thus, this concept includes not only the financial regulatory system in the narrow sense, but also any explicit and implicit rules, conventions and norms which create common standards to govern the behaviour of financial market participants. Using this key concept, the chapter sheds light on the financial aspect of the post-war Japanese economy and its crisis.

Financial mode of *régulation* in post-war Japan

The distinctive features of the post-war Japanese financial system are said to include the financial authorities' strong protection of banks, the important role of public financial intermediation, the bank-based corporate finance structure based on the predominance of indirect finance, and the main bank system (MBS). In addition, there was a complementarity among these elements which enabled the Japanese financial system to function smoothly and to support the investment-led accumulation regime. This section examines the financial mode of *régulation* in post-war Japan in terms of the three key concepts mentioned above and describes how they complement each other.

The post-war financial regulatory system

In post-war Japan, along with maintaining orderly credit conditions, one of the purposes of financial regulation was to foster economic growth, a role seemingly unique to Japan. It is often believed that the coordination of fund allocation through credit rationing under the so-called 'artificial low interest rate policy' played an important part in fostering growth.[3] According to this view, during the high growth period, this policy reduced investment fund costs for firms, and it gave priority to basic industries such as iron, steel, and shipbuilding in fund allocation. Moreover, public financial intermediaries such as the Japan Development Bank (JDB) played an important role in fund allocation.[4] In addition, the corporate bond issuing market was placed under rigid controls as part of the artificial low-interest-rate policy, so satisfactory development of the bond market was obstructed. Consequently, firms had to depend on borrowing to raise funds, and the 'bank-based financial system' was established.

As explained in the classic discussions by McKinnon (1973) and Shaw (1973), a decrease in the national saving rate retards production activity under conditions of 'financial repression', in which real deposit rates become negative because of high inflation. In contrast to financial repression, the government may execute a policy of so-called 'financial restraint' holding down nominal interest rates on deposit accounts while maintaining positive real deposit rates in order to create rents for the private business and/or banking sectors. Recently, some economists have argued that the post-war Japanese financial regulatory system, by realising moderate financial restraint, helped to improve the efficiency of financial intermediation and promote economic growth, making an important contribution to the formation of the MBS (Patrick 1994; Hellmann, Murdock and Stiglitz 1996).[5]

Another purpose of financial regulation is maintaining orderly credit conditions. In post-war Japan, the financial authorities used mainly competition-restrictive regulations and various safety-nets to maintain the stability of the financial system. The authorities implemented a 'convoy system' to protect even the most inefficient banks and ensure profitability by imposing severe restrictions on new entries into the banking industry, the opening of new branches, the development of new financial products, and the setting of deposit rates. As a result, financial disturbances were avoided. In exceptional cases when a bank did go bankrupt, stronger banks provided rescue loans or, under the guidance of the financial authorities, absorbed it.

Structure of corporate finance and corporate governance

Recent literature, focusing on the structure of corporate finance, usually classifies financial systems of various countries into those that are capital-market based and those that are bank based, then compares their relative efficiency. As seen in Table 6. 1, internal funds have been a main source for firms in many advanced capitalist countries throughout the whole post-war period. But their weight has been relatively low in Japan. As for external funds, securities are highly important in the capital-market based structures of corporate finance, such as that of the United States. In contrast, Japan, along with Germany and France, has a bank-based financial structure in which borrowed capital assumes greater importance.

It is often pointed out that the bank-based financial systems function more efficiently than the capital-market-based financial systems. In the market-based systems, the sales of bonds and stocks influence firms. In contrast, the bank-based systems presuppose that financial institutions and government have a say through their participation in corporate management by financial

Table 6.1 International comparison of the structure of corporate finance (percentage)

	Japan				United States			
	Internal	*External*	*Borrowing*	*Securities*	*Internal*	*External*	*Borrowing*	*Securities*
1962–64	39.4	60.6	46.6	11.0	76.0	24.0	11.3	7.9
1965–69	50.1	49.9	43.2	5.6	67.9	32.1	18.8	13.9
1970–74	41.6	58.4	50.0	5.7	55.1	44.9	25.6	18.0
1975–79	50.6	49.4	41.5	7.5	69.7	30.3	16.3	14.0
1980–84	59.0	41.0	35.0	6.2	74.2	25.8	15.5	9.5
1985–89	52.3	47.7	32.1	11.0	85.4	14.6	14.0	- 1.3

	West Germany				United Kingdom			
	Internal	*External*	*Borrowing*	*Securities*	*Internal*	*External*	*Borrowing*	*Securities*
1962–64	66.5	33.5	22.8	5.0	73.2	26.8	16.5	10.3
1965–69	68.8	31.2	20.8	4.1	74.1	25.9	14.6	11.3
1970–74	58.5	41.5	28.1	3.2	62.2	37.8	34.2	3.6
1975–79	72.6	27.4	22.3	1.6	79.1	20.9	16.4	4.5
1980–84	75.4	24.6	21.6	3.0	82.5	17.5	16.3	1.2
1985–89	78.6	21.4	16.5	4.9	63.0	37.0	26.1	10.9

	France		
	Internal	*External*	*Borrowing*	*Securities*
1962–64	54.3	45.7	35.6	10.2
1965–69	64.3	35.7	27.9	7.8
1970–74	46.8	53.2	34.7	10.3
1975–79	48.2	51.8	37.3	12.8
1980–84	41.9	58.1	41.9	13.6
1985–89	49.9	50.1	27.2	23.0

Source: Ito (1995: 145).

Notes: Trade credits are excluded. For West Germany, includes personal and public enterprises.

institutions and government. Whereas investment and production plans in bank-based systems are made according to long-term projections, in market-based systems corporate managers tend to have a somewhat myopic sense of judgement, and research and development and other productive investments based on long-term horizons are retarded. In addition, in countries with bank-based systems, bankers are very concerned about the long-term stability and growth of firms because of the close link between finance and industry. Therefore, these countries are more amenable to State interventions such as expansionary macroeconomic policies and industrial strategies. It seems that this is one of the factors which brought good economic performance in bank-based systems (see Zysman 1983; Pollin 1995).[6]

Corporate managers in Anglo-American type economic systems, in which firms raise funds through capital markets, are generally disciplined by stockholders' power and hostile take-overs. But in bank-based systems such as Japan's, the power of shareholders is extremely limited. In addition, the convention of interlocking shareholdings among firms strengthens the autonomy of corporate managers from shareholders. Therefore, in Japan, main banks have monitored corporate management on behalf of shareholders. Corporate managers accepted monitoring by main banks in exchange for full autonomy within their companies (Teranishi 1994: 78–80).

Existing research posits the following stylised facts regarding main banks: (a) main banks provide the largest share of loans to their customer firms; (b) there are interlocking shareholdings linking main banks and customer firms, with a corporation's main bank being its largest shareholder among banks; (c) the relationship between a main bank and a firm is generally long-term and stable; (d) the main bank maintains a personal relationship with client corporations by dispatching managers; (e) in addition to lending money, the main bank maintains a total transaction relationship with the customer firm by offering payment services, conducting the trustee business and so on; and (f) the main bank undertakes positive rescue operations if customer firms fall into financial distress. Many studies have both empirically verified the existence of these practices and applied theoretical analysis to describe main bank functions.[7]

Many researchers have recently analysed the Japanese MBS by focusing on its information production function (see Schoenholtz and Takeda 1985; Horiuchi and Fukuda 1987; Sheard 1989). According to this view, the main bank as an information producer screens and monitors the management conditions of customer firms on behalf of many suppliers of funds, and it transmits the information to other banks. This mechanism enables banks as a whole to save screening and monitoring costs. Further, in Japan, the main bank is both a creditor and a stable shareholder for firms. As a stable shareholder, the main bank usually defends customer firms from hostile takeovers. Once a firm falls into financial distress, the main bank actively intervenes in corporate management by means of rescue lendings, dispatch of managers, formulation of a recovery plan, and so on. Hence, in Japan, it has been main banks instead of the takeover market which monitored and disciplined corporate managers.[8] If information production activities of main banks have succeeded in reducing agency costs resulting from the asymmetry of information, as this view argues, it may have reduced capital costs accompanying external financing, and fostered the investment-led growth of the high-growth period (see Hoshi, Kashyap and Scharfstein 1991; Ikeo and Hirota 1992; Okazaki and Horiuchi 1992).

According to Aoki, Patrick and Sheard (1994), in order for the MBS to function effectively and remain stable, an adequate range of rents, or 'main bank rents', must be guaranteed for banks that undertake appropriate monitoring and rescue activities. One of the sources of such rents is the total transaction relationship listed above as stylised fact. The main bank is able to gain lucrative fees from transaction relations other than loans such as deposits and bond trusteeships. Another source of main bank rents is the protection of financial institutions by the regulatory authorities. Until recently, there were strict regulations on interest rates, new entries into banking business, and issuing bonds. The important rents generated by these regulations created strong incentives for banks to properly monitor customer firms and to rescue financially distressed firms. Further, private financial institutions could offer stable supplies of funds because they had confidence that the government and the Bank of Japan (BOJ) would protect them from bankruptcy.[9]

There were fears that the convoy system, by creating rents and protecting weak institutions, involved a high moral risk, but the regulatory authorities minimised such risk through strict auditing and detailed administrative guidance. In this sense, it can be said that there was, in the Japanese financial system, a complementarity between the structure of corporate finance and corporate governance on the one hand and the regulatory system of the authorities on the other hand. In this way, the MBS may have contributed to economic development in post-war Japan by reducing monitoring costs and social costs accompanying firm failures.

Post-war financial mode of régulation *and high economic growth*

In the post-war Japanese financial system, the financial authorities have maintained orderly credit conditions by means of interventions in the behaviour of individual financial institutions, using various competition-restrictive regulations and administrative guidance measures under the convoy system. Moreover, the authorities rescued financial institutions verging on bankruptcy under the principle of 'preventing any banks from failing', and therefore the authorities bore at the least a part of the risk. In addition, the authorities used the artificial low-interest-rate policy to create the state of moderate 'financial restraint', and thereby produced rents for the banking sector and the corporate sector. Through this mechanism, the post-war financial regulatory system gave banks and firms incentives to behave appropriately, and contributed to the stability and the development of the economy. The strict regulation of bond issues under this artificial low-interest-rate policy was one of the factors which encouraged the creation of the bank-based corporate finance structure. Consequently, main banks, the major sources of funds for firms, came to carry out the function of corporate monitoring.

In short, the financial mode of *régulation* in post-war Japan may be characterised by the disciplining of corporate management by the MBS and the socialisation of risks by the government and the BOJ. The financial system operated by this mode of *régulation* enhanced the efficiency of corporate management by reducing the agency costs accompanying capital procurement. It also supported the financial aspect of the investment-led accumulation regime by guaranteeing a stable supply of capital investment funds, including rescue lending, from public and private financial institutions. Therefore, it can be said that the post-war financial mode of *régulation* was compatible with the accumulation regime in the high-growth period.

It is worth noting that the post-war financial mode of *régulation* mitigated various social conflicts in the financial market. A firm and a bank usually belonged to the same industrial group, and they retained a close link through interlocking shareholdings. Main banks monitored firms in exchange for receiving a stable supply of funds. As a result, firms could conduct heavy investment and improve managerial efficiency. At the same time, the convoy system mitigated conflict between large financial institutions and smaller ones. The financial authorities set interest rates so that weak smaller financial institutions could survive, and gave priority to financial institutions for small business – *sogo* banks, *shinkin* banks and credit unions – in approving the establishment of new branches. These regulations protected individual financial institutions from bankruptcy and successfully promoted the stability of the financial system as a whole. In addition, there was little competition between the large and the smaller financial firms in the loan market because of the high corporate demand for capital to fund investment.

So, in the post-war financial mode of *régulation*, there existed institutional complementarity among three elements: ① active regulation and intervention by the Ministry of Finance (MOF) and the BOJ; ② the bank-based financial system; and ③ the system of corporate monitoring by the main banks (Figure 6.1).[10] First, regulation and intervention by the financial authorities influenced the formation of the bank-based corporate finance structure by restricting the development of the corporate bond issuing market ①. Further, the authorities created rents for the banking sector and the corporate sector by means of competition-restrictive regulations, the provision of safety-nets, the artificial low-interest-rate policy and so on. These regulatory arrangements

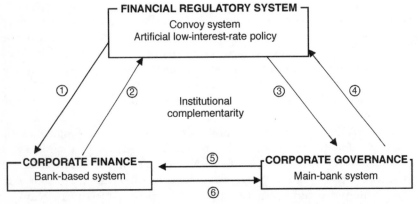

Figure 6.1 Institutional complementarity in the post-war financial mode of *régulation*.

gave institutional support to the formation and development of the MBS and the stable supply of funds under that system. In addition, the authorities controlled the moral hazard of financial institutions, using administrative guidance ③. Corporate monitoring by the main banks presupposed the existence of the bank-based system ⑥, while the establishment of this monitoring system further strengthened the bank-based system ⑤. So long as the system of corporate finance and corporate governance based on the dual MBS and bank-based system functioned effectively and promoted high growth, the authorities' strict regulations and interventions were not questioned, and were in fact legitimated ②, ④. In this way, the post-war Japanese financial system functioned smoothly, because its institutional and structural elements operated in harmony.

Collapse of the post-war financial mode of *régulation*

With the transition from the high-growth economy to the low-growth economy, the old financial mode of *régulation* began to decline. Financial deregulation after the 1980s facilitated the change in the behaviour of financial institutions, and exerted a strong influence on structural change in corporate finance. In addition, it has recently often been pointed out that the corporate monitoring function of the main banks is declining because firms are turning away from banks in fund raising. For these reasons, the complementarity among elements of the financial mode of *régulation* has disappeared, and various social conflicts in the financial market have intensified. At present, Japanese capitalism may have entered into the phase of a 'structural crisis' due to the loss of compatibility between the financial mode of *régulation* and the accumulation regime, and it is being forced to reform its financial mode of *régulation*.

Decline of the old financial regulatory system

In the late 1970s, the financial mode of *régulation* that had supported high growth for an extended period began to decline. First, the financial regulatory system became less valid, and then the system lost its ability to adjust to economic transformation. The crucial moments in this systemic weakening were the mass flotation of government bonds and the globalisation of financial transactions.

After the mid-1970s, budget deficits increased because tax revenues decreased as economic growth slowed. This fact is affirmed by the expansion of financial deficits in the public sector (Figure 6.2). The government floated a large volume of government bonds to cover these deficits, and it also fostered the development of the large secondary market of government bonds in Japan. In this situation, if interest rate regulations as usual had been maintained, investors would have shifted their assets from regulated bank deposit accounts to the repurchase agreement bond market (the *gensaki*

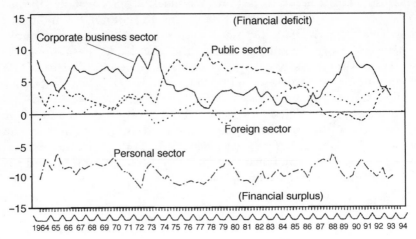

Figure 6.2 Sectoral deficits and surpluses (percentage of nominal GNP). Source:
        Nippon Ginko Kin'yu Kenkyujo (1995: 33).
Note: Three-period moving average of seasonally adjusted figures, with weight of 1: 2: 1.

market), a middle-term and long-term government bond market in which
financial assets had higher yields. As a result, the banks' share in financial
intermediation would have inevitably fallen. This phenomenon is generally
called financial disintermediation. In this case, it was favourable even for
banks to deregulate deposit interest rates in order to compete with expanding
security markets. In this way, the mass flotation of government bonds
necessarily produced pressure to deregulate deposit rates.

    Moreover, maintaining strict domestic regulations during the international
integration of financial markets would have driven financial transactions
overseas, bringing a hollowing out of domestic financial markets. In addition,
pressure from foreign countries, especially the US, to relax financial
regulation increased as Japan became more important in the world economy
and international capital flows grew. This institutional international conflict
was a second factor which facilitated the deregulation of interest rates.[11]

    These factors led to the gradual relaxation of regulations on interest rates
throughout the 1980s. Time deposit rates were completely liberalised after
June 1993, and liquid deposit rates were also liberalised after October 1994.
In addition, the mass flotation of government bonds after 1975 fostered the
transformation of the secondary bond market. Thereafter, various regulatory
measures on the issue and trade of bonds were gradually relaxed and
abolished. Consequently, it is to be expected that the rents which banks
enjoyed under the old regulatory system will decrease through the shrinking
of interest margins and other factors resulting from financial deregulation. As
a matter of course, the decrease of rents reduces the main banks' monitoring
capacity and incentive to undertake rescue operations for customer firms.
Further, corporate borrowers tend to turn away from banks as a result of

the deregulation of the corporate bond market, weakening the bank-based corporate finance structure.

It is important to note that the decreased main bank rents resulting from financial deregulation induced banks to indulge in greater risk-taking. This indicates that the financial authorities will need to reconsider their means of supervising and regulating financial institutions. Before liberalisation, various regulations and administrative guidance measures were used to control the moral hazard of financial institutions. But deregulation decreased main bank rents, thus reducing the capacity of the old system to discipline financial institutions. In addition, government-led rescues of bankrupt financial institutions are no longer feasible. In this way, the relaxation of competition-restricting regulations in accordance with financial deregulation makes it necessary to establish a new system to discipline management in financial institutions.

Firms' movement away from banks and weakening of the main bank system

In contrast to the expansion of public-sector budget deficits owing to slow growth, the financial deficits of the corporate sector nearly disappeared as capital investment stagnated (Figure 6.2). Consequently, the capital ratios of large companies, which had been falling until the mid-1970s, began to rise from the beginning of the 1980s. But financial deficits in the corporate sector expanded again in the late 1980s, during the boom caused by the increase in capital investment. However, the level of dependence on bank lending by firms remained low in this period because financing methods diversified and funds obtained through securities such as corporate bonds and stocks increased. In particular, the flourishing of equity-related financing by means of the issuing of convertible and warrant bonds facilitated the firms' movement away from banks. This increased element of securities in corporate finance resulted from the gradual advance of deregulation in security markets in the course of financial deregulation and internationalisation. The rise of stock prices at that time was one of the factors that accelerated this trend.

Table 6.2 shows the transition of the finance structure of large firms with more than 1 billion yen in equity. After the mid-1980s, the weight of internal funds rose notably. The proportion of borrowing fell remarkably, and fund raising through issuance of stocks and corporate bonds has been increasing. It may be said that the bank-based financial system which has characterised Japanese corporate finance structure is breaking down. The firms' movement away from banks, caused by the accumulation of internal funds in firms and the diversification of financing methods, is conducive to the dissolution of main bank relations. Firms are now able to invest without depending on borrowing. On the other hand, banks cannot but agree to finance projects that they previously would have rejected if they want to secure their positions as main banks. As a result, the main banks' disciplining function with respect to corporate management is weakened and it is expected that the resulting

Table 6.2 The financing structure of main enterprises

Years	Internal funds	Borrowings	Short-term borrowings	Long-term borrowings	Bonds	Capital increase	Trade payables
1960–64	22.9	33.8	20.3	13.4	6.8	10.8	16.2
1965–69	37.5	36.9	17.2	19.7	5.2	3.8	22.7
1970–74	35.1	41.6	19.3	22.4	5.1	3.2	21.9
1975–79	45.8	26.5	16.9	9.6	10.6	8.0	17.7
1980–84	55.3	16.4	9.9	6.5	8.5	10.4	9.6
1985–89	45.2	6.4	5.3	1.1	17.4	15.8	5.0
1990–94	87.3	5.2	−2.8	8.0	11.1	4.6	−7.1

Source: Shimizu and Horiuchi (1997: 100).

excessive finance will reduce the efficiency of corporate management. Some researchers have pointed out that there is a danger that 'soft budgeting constraints' on capital use may occur in many Japanese firms as a result of the relaxation of discipline by main banks (see Ikeo 1994b; Sheard 1994a). It seems that the excessive investment in the late 1980s occurred together with excessive lending by banks. As Ikeo argues, the systematic lowering of efficiency in Japanese firms is inevitable, as long as a new corporate monitoring system is not established in place of the MBS.

Collapse of the financial mode of régulation *and the contemporary crisis*

As argued so far, the decline of the old financial regulatory system was one of the factors that undermined the bank-based corporate finance structure and the MBS. At the same time, the breakdown of the bank-based system weakened corporate monitoring, previously carried out by the MBS. In turn, the increasing financial instability that has resulted from the decline of main banks has created additional pressure to reconsider the old regulatory system. In the course of financial deregulation during the 1980s and after, the institutional complementarity among the elements which composed the financial mode of *régulation* (Figure 6.1) disappeared. As these elements became less and less consistent, the capacity of the existing financial mode of *régulation* to support the accumulation regime decreased.

In the course of financial deregulation, the relaxation of competition-restrictive regulations induced excessive risk-taking by banks because it reduced main bank rents. At the same time, the monitoring capacity of main banks weakened because of the firms' movement away from banks. These phenomena show that the post-war financial mode of *régulation* itself, characterised by the disciplining of corporate management by main banks and the socialisation of risk by the public authorities, became dysfunctional. While the old financial mode of *régulation* collapses, a new mode of *régulation* has not yet been established. This lack of coordination in the financial system destabilised the real economy by encouraging greater risk-taking by both banks and firms, and brought about the abnormal event, expansion and bursting of asset-price bubbles in the late 1980s.

In this way, the recession that began in the early 1990s in Japan is led by the financial sector. Miyazaki (1992) argues that it is different from previous recessions, which had resulted from the insufficiency of effective demand. Even if the current depression itself is cyclical, it may be a symptom that Japanese capitalism has already fallen into a 'structural crisis' because of the malfunctioning of the existing financial mode of *régulation*. Even in the late 1990s, there has been no vigorous recovery, and stagnation continues. Thus, adopting Keynesian low-interest-rate policies is not enough to overcome this crisis; it is necessary to create a new mode of financial *régulation*. The present financial regulatory system, characterised by restrictions on competition and protection of financial institutions, must be reconsidered. It is also necessary to construct a new corporate monitoring system to fill the gap left by the decline of the MBS (see Nabeshima 1997).

During the process of the collapse of the post-war financial mode of *régulation*, conflicts among financial market participants intensified. Firms began to choose alternative forms of raising funds, weakening the close link with banks that had once existed. It is feared that this will weaken the monitoring function of the main banks, thus aggravating the agency problem between lenders and borrowers. The relationship between large and small financial institutions also changed. City banks and other large financial institutions, which lost their traditional corporate clientele due to the firms' movement away from banks, expanded loans for small and medium-sized companies in a search for new profit opportunities. Therefore, competition for loans between large and small financial institutions intensified. Some small financial institutions, their usual corporate client bases eroded, moved toward high-risk, high-return loans in sectors such as real-estate and non-bank financial companies. As a result of the burst of asset-price bubbles, they hold a lot of bad loans and verge on bankruptcy. In short, the destabilisation of the financial system that has followed the collapse of the old financial mode of *régulation* is a phenomenon caused by the intensification of social conflicts in the financial market.[12]

Conclusion

Asymmetric information and fundamental uncertainty are the inevitable plague of capitalist economies. In the real world, in which these problems cannot be avoided, various economic and social institutions act as the anchor for economic agents to make decisions and stabilise their expectations. The very existence of a stable institutional structure, promotes accumulation activities in capitalist economies.

The financial mode of *régulation* in post-war Japan has worked effectively because of the institutional complementarity that unites active intervention and regulation by the financial authorities, the bank-based corporate finance system, and corporate monitoring by main banks. Furthermore, this complementarity supported the monetary aspect of the accumulation regime during the high-growth period. However, the post-war financial mode of *régulation* became incompatible with the accumulation regime because the institutional complementarity disappeared during the transition to the low-growth economy. At present, Japanese capitalism is entering the phase of structural crisis. Therefore, in order to construct a new growth regime, it is essential to create new conventions, rules, and institutions to deal with asymmetric information and fundamental uncertainty: a new financial mode of *régulation* which conforms with macroeconomic structural changes to coordinate conflicts and enhance the stability of the financial system and economic growth.

Equitable and efficient credit allocation is evidently impossible if defending the old financial system or entrusting economic activities to the market. It is urgently necessary to arrange, by means of public regulations, that non-financial and financial firms conform to various social goals. We need to to realise the 'socialisation of investment' advocated in Keynes's *The General Theory*, in a modern way.[13] Agency problems may occur not only in the private economic sector but also in the process of planning and implementing state policies (Epstein and Gintis 1995b). Therefore, the new financial mode of *régulation* must resolve agency problems in both state and market.

Part III

What crisis and what futures?

7 The wage labour nexus challenged

More the consequence than the cause of the crisis

Robert Boyer and Michel Juillard

Introduction

Since the 1980s, academics and managers have come to admire the efficiency of certain Japanese economic institutions, in particular the employment system (JES), built upon employment stability, on job training and on seniority wage. A famous MIT report argued that employment stability was essential to the deployment of lean production and advocated the adoption of such a device by car industry firms all over the world (Womack *et al.* 1990). During the 1990s, outside Japan, most labour economists and managers have come to a totally opposite conclusion: life employment is obsolete and decaying under the pressure of numerous and converging factors. The recession that began early in 1991 would be clear evidence for the need for a shift towards a market-led capitalism, inspired by American economic institutions (Dornbusch, 1998). The longer the time taken to decide and implement this reform, the more severe the adjustment costs will be.

This chapter challenges this vision and argues that overemphasising the so-called intrinsic rigidity of life employment leads to a misreading and misrepresentation of the many tools available to cope with economic fluctuations, uncertainty and technical change: in fact, the Japanese economy exhibits a rich variety of such tools. Facing the atypical evolution of the 1990s, a central issue is the following: have the numerous revisions in the processes of hiring, training, wage setting and career pattern at the firm level constituted a shift or even a drastic transformation into macroeconomic evolution of employment, hours and wages? It is especially difficult to diagnose structural changes in historical real time: the complexity of the interactions operating since the 1990s and the lack of adequate statistical information for such a recent episode make the challenge even harder. The current situation demands a more hypothetical study. Do the current trends add up to a non-reproductive cycle? Do economic adjustments reinforce the past institutional architecture or do they stabilise it? Have firms and workers interest in discarding the past configuration. A brief conclusion points out that the WLN is in flux, but this is more a consequence than a cause of the adverse evolution of the 1990s. A crisis of the whole *régulation* mode is quite likely, but this does not necessarily involve a brusque collapse or a progressive convergence towards a typical market-led configuration.

Inefficiency and rigidity of the Japanese wage labour nexus: largely a myth

Within the American Fordist Wage Labour Nexus (WLN), business cycles or unexpected events are associated with hours variation and significant employment evolution. During recessions, layoffs are the first, frequently used tool, the more likely the longer the time horizon of collective agreements that set wage formation according to a given set of indexing variables. When one observes the Japanese labour markets in this light, there seem to be many factors blocking adjustments. However, the Japanese Wage Labour Nexus (JWLN) has numerous alternative ways of adapting. They might damage static efficiency by implying a short-term quasi immobility of labour in large firms but this in fact provides a strong incentive for product innovation and dynamic efficiency, i.e. cumulative productivity increases. This theme has largely been investigated by Chapters 1, 2, and 3. The following section focuses upon the capacity to react to recessions and macroeconomic shocks.

A series of adjustment processes during recessions

In the 1990s, the new forms of world competition and slow Japanese growth put strong emphasis on how the JWLN responds to stagnation and major financial uncertainty. Even if the Golden Years broke records in terms of the average speed and regularity of growth, firms relied upon built-in adapters to respond to recessions which are specific to the JWLN. In combination, these devices allow significant room to manoeuvre (Table 7.1). If the recession is rather mild, the firms may first reduce overtime and terminate the contract of temporary employees, which corresponds to phases I and II. If the slowdown is more significant and lasting, then they reduce the hiring of new graduates, begin to transfer some employees to other business within the same company group or outside the company, or strengthen the sales department (phase III). When the recession is still more severe, firms reduce working hours, temporarily close some plants or factories and launch restructuring operations (phase IV). If the situation worsens, firms completely stop recruiting, ask for voluntary redundancy and try to get into new business with a counter-cyclical demand or more promising future (phase V).

Compulsory redundancies are therefore the last-resort method to restore the firm's viability (phase VI). They are undertaken in Japan only when the situation is desperate, if for example the main bank is taking control of the company after a series of dramatic loses (Aoki 1988, 1993). Note, in passing, that previously the managers have cut their own salaries – an important difference in approach to Anglo-Saxon managers who frequently vote

Table 7.1 Compulsory redundancy is the last-resort instrument in Japan

Phase		
I	1.	Reduction of overtime
II	2.	Terminate the contracts of temporary employees
III	3.	Reduction of hiring of new graduates
	4.	Temporary assignment to another business area or group company
	5.	Transfer to other business
	6.	Strengthen sales
IV	7.	No overtime
	8.	Temporary factory closure
	9.	Restructuring
V	10.	No recruiting
	11.	Voluntary redundancy
	12.	Introduction of other new business
VI	13.	Compulsory redundancy

Source: Compilation from various company statements and academic research papers.

themselves hectic income increases at the very moment of firing workers to compensate when profits are insufficient, or even just lower than expected (Dore 1994).

In Japan 'mass lay-off should be regarded by management has a sign of its own failure' (Takezawa 1995: 22) and, on the other side, trade union officials consider employment stability to be their best post-war achievement, followed by improvement in working conditions – wages reflecting living expenses and length of service come in sixth (*ibid*.: 23). It is important to recognise that in Japan employment stability is at the core of a capital labour accord which was progressively built through history and reinforced after the first oil shock (see Chapter 1). This cannot be interpreted as a pure irrationality, since it is the building block for cooperation, acceptance of internal mobility and technical change, i.e. some of the core strengths of JWLN.

Of course, many social democratic countries, notably Sweden, had already established an equivalent compromise, concerning full employment rather than employment stability, before the 1990s. But these active government policies have been blown out by the inability of the existing *régulation* mode to cope with financial deregulation, changing forms of world competition and the discrepancy between the national style of *régulation* and the depressive forces brought by market-oriented *régulation* (Mjoset, 1995; Amable, Barré, Boyer, 1997). Under the same pressures, could the JLWN go down the same track?

Has the Japanese employment system come to an end?

'*Régulation* Theory' has developed a precise taxonomy for economic and social crises (Introduction; Boyer and Saillard 1995: 540–1). They may result from a purely exogenous transformation, or be the direct consequence of the ongoing *régulation* mode. Clearly, the trends observed in Japan since the early 1990s are not compatible with these two forms of crisis: the bursting of the bubble economy is a largely endogenous and domestic phenomenon (Chapter 6), while the macroeconomic evolution from 1991–99 does not exhibit a typical business cycle at all (Chapter 8). The crisis is thus, a crisis of the *régulation* mode, but it is important to diagnose its precise origin; either an internal lack of coherence in the JWLN, or incompatibility with the evolution of other institutional forms. These two hypotheses are investigated below.

Economic slow-down puts new pressures on most institutional forms

Back in the 1960s and 1970s, the JWLN configuration was calibrated and tuned in order to cope with the economic fluctuations associated with the *régulation* mode. 'Each society has the economic fluctuations of its economic structures', to quote the famous statement by Ernest Labrousse which was taken on board by *régulation* theory (RT) (Boyer and Saillard 1995: 21–9). The JES was then fully functional as far as the prevailing accumulation regime was concerned (Figure 7.1(a)). The virtuous circle linking on-the-job training, polyvalence, employment stability and workers' involvement used to allow rapid productivity increases and, after 1973, a renewal of products in order to maintain and extend the competitive advantage of the Japanese economy. Given the high growth rate and minor economic fluctuations, job stability was no constraint, but rather an ingredient for a high profit and high investment economy.

But the Japanese economy has become more and more dependent on the state of the international system and the evolution occurring in the United States. On one side, the yen was becoming a key currency around the mid 1980s and consequently, its exchange rate was no longer governed by the competitiveness of Japanese manufacturing but by the vagaries of international finance. On the other side, during the 1980s, just because banks and the financial system were piling up large reserves, minimal reforms took place under the general pressure towards financial deregulation. This led to an unprecedented speculative boom in which housing prices (OECD 1994: 76–119), stock market indexes and levels of private debt rocketed sky high. When the bubble burst, there were a lot of 'non-performing assets' burdening the financial situation of the banks and the manufacturing sectors.

Given this new context, the JWLN is submitted to unprecedented strains. Usually recovery was triggered by an export boom. In the 1990s, this source of growth was blocked by the very high yen/dollar exchange rate and by the de-localisation of production facilities abroad. This is bad news for the companyist compromise, since most Japanese exports originate from large corporations. Similarly, firms prefer to reorganise their balance sheet by reducing their debt instead of buying new equipment goods. This propensity is reinforced by the over-capacity inherited from the bubble years. Finally, the

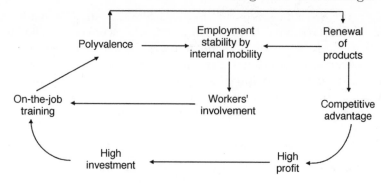

(a) Virtuous circle of Japanese wage labour nexus

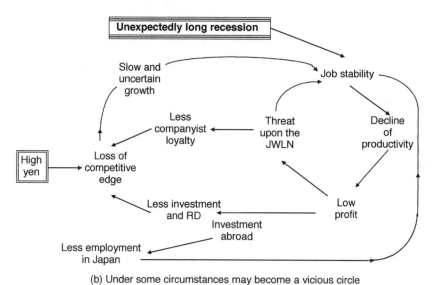

(b) Under some circumstances may become a vicious circle

Figure 7.1 From a virtuous circle to a structural destabilisation.

rapid adjustment of the real wage makes Japanese households cautious in their consumption decisions, whereas the relative recovery in the construction of private houses is not sufficient to compensate for other deflationary pressures. All these factors add up in explaining the absence of a strong recovery, in spite of four large public spending programs.

Thus, a vicious circle could now develop between the *régulation* mode and the WLN (Figure 7.1.(b)). An unexpectedly long recession reveals the static inefficiencies possibly associated with employment stability: productivity must be kept down in order to continue to provide the required level of jobs for core workers. Consequently, the profit rate is lower, even if it does not collapse, which in turn explains why investment is sluggish and why some firms cut their efforts in R&D expenditures. The structural component of the competitive advantage is therefore eroded. Similarly, the persistently high yen has a deflationary impact upon exports, weakening the price competitiveness of Japanese manufacturers. Under these very specific circumstances, some companies, especially foreign ones, may be tempted to renege on the implicit compromise of employment stability. Is this trend general or limited to some specific firms? A brief survey of the transformations occurring in the contemporary JWLN helps to answer this question.

Case for an epochal change: many firms look for new human resource management

Until now, analyses have focused upon major, society-wide transformations in institutional forms and macroeconomic regularities. But according to RT, a sharp discontinuity as acute as the great American depression is quite exceptional. Basically, a structural crisis can be diagnosed by the inability of existing institutional forms to channel the accumulation regime and the everyday economic behaviour of firms and wage earners. To derive possible global outcomes, it is therefore necessary to extract minute details of the JWLN from transformations occurring at firm level.

Division of labour experiences two major movements. On one side, white-collar employees are the main target for restructuring, contrary to what happened during *yendaka*. *De facto*, blue-collar work had been permanently rationalised but very rarely administrative and related work. In the 1991 recession, managerial, clerical, and sales work shifted from scarcity to oversupply (Japan Institute of Labour 1994: 2). On the other side, during the bubble years, some manufacturing firms pushed automation to a degree which nowadays appears excessive.

Labour mobility is enhanced by various measures: early retirement for top managers, restructuring the plant for Nippon Steel and Mazda, reorganisation of administrative work in Toyota, pressure for obtaining productivity from white-collar workers in Matsushita. Note that early retirement does not mean inactivity since most wage earners may continue to work for smaller companies. The 1994 reform of the financing of pension funds aims to extend the duration of activity over a life-time horizon. Again the dualism of the JWLN is important. A more surprising change relates to the routines for hiring new workers. Firms as important as Toyota do not ask any more for the name of the applicant's university, which seems to imply the development of specific selection strategies centred upon the precise needs of the firms and the talent and competence of the applicants.

Wage formula used to be fairly complex and specific to each firm in order to fit the productive organisation requirements, which may differ from one firm to another (Hanada 1992; 1994; Shimizu 1999). The transformations are twofold. For instance, Toyota's wage formula is drastically simplified while retaining the principle of seniority and remuneration of ability. Honda has implemented a totally opposite reform since pay according to seniority is banished and replaced by individual performance related pay. For Fujisu Daiei, the strategy is to negotiate individually annual wage increases in relation to competence. Some other companies do not seem to implement any major change for blue-collars' wages but rationalise the pay system for managers and clerical work (Nissan, Mazda). A final remark: some firms belonging to an internationalised group consider organising a competition between Japanese and foreign plants in order to get the same production done (Nissan, Kyushu). This means that in the long run, Japanese workers might be submitted to the same threat as the American and Canadian ones, facing possible de-localisation of production to Mexico.

The case study of Mazda allows a comparison to be made between the present period and two previous recessions (Boyer and Juillard 1995: 47; 1997). Given the fact that the ordering from 1 to 13 (see Table 7.1) reflects the severity of the reduction of sales, the 1991 recession is unprecedented; the firm was obliged to stop hiring and announced a program of job reduction for the years 1994 to 1996. No compulsory redundancy was required, but some recovery in sales did help. More generally, previously successful exporting firms experience unprecedented difficulties which induce them to screen out all their previous labour management routines.

From a more structural point of view, one could argue that the flux within the JWLN is so strong and permeating that new forms are bound to emerge from this trial and error process (Table 7.2). These numerous changes in labour management call for some interpretations. Do they represent a new epoch in the permanent (or more precisely recurrent) adaptation of the JWLN to changing internal and international circumstances, in such a manner as to avoid transforming the whole architecture? Or on the contrary, do these changes point out a radical move toward a totally new system and possibly a move towards an Anglo-Saxon WLN, governed by market relationships?

It is time to see whether all these changes observed at the level of scattered firms or anecdotal evidence alter the main macroeconomic regularities associated to the JWLN.

Do these changes show up in aggregate relations?

Let us take seriously the hypothesis that the capital labour compromise is irreversibly eroded by all the factors previously described. Then, the last four years from 1991 to 1995 would mean a phasing out of past determinants in employment, hours and wages, faster adjustments of both employment and hours and more competitive forces for wage formation. In order to check this prognosis, some recursive estimates have been run over the period 1965–95, using semestrial data extracted from OECD statistics.

Table 7.2 The old and the emerging wage labour nexus

The JWLN	→	Current disequilibria/tensions	→	New forms
1. Similar status for white and blue collars	→	Low productivity of white collars, high pressures on blue collars	→	Rationalisation of white-collar jobs, reductions of middle management
2. Synchronisation of hiring from Universities and schools delivering standardised basic knowledge	→	Need for a continuous hiring process of more diverse talents	→	1. 'Recruit the person needed when needed' 2. Look for specific competence and do not follow conventional university hierarchy
3. Professional training by internal mobility	→	Some skills nurtured by the firm may become obsolete	→	More eclectic approach to competence: in-house training, diverse background hired at mid-career, creation of professional tracks for specific skills
4. Institutionalised wage system based on collective competence enhancement	→	Excessively complex systems resulting from historical stratification	→	Either drastic simplification (Toyota) or bargaining of individual annual wage (Honda)
5. Synchronisation of wage increases across firms and industries	→	Due to industrial restructuring the productivity performances and abilities to pay are more diverse	→	Wage earners expect more wage differentials and enterprise unions may follow
6. Job stability for core workers but large variations in hours and for temporary workers	→	Reduction of stable jobs due to the new pattern for macroeconomic evolution	→	Add a professional labour market to the internal career Restrict job stability to core competence for the firms
7. Organised mobility within the large firm during the whole career including downwards	→	Growth slow-down makes adjustments more difficult Excessive diversification of production in reaction to job preservation	→	Mix internal mobility along with more active labour markets (mid-career change)

Employment: paradoxically more stability after 1973, but apparently no reversal after 1991

Employment in the manufacturing industry is assumed to adjust to significant lags according to expected and unexpected levels of production. Logically, firms should use hours to react to unexpected variations in production but expand employment if the growth in production is expected and still more considered as permanent. By lack of direct measure, expected output is estimated by a three semesters lagged auto-regressive model (Box 7.1). This is a simplified estimate based on the econometric study run by M. Hashimoto (1993: 153). Instead of estimating employment, hours and inventories, only the variables related to the JWLN are considered here.

Previous research had already pointed out the very slow adjustment process typical of the Japanese manufacturing sectors, with still more sluggish processes after 1973 (Boyer 1992: 46). These two results are confirmed here with other data. Three major conclusions emerge.

1. On an annual basis, the speed of adjustment of employment is extremely low since the lagging term is around 0.966. Japan is quite exceptional

---

Box 7.1 Econometric analysis of manufacturing employment

In order to get an idea about the adjustment mechanisms affecting employment, we estimate the following equation:

$$N_t = 0.159 + 1.783N_{t-1} - 0.817N_{t-2} + 0.004Q_t^* + 0.117Q_t^u + e_t$$
$$ (1.90) \quad (24.0) \qquad\quad (-11.3) \qquad\quad (2.1) \qquad\quad (4.32)$$

$$R^2 = 0.99 \quad D.W. = 1.99 \quad (t\text{-statistics in parentheses})$$

where N_t represents the logarithm of employment in period t, Q_t^*, the logarithm of expected production in period t, and Q_t^u, the logarithm of unexpected shocks in the same period, such that $Q_t = Q_t^* + Q_t^u$. Data run on a semester basis from 1965:1 until 1994:2.

Expected production is computed on the basis of the forecast of the following autoregressive model:

$$dQ_t^* = 0.01 + 1.50dQ_{t-1} - 1.211dQ_{t-2} + 0.501dQ_{t-3}$$
$$ (1.8) \qquad (14.1) \qquad\quad (-8.0) \qquad\quad (4.81)$$

$$R^2 = 0.79 \quad D.W. = 1.93$$

Unexpected shocks are computed as $Q_t^u = Q_t - Q_t^*$.

The graph of the Cusum statistic (Figure 7.2) indicates that this relation is most likely not structurally stable.

among OECD countries; no real surprise considering that the companyist compromise deals precisely with the issue of employment stability (see Chapter 1). Smaller firms also appear to adjust slowly to the variation in their environment. Nevertheless it is surprising, and not very convincing, that the impact of unexpected output is higher than that of expected output (0.117 versus 0.004). M. Hashimoto had already obtained such paradoxical results, i.e. the same impact for both shocks.

2. Running recursive regressions of the same relation, backward and forward, it turns out that the relation is probably not structurally stable all through the period (Figure 7.2, Box 7.1). The breakdown of the relation is likely to take place around 1974, i.e. after the first oil shock, which confirms some previous estimates. Elasticity in response to production shocks is particularly volatile, first it increases until 1974 and then decreases and stabilises according to forward estimates. The lagged coefficient for employment is higher after 1974, which implies a larger employment stability. The result interestingly contradicts conventional theory: given a clear slow-down in the growth rate and larger fluctuations firms should have tried to make their employment system more flexible. In fact what occurred was the contrary; here, life employment was reinforced in exchange for the acceptance of technical change, innovation and wage moderation.

3. No clear breaking-down had already happened after the 1991 recession. Statistical tests do not diagnose any structural change for the most recent period. The evidence gathered earlier about human resources management implies that there would be a higher speed of adjustment. By contrast, the first oil shock reaction was to strengthen job stability.

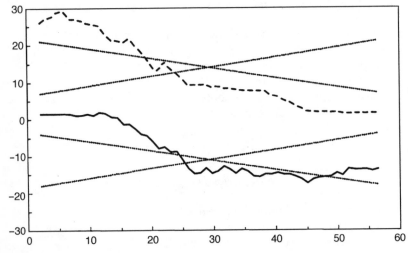

Figure 7.2 Cusum test for employment.

For the time being (i.e. only six semesters, the results still hold adding some estimates for 1994–95), there has been no renewed flexibility in terms of total employment manufacturing.

Some more desegregated statistical data confirm that employment tenure has not been eroded during the 1990s (Morishima 1995: 30). For both blue and white collars, large firms and smaller ones, the fraction of workers employed for more than 20 years has increased. Of course, given the succession of cohorts, an increase in flexibility might take place for incumbent workers only, shown by the fact that the fraction of workers with less than two years' seniority has increased from 1982 to 1992 between 2 or 3 per cent for each category. Clearly, if life-time employment is being eroded, it will take a long time, i.e. the successive generations of workers and the transformations of companies' human resources management. This could explain why these new policies do not yet have a visible effect on macroeconomic statistics.

Hours: significant flexibility used during the 1990s

When the same econometric exercise is repeated for hours, different results emerge but they seem to confirm again the strength of the companyist compromise. Of course, extra hours used to deliver an extra income to workers but it is clear that they have to be varied according to the demand addressed to the firm. There is thus a strong difference from European countries or North America, where work duration is the outcome of public legislation and/or collective bargaining.

Globally over the period, hours are more flexible than employment (Box 7.2). On one side, inertia of hours is smaller than inertia in employment (0.878 against 0.966 over one year period) and on the other side, the impact of unexpected output shocks is higher (0.185 against 0.117). This is a conventional property since it is easier to vary hours for workers already hired than to hire new workers, due to screening, hiring and training costs. This hierarchy is all the more important, the more uncertain the economic environment (Topel 1982). This is specially so for the Japanese WLN (Hashimoto 1993), near employment stability must be compensated for by more freedom to adjust hours.

Contrary to the situation with employment, there is seemingly no structural change for hours over the whole period 1963–93 (Figure 7.3, Box 7.2). Apparently, the elasticity of hours to deal with unexpected shocks of output is increasing at the end of the period but this does not yet show in statistical tests. Two opposed explanations can be given for such a finding: either it is an unfortunate property of the statistical tests, or it is the emerging, but still embryonic, evidence of a new pattern for hours management. It is especially difficult to detect structural changes in real historical time, a core difficulty for RT both from econometric (Juillard 1995) and from theoretical standpoints (Chartres 1995).

Box 7.2 **Econometric analysis of manufacturing average monthly hours**

We estimate the following equation:

$$H_t = 0.561 + 1.236H_{t-1} - 0.358H_{t-2} - 0.007Q_t^* + 0.185Q_t'' + e_t$$
$${}_{(3.47)}\phantom{ + 1.236H_{t-1}}{}_{(12.7)}\phantom{ - 0.358H_{t-2}}{}_{(-3.64)}{}_{(-1.92)}{}_{(5.43)}$$

$$R^2 = 0.97 \quad D.W. = 2.45$$

where H_t represents the logarithm of average monthly hours in period t, Q_t^*, and Q_t'' are as previosly defined. Data run on a semester basis from 1965:1 until 1994:2.

The graph of the Cusum statistic (Figure 7.3) indicates that this relation is most likely structurally stable.

These results are not so surprising after all since they express the core of the post-Second World War capital labour accord. When production slows down and stagnates in the 1990s, firms have an interest in, and are entitled to, drastically reduced working hours, since working time has always been flexible at the requirement of firms. Incidentally this is a direct consequence of the Toyotist model according to which production is demand-pulled and no longer technology-pushed (Coriat 1991). Working time must be adapted accordingly. On the other side, young workers have expressed a desire to have more personal time, whereas in the 1980s some unions had demanded larger

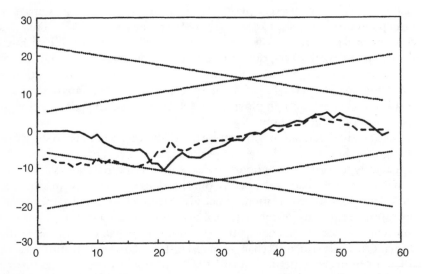

Figure 7.3 Cusum test for hours.

hour reductions to compensate for the reluctance of younger generations to take on manufacturing work. There is therefore room for drastic adjustment of hours, at the possible cost of less household income and therefore less consumption and domestic demand, if Japan were still a wage-led economy (Bowles and Boyer 1995). But it is far more likely that an export-led growth regime will come to prevail (see Chapter 3).

This flexibility in varying hours is usually reinforced by wage formation being highly sensitive to the macroeconomic context and the firms' financial position. Does the post-oil-shock wage formation still apply in the 1990s?

Wages: in-built flexibility muddles through the 1990s

Ideally, testing the stability of the JWLN involves econometric testing of wage formation according to the size of the firm and the status of workers (sex, education level), since this segmentation has been proved significant and important in explaining average wage formation (Ebizuka, Isogai and Uemura 1997). Here, the tests have been carried out only on the average wage following previous studies (EPA 1994: 176).

Over the whole period, the econometric tests do not reject the basic hypothesis derived from the JWLN. Any imbalance on the secondary labour market has an impact on wage formation. For instance, during the bubble years, labour scarcity triggered nominal wage increases, but conversely the slack which appeared afterwards curbed nominal wages. In addition, within the companyist sector, wage earners benefit from a form of profit or productivity sharing. During the 1990s, the phasing out of productivity induces a quasi-stagnation of the real wage (OECD 1995) and builds in another flexibility. These two factors satisfactorily explain the evolution of the Japanese average wage and point to more adaptability than typical Fordist formulae. This is an implicit advantage for the resilience of employment stability which would not be viable if wages were highly rigid.

The wage formation seems stable all over the period, with no clear breaking-down of the econometric relation (Figure 7.4, Box 7.3). Recursive estimates for the coefficient of labour market imbalance show first an increase at the end of the 1960s and then a decline after the first oil shock. Wage indexing is more difficult to interpret perhaps because such a mechanism is only indirect, contrary to what was observed in typical Fordist WLN. Note that the under-indexing implies that when consumer price slows down, wage earners may benefit from an extra real income, which provides a self-equilibrating mechanism against possible debt deflation depression 'à la I. Fisher' (Japanese industrial prices tend to decrease and consumer prices tend to be stable since the 1990s).

Contrary to previous findings by Japanese *régulationists* (Toyama 1994; Hirano 1994) it is difficult to perceive any strengthening of productivity sharing after the first oil shock, since econometric evidence is weak. Again this could be interpreted as due to the importance of employment stability,

Box 7.3 **Econometric analysis of wage determination**

The results of estimation are as follows:

$$\overset{\circ}{WM}_t = -0.016 + 0.067\,V_t/U_t + 0.769\,\overset{\circ}{PC}_{t-1} + 0.222\overset{\circ}{\Psi}_{t-1} + e_t$$
$$\underset{(-3.78)}{} \quad \underset{(6.28)}{} \quad \underset{(8.46)}{} \quad \underset{(2.82)}{}$$

$$R^2 = 0.84 \quad D.W. = 2.81$$

Where $\overset{\circ}{WM}_t$ indicates the growth rate of manufacturing nominal wage in period t, V_t/U_t is the ratio of the number of vacancies to the number of unemployed people, $\overset{\circ}{PC}_{t-1}$ is the rate of growth of the consumption price index in the previous period and, $\overset{\circ}{\Psi}_{t-1}$, the growth rate of apparent labour productivity in the previous period. The estimation was done on semester data from 1965:2 until 1993:2.

The graph of the Cusum statistic (Figure 7.4) indicates no suspicion of structural instability.

over wage increases for salarymen after the first oil shock. Nor is there any sharp break-down in the 1990s, which tends to invalidate the idea that there was a general change in wage formation, as was observed in scattered companies. Either they are atypical isolated cases or they have not yet had enough time to affect wage formation at the macroeconomic level. In any

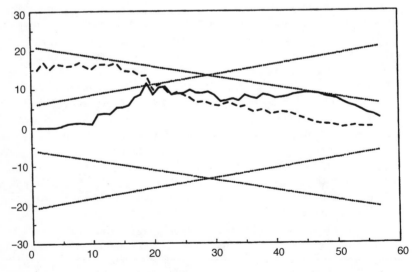

Figure 7.4 Cusum test for wage formation.

case, the vision provided by the business press seems quite over pessimistic, when seen against the macroeconomic record.

We are left with a puzzling paradox: drastic changes in the JWLN are taking place everywhere except in macroeconomic statistics! In any case, it is important to note that other research appears to confirm the view that the Japanese employment system has been less severely affected than financial and economic journals would represent. Internal mobility has been intensively used (Dirks 1999), in some cases the adjustment of employment has slowed down because it is the core of the companyist compromise (Morishima 1995), and the service sector displays structural flexibility due to a large variety of complementary labour contracts (Ribault 1999). Clearly, the Japanese employment system is in transition, but not in total or rapid transformation (German Institute for Japanese Studies 1997), and Japanese business management style is hybridising, by mixing contractual principles with conventional methods (Hasegawa and Hook 1998). The notions and tools of RT provide a tentative explanation for this discrepancy between seemingly stable macroeconomic regularities on the one hand, and organisational and institutional transformations on the other.

An unprecedented crisis of the *régulation* mode

Each structural crisis is largely specific to an accumulation regime and a *régulation* mode, the cumulative collapse of the 1929 crisis in the United States being an impressive exception, as then all the criteria for a structural crisis converged at once. The section below investigates three features of the contemporary Japanese economy: loss of stability of economic adjustments, counterproductive effects of tentative institutional reforms, and inability of private agents as well as public authorities to work out new compromise in response to the crisis.

1991–99: A non-reproductive cycle?

An economic fluctuation can turn from expressing a typical business cycle to triggering a cumulative depression when the production slow-down, the rise in unemployment, the stiffening of competition due to over-capacity and the financial bankruptcies, far from solving previous imbalances, end up exacerbating them. In more analytical terms, the recession no longer contributes to the self-equilibrating process of the profit rate. This is then a non-reproductive cycle (Bowles, Gordon and Weisskopf 1983) and it forces capitalists and workers to try to find ways out of the crisis through structural changes in the institutional forms.

If this framework is applied to the Japanese situation of the 1990s, the following hints emerge:

- Given the large flexibility associated with the JWLN, the economic slow-down has been associated with a parallel and highly synchronised evolution of productivity and real wage. The recession and stagnation does not seem to have created any strong imbalance in income distribution between wage and profit. This is important compared with the oil shock, for instance, which had induced a drastic and permanent decline in profit shares. The bursting of the speculative bubble did not trigger a cumulative erosion of profit share, but mainly decline and then stabilisation.

- One of the key determinants of an accumulation regime is the level and stability of the profit rate (see Chapter 8). In this respect, the present situation is far less severe than that observed after the first oil shock: the profit rate decreased from 28 per cent in 1970 to 14 per cent in 1976, i.e. it was halved. No surprise then if the accumulation rate was also halved, along with the growth rate, in accordance with the common teachings of post-Keynesian growth theory as well as classical and Marxian analyses. The profit rate recovered mildly, around 16 per cent, only at the end of the bubble years. Conversely, the profit rate in the present crisis has been declining moderately. The implicit growth rate associated with such a low profit is lower than previously, but there no cumulative forces appear to be in operation, which would imply a constant decline of profitability.

Thus, from a purely classical or Marxian point of view, the cycle beginning in 1991 is not at all exceptional and does not point towards a cumulative depression. Of course, some financial losses are not apparent and may trigger deflationist forces in the future, but they have been mitigated by the noticeable flexibility of the JWLN.

Diverging evolution between the wage labour nexus and other institutional forms

According to RT, a spectacular economic collapse is not a necessary condition to provoke structural crisis. Institutional forms are in fact continuously eroded by the very fact that the *régulation* mode is functioning. Therefore in the long run, the accumulation regime is not viable because of the vanishing of its prerequisites. A period of stagnation and slow decay of economic institutions is also a possible trajectory, which indicates that the previous accumulation regime is over.

What is the relevant evidence for the contemporary Japanese economy?

- Due to over-capacity in many manufacturing and service sectors, the well-ordered oligopolistic competition of the golden years has been replaced by creeping price wars. For instance in the distribution system new forms of organisation have stiffened competition and eroded the old system of mark-up pricing on top of official manufacturing prices.

Similarly, consumption has shifted from the search for status goods towards a more practical concern for quality and price. Consequently a slow and still embryonic process is under way in order to redraft the forms of competition. The pressures from American and European negotiators and World Trade Organisation reinforce these trends.

- The relationship with the world economy is changing too. First, manufactured goods exports are replaced by the overseas production of Japanese transplants, which in the long run could bring into Japan the same disease which eroded the competitive edge of the United Kingdom in the last century and the United States since the 1960s. Second, the exchange rate has ceased to be a policy instrument, given the importance of international financial markets. Therefore, the under-evaluation of the yen which benefited Japan's competitiveness back in the 1960s is replaced by an over-evaluation against the Dollar during the early 1990s. Hence, a likely de-industrialisation of Japan and the rising importance of the financial sector, that may bring a significant shift in macroeconomic trends.
- The links between the State and the economy have somehow changed. Even if Keynesian counter-cyclical policies have never played a major role in the dynamism of the Japanese economy, they used to exert some influence in smoothing short-term macroeconomic evolution. Surprisingly, many reflationary programs have been put into action throughout the period; in August 1992 (+ 2.3 per cent of GDP), April 1993 (+ 2.8 per cent), September 1993 (+ 1.3 per cent), February 1994 (+ 3.3 per cent), September 1995 (1.1 per cent) and, after a period of budgetary austerity in march 1997, the largest expansionary program took place in April 1998 (3.4 per cent). None of these plans has yet succeeded and levered the economy out of the stagnation (OECD 1998: 76–81). Basically, real income of households is limited, firms are restructuring their balance sheet and exports are limited by the current state of the world economy (de-connecting exchange rates from external trade, surge of foreign direct investment, emulation of competitors by the previous success of Japanese manufacturers). Thus, given the duration of the stagnation, public debt as a proportion of GDP is increasing: public finance is no longer self-balancing. This is indirect evidence suggesting a structural crisis of the *régulation* mode.
- The WLN is subject to contradictory forces. On one side, many firms have to innovate and reform their labour management, wage formula, skill training, etc. and the list of change is impressive. On the other side, no radical innovation has replaced the old configuration. Life-employment is a good example of this contradictory evolution. Whereas in 1994 many observers were forecasting a fast transformation in the direction of more flexibility, especially in terms of employment, the life-employment, supposedly dead or dying, JWLN was still used by many companies, including reluctant foreign multinationals. It is transforming itself but not collapsing. The way forward largely depends on the strategy

developed by the various economic actors: companies, new generations of workers, banks, public authorities and foreign governments.

Have firms and wage earners a common interest in breaking down the previous compromise?

According to a third definition of structural crisis, an accumulation regime and a *régulation* mode are bound to vanish when political, financial and economic actors are unable to manufacture any new compromise that would promote a new development mode. The issue is too ambitious to be dealt with fully here, given space restrictions and the complexity of Japanese politics. Therefore the analysis will focus upon the JWLN. Do companies and wage earners have interests in keeping the old configuration or do they automatically end up trying to formulate a new one? Basically the answer is not evident; unexpected events might tilt the balance of costs and advantages.

- Companies have an interest in keeping the JWLN if on-the-job training remains an active source of technical change, if coordination remains an important issue in some modern manufacturing sectors, and if the competency built upon the manufacturing of a product can be mobilised in the next production generation of this product or of related goods. On the contrary, firms will try to abandon the JWLN and especially life-employment in large companies if the stagnation period is long, if economic fluctuations remain large and difficult to forecast, if the Toyotist productive paradigm becomes obsolete and finally if younger workers are unwilling to enter the old companyist WLN.
- On the other hand, wage earners will be eager to keep the JWLN if they adopt a longer time horizon and not the short-termism typical of market-led economies, if they are still very risk averse and do not want to confront the basic uncertainty of a typical labour market, if large companies continue to provide a significant proportion of social benefits on top of general welfare (Chapter 5) and if no professional training system delivering transferable skills can be activated. Conversely, if new generations prefer to maximise revenue instead of security, if excluded minorities and the majority of women progressively challenge the ostracism they are victims of, if a new elite of professional, possessing very special and scarce skills decide to express fully their bargaining power then the JWLN could be replaced by other labour market institutions including, for instance, active professional markets. These trends nevertheless seem less evident in Japan than in other developed countries such as the US and France (Beffa, Boyer and Touffut 1999).

In either case, this is not a matter of months or even years but of one or several decades, the time required for any new mode of *régulation* to emerge and be put into action.

Conclusion: crisis of the *régulation* mode with uncertain prospects

Contrary to a quite conventional view, the minor role that external mobility and labour market adjustment plays in large companies does not mean an intrinsic and absolute rigidity. The JWLN allows a lot of responsiveness for firms facing economic fluctuations, uncertainty and technical change.

A puzzling paradox emerges from the present chapter: whereas many firms struggle to reform their labour management, either marginally or more drastically, these changes occurring at the micro level do not show up in macroeconomic statistics. During the 1990s, hours, wages, employment and unemployment tend to evolve more or less in line with the past; there is a functional synergy between companyism and the large pool of secondary jobs. The available evidence does not provide the means to discriminate between two opposing interpretations: either the institutional changes are actually minor and will remain so in the future with only a marginal redesign of the JWLN, or it is too early to diagnose the structural transformation that is already taking place but will become fully apparent in the course of one or two decades.

In spite of very active strategies designed to innovate and transform the Japanese employment system, conceptually it is difficult to perceive a follower. In particular, it does not seem that companies have an interest in totally abandoning the old system, whereas new cohorts of workers do not necessarily ask for totally new labour contracts but more likely for various adjustments to their aspirations and the present macroeconomic conditions. For instance, replacing the mix of companyist and secondary WLN by a professional market, similar to the German one, is not an easy task since it calls for an entire redesigning of the education system, firm organisation, wage formula, labour market and many related institutions.

This evidence leads to the conclusion that contemporary Japanese economy faces a crisis of the post-Second World War *régulation*. The strains upon the WLN are not its cause but the consequence of this crisis. Nevertheless, an old institutional structure is slowly decaying and large corporations and politicians are experiencing many difficulties in working out socially admissible compromises, which would deliver a more relevant *régulation* mode, tuned to the new financial, international and technological trends. Therefore, according to a Gramscian vision, an old system does not want to die, but a new one is unable to emerge. This explains the duration of the Japanese crisis and the crucial role of new political alliances, a quite general result indeed (Palombarini 1997; 1999). The fate of the WLN is largely undecided. It is open to the complex process of interactions between domestic alliances and international pressures and challenges . . . and this is not the first episode in Japanese history since the Meiji.

8 Growth, distribution and structural change in the post-war Japanese economy

Hiroyasu Uemura

Introduction

The Japanese economy has experienced very dynamic economic growth and several changes in growth pattern in the post-war period. The changes have been caused by the institutional transformation of the Japanese economy as well as shifts in the international environment. The aim of this chapter is to analyse growth patterns in the post-war Japanese economy, especially from the viewpoint of growth, distribution and structural change. A macroeconomic model based on Kalecki and Kaldor is used to analyse the relationship between growth and distribution. In this framework, investment is the driving force in the dynamics of capital accumulation. This involves 'putting the horse before the cart' (Gordon 1995a). The institutional arrangements of the Japanese economy will be examined in the framework of *régulation* theory, to create a bridge between macroeconomic analysis and the institutional analysis of 'the Hierarchical Market-Firm Nexus (HMFN)' examined in detail in Chapter 2.

First of all, this chapter proposes a structuralist model of economic growth that is closely linked to the institutional coordinating mechanisms of investment, labour productivity and wages. The framework is largely based on the recent development of structuralist macroeconomic models (Rowthorn 1982; Bowles and Boyer 1990; 1995; Marglin and Bhaduri 1990; Taylor 1991). Generally speaking, the relationship between growth and distribution is not uniquely determined, and it may form a certain regime, depending on institutional coordinating mechanisms in investment, labour productivity and wages. In this sense, institutional arrangements play a crucial role in determining growth patterns in all countries.

Next, the study conducts a long-term economic analysis of the Japanese economy, focusing especially on structural shifts in the growth pattern by using various macroeconomic data and econometric tests. During the high economic growth of the 1960s, the Japanese economy exhibited vigorous 'profit-investment-led growth' through the mass production and mass consumption of consumer durable goods, supported by specific institutional arrangements in the relationship between banks and companies. Wage shares fluctuated counter-cyclically, because the growth of product wages lagged behind productivity growth during expansions, and the deceleration in productivity growth was much greater than that in product wages in contractions. This was caused by increasing returns to scale and labour hoarding, the latter being a common phenomenon in large firms which maintained the long-term employment of core workers. High economic growth came to an end around 1970 because of rising wages and the saturation of domestic demand for consumer durable goods.

In the first half of the 1970s, the Japanese economy experienced sharp falls in the profit rate and the rate of capital accumulation, but firm organisations and subcontractor networks were effectively restructured to adjust to new cost conditions after the first oil shock. Thus, the HMFN was fully established with 'structural compatibility' between its components, and the Japanese economy started to show a new growth pattern. Efficient production systems realised high competitiveness in manufacturing industries and made it possible to increase exports, and the large volume of exports promoted vigorous investment. This growth pattern can be called 'export-investment-led growth'. It must be emphasised in this chapter that the HMFN sustained the expansion of exports in a way that helped integrate workers into firm organisation, coordinated wages flexibly responding to changes in the terms of trade, and promoted vigorous investment. In addition, the appreciation of the dollar promoted the exportation of industrial products in the first half of the 1980s. As a result, the export goods sector achieved 'cumulative causation' on the bases of the expansion of export and of investment.

In the first half of the 1980s, heavy investment coupled with an undervalued yen led to the creation of excess capacity. Then, even more excess capacity was created in 'the Bubble Boom' in the second half of the 1980s. Therefore, the rapid depreciation and scrapping of capital stock after the collapse of the Bubble Boom can be characterised as the prolonged adjustment of excess capital accumulated over the 1980s. In fact, the profit rate started to fall even before the collapse of the Bubble Boom, and it fell sharply in the recession in the 1990s. In these circumstances, one of the most important questions is whether the Japanese economy can maintain its growth potential and job-creating mechanisms.

Structuralist model of growth and distribution

The structuralist macroeconomic theory usually seeks to synthesise Kalecki and Kaldor based on the analysis of long-term institutional evolution. A particularly common perspective is to attempt to build a framework of macroeconomic dynamics by synthesising the logic of effective demand and the logic of capital-labour conflict under certain historical and institutional conditions. The structuralist macroeconomic model used here also comprehends the analysis of institutional evolution in 'the wage-labour nexus'. The determinants of the profit rate and of investment and income distribution are considered from the resulting perspective.

Profit rate

The pursuit of profit is the driving force in the capitalist economy, and the profit rate is a key category in analysing the accumulation of capital. The basic formula for determining the profit rate is given by the national account, as follows:

$$
\begin{aligned}
r &= \frac{p_x \Pi}{p_k K} \\
&= \frac{\Pi}{Y} \frac{Y}{X} \frac{X}{\bar{X}} \frac{\bar{X}}{K} \frac{p_x}{p_k} \\
&= \pi \cdot \beta \cdot u \cdot \sigma \cdot p \\
&= (1 - w_s) \cdot \beta \cdot u \cdot \sigma \cdot p \\
&= [1 - (w/p_x)/\lambda_n] \cdot \beta \cdot u \cdot \sigma \cdot p
\end{aligned}
\tag{1}
$$

The basic notations are as follows. r = profit rate, Π = real profit, π = profit share, X = real output (= real GDP), $\bar{X}$ = potential real output, Y = real national income (= real GDP − depreciation), K = real capital stock, β = the national income–GDP ratio, u = capacity utilisation, σ = the potential output–capital ratio, p_x = the prices of output (= GDP deflator), p_k = the prices of capital, p = the ratio of output prices to capital prices, w_s = wage share, w = nominal wages, λ_n = net labour productivity ($\lambda_n = Y/N$; N = employment).

Equation (1) is an identity at the macroeconomic level but there are several causal chains behind it. As Kalecki pointed out, investment is induced by the expected rate of profit, and, in turn, profit is realised by investment expenditure. Therefore there is a dynamic interaction between investment and profit that determines the level of capacity utilisation. Wages play a triple role, that is, 'a source of consumption demand, a component of unit labour costs and hence a deduction from profits, and an instrument in capital's labour-disciplining strategies' (Bowles and Boyer 1990). Therefore, the level of wages indirectly influences capacity utilisation and labour productivity. As argued in Chapter 2, the labour-disciplining effect may take various forms when the wage-labour nexus is highly institutionalised. Furthermore, the potential output–capital ratio is influenced by technological and organisational conditions in the production process and industrial structures.

Investment and savings

Investment is the driving force behind the dynamics of capital accumulation. According to the Kaleckian understanding of investment decisions under oligopolistic conditions, it may be assumed more specifically that investment responds to changes in both profit rate and capacity utilisation (Rowthorn 1982; Marglin and Bhaduri 1990; Taylor 1991). A simple linear investment function may be defined based on the gross profit rate, r^*, and capacity utilisation, u, as follows:

$$\frac{I}{K} = g_o + g_r \cdot r^* + g_u \cdot u \tag{2}$$

Here, I is real gross investment. $r^*(= r\eta)$ is the gross profit rate, where $\eta = (\Pi + D)/\Pi D$ is depreciation. Equation (2) states that the (gross) rate of capital accumulation, I/K, responds to (a) investment climate, in other words, the state of business confidence in the long term, (b) the (gross) profit rate, r^*, and (c) capacity utilisation, u. Investment climate, which is represented by g_o , is determined by institutional and social factors constituting the environment of capital accumulation rather than merely subjective factors. Above all, the overall stability of the financial system is necessary for this to be stable at a high level. The sensitivity of the (gross) accumulation rate to the profit rate, g_r, plays a very active role and varies with the changing expectations in the process of capital accumulation. Finally, the direct response of the (gross) accumulation rate to capacity utilisation, g_u, can be explained as an adjustment to maintain the normal capacity utilisation in oligopolistic circumstances.

As for saving, the Kaldorian saving function may be used (Kaldor 1978b). Namely, it comes from both wage incomes and profit incomes at the saving rates, s_w and s_r, respectively, as follows.

$$S = s_w \cdot W + s_r \cdot \Pi^* \tag{3}$$

where S = gross savings, W = real wage incomes, $\Pi^* (= \Pi\eta)$ = gross profit (including depreciation), s_w = the saving rate from wage incomes, and s_r = the saving rate from profit incomes. In the Kaldorian framework, $s_w < s_r$ is usually assumed, based on the understanding of different saving patterns between different income classes.

Investment and saving functions give excess aggregate demand. ED stands for the excess demand which is normalised by nominal capital stock, $p_k K$.

$$ED = g^* + (-p_x S + G - T + NEX)/p_k K \tag{4}$$

where $g^* (= I/K)$ is the gross accumulation rate, G = government spending, T = tax., NEX = net export. G, T and NEX are in nominal terms. The excess aggregate demand function can be written as a function of both $\pi^* (= \pi\eta\beta = (\Pi + D)/X)$ and u.

$$ED = g_o + g_r r^* + g_u u - (s_w W + s_r \Pi^*)(p_x/p_k K)$$
$$+(G - T + NEX)/p_k K$$
$$= g_o + g_r \pi^* u\sigma p + g_u u - s_w(1 - \pi^*)u\sigma p - s_r \pi^* u\sigma p$$
$$+(G - T + NEX)/p_k K \tag{5}$$

where π^* may be called 'gross profit share'. Therefore, the market-clearing condition can be written so that investment demand equals saving, namely, $ED = 0$. Under this condition, investment determines saving. The partial derivatives of ED may be obtained as follows.

$$ED_{\pi^*} = -(s_r - s_w - g_r)u\sigma p + \partial(NEX/p_k K)/\partial\pi^* \tag{6}$$

$$ED_u = g_r \pi^* \sigma p + g_u - [s_w(1 - \pi^*)\sigma p + s_r \pi^* \sigma p] \tag{7}$$

The effect of the change in profit share on capacity utilisation is determined by totally differentiating the equilibrium condition in the commodities market, as expressed by equation (5) and $ED = 0$.

$$du/d\pi^* = -ED_{\pi^*}/ED_u \tag{8}$$

In investigating the medium-term process of capital accumulation, it is assumed that capacity utilisation may be adjusted to narrow the gap between demand and supply in the commodities market, namely, $ED_u < 0$ (Keynesian stability condition). Under this condition, if $ED_{\pi^*} > 0$, the growth pattern is 'profit-led', and if $ED_{\pi^*} < 0$, it is 'wage-led' (Bowles and Boyer 1995).

Wage share, labour productivity and product wages

The determination of the wage share is a highly complicated process, because it depends on a lot of institutional factors. However, it is possible to identify some factors which determine the wage share.

$$w_s = (w/p_x)/\lambda_n \tag{9}$$

The wage share is determined by net labour productivity and product wages. It is very difficult to specify all the factors that determine labour productivity ($\lambda = X/N = \lambda_n/\beta$), but it is possible to identify several, including capacity utilisation, the unemployment rate (or employment rate), and the accumulation rate, which have their own time horizons.

$$\lambda = \phi(u, h) \cdot \lambda_0 \exp(\hat{\rho}(g)t), \quad \phi_u \geq 0, \quad \phi_h \leq 0, \quad \hat{\rho}_g \geq 0 \tag{10}$$

Equation (10) shows three factors which have an influence on labour productivity. First, in the short period, capacity utilisation, u, has a positive effect on labour productivity, λ. This effect is very strong in an economy such as Japan's that persists in 'labour hoarding' during recessions. Second, a decrease in the employment rate, h, might have a positive effect on labour productivity by the strengthening of the labour-disciplining effect of job-loss, which can be called 'the reserve army effect' (Bowles and Boyer 1990). This is not, however, always effective because the effect may be weakened in a highly institutionalised labour market. In this case, there may exist a 'functional equivalent' of the reserve army effect (see 'institutionalised job-loss costs' in Chapter 2). Third, in the long term, the growth rate of capital, g, also has a positive effect on productivity growth ($\hat{\rho}$ = the long-term growth rate of labour productivity). This is usually called 'the Kaldor-Verdoorn law', which can be understood to represent 'dynamic increasing returns to scale' (Kaldor 1978). As a result of those processes, the growth rate of employment is determined ($\hat{N} = \hat{X} - \hat{\lambda}$).

The factors determining nominal wages, w, and the relationship between nominal wages and prices depend on institutional conditions in the labour market as well as 'the wage-labour nexus' as a whole. Nominal wages, w, usually seem to be influenced by consumer prices, the employment rate, and labour productivity, but how those three factors influence wage determination depends on institutional arrangements in the labour market. The strength of the reserve army effect and the mode of institutionalised wage setting are the keys to understanding the determination of nominal wages.

Overview of economic growth in the post-war Japanese economy

Trends of macroeconomic variables

Through the dynamic patterns of macroeconomic variables: real GDP, profit rate, accumulation rate, wage share, capacity utilisation, the potential output–capital ratio and relative prices, it is possible to obtain an overview of the dynamics of economic growth in post-war Japan.

The average growth rate was about 10 per cent in the high-growth era, as the Japanese economy experienced the 'Izanagi Boom*' in the second half of the 1960s (EPA 1998b). The growth rate peaked in 1969, and fell sharply at the beginning of the 1970s before the oil shock. In the late 1970s and the 1980s, it was about 4 per cent on average, and the 'Heisei Boom'(= Bubble Boom) occurred in the second half of the 1980s. Then, the economy turned into a recession in 1991, and the growth rate stagnated at about 1 per cent during the recession in the 1990s.

The profit rate, r, calculated as net profits divided by the gross capital stock at current prices was quite high in the period of high economic growth, and was at its peak in 1969 (Figure 8.1). Since then, it has been falling generally. The Japanese economy has experienced two sharp falls in the profit rate in the post-war period. First, it started to fall at the beginning of the 1970s, before the first oil shock, and fell very sharply after it. Second, it fell at the end of the

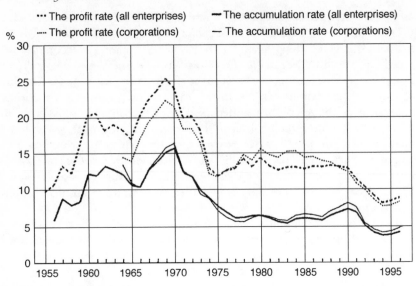

Figure 8.1 The profit rate and the accumulation rate. Source: Economic Planning
  Agency, *Annual Report on National Accounts* and *Gross Capital Stock of Private
  enterprises*.

Note: In calculating the accumulation rate, the data of gross capital stock are adjusted to remove
the effect of the privatisation of NTT and Japan Tobacco Industry in 1985, and JNR in 1987, etc.

1980s and the 1990s. The factors causing the falls in the profit rate in those
periods are revealed by analysing changes in the components of the profit rate
(Table 8.1). At the beginning of the 1970s, the decreases in profit share,
capacity utilisation and the potential output–capital ratio were the
contributing factors, and the falls in profit share and capacity utilisation
became remarkable in the process of the downturn in the first half of the

Table 8.1 Changes in the components of the profit rate

	$r\,(\%)$	$\hat{r}$	$\hat{\pi}$	$\hat{\beta}$	$\hat{u}$	$\hat{\sigma}$	$\hat{p}$	$\hat{\lambda}_n$	$\widehat{(w/p_x)}$
1965	16.9								
1969	25.3	12.48	8.74	0.05	1.85	−2.82	4.08	11.54	7.58
1973	18.3	−6.90	−4.67	0.54	−0.45	−4.22	1.69	7.04	9.85
1975	11.8	−17.67	−13.43	−0.86	−4.21	−1.92	1.08	1.01	5.81
1980	14.4	4.31	5.15	0.16	1.15	−3.01	1.34	3.47	2.05
1985	12.9	−2.14	−0.63	−0.12	0.06	−3.17	1.98	2.39	2.61
1988	13.4	1.29	1.71	0.07	0.28	−2.44	1.83	3.53	2.96
1994	8.3	−6.32	−4.63	−0.28	−0.84	−2.48	1.38	0.98	2.56

Notes:
Years shown in the table are the several turning points (peaks and troughs, etc.) of the profit rate.
 ˆ means the annual rate of change (%) of a variable from its level at the previous turning point.

$$\hat{r} \doteqdot \hat{\pi} + \hat{\beta} + \hat{u} + \hat{\sigma} + \hat{p}$$

1970s. In the fall in the profit rate around 1990, the fall in the potential output–capital ratio contributed a lot and both profit shares and capacity utilisation fell sharply in the recession in the 1990s. The rise in the ratio of output prices to capital prices has pushed up the profit rate during periods of expansion and has prevented it from falling in contractions.

The (net) accumulation rate, g, is calculated on the basis of the percentage growth rate of gross capital stock of private enterprises (Figure 8.1). It was fluctuating in a very dynamic way, mostly following the profit rate with a one-year lag in the 1960s. The accumulation rate reached a peak in 1970, then declined sharply in the first half of the 1970s. It increased again in the second half of the 1980s during the 'Bubble Boom', although the profit rate was rather stagnant. Then it fell quite sharply at the beginning of the 1990s, and has been at a very low level in the long-lasting recession. As a result of Granger causality test there was a close interaction between the profit rate and the accumulation rate in the period of high economic growth, especially as the accumulation rate followed the lead of the profit rate. In the 1970s and 1980s, however, the accumulation rate came to move independently of the profit rate, while the profit rate followed (Isogai, Uemura and Ebizuka 1999). The factors that influenced the accumulation rate itself in the 1980s are investigated in detail later in the chapter.

Wage share, $w_s (= 1 - \pi)$ is seen in Figure 8.2. The share of incomes of unincorporated enterprises accounted for a high percentage of national income in the high-growth era, so the result of calculations of wage share levels depended largely on how they dealt with the incomes of

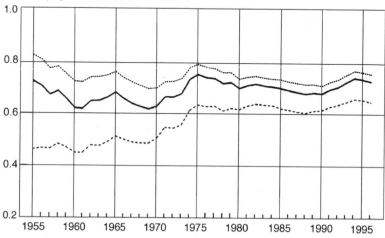

Figure 8.2 Wage share. Source: Economic Planning Agency, *Annual Report on National Accounts*.

unincorporated enterprises. In terms of 'employee incomes/(national income − unincorporated enterprises' incomes)', wage share slightly decreased in the period of high growth, rose considerably in the first half of the 1970s, and then stagnated again after 1975. This reflects structural shifts in the institutional arrangements of wage bargaining. Wage share has been quite stable since the late 1970s, and been fluctuating counter-cyclically over the post-war period in the Japanese economy for reasons given below. Net labour productivity λ_n, fluctuates pro-cyclically, because the job security of core workers results in 'labour hoarding' during contractions and a subsequent easing of labour costs during expansions. Furthermore, the economy realises 'increasing returns to scale' in expansions. Therefore, product wage, growth lags behind productivity growth in expansions, and the deceleration in productivity growth was much larger than that in product wages (Figure 8.3). This makes wage share fluctuate counter-cyclically in the Japanese economy.

Nominal wage growth was highly sensitive to the unemployment rate in the second half of the 1960s, so 'the reserve army effect' was sufficiantly strong (Chapter 2). However, this was not the case even with quasi-full employment in the late 1980s. Therefore product wages increased almost in line with labour productivity over the 1980s, and this was quite compatible with the export-led growth. This was ensured by complex wage coordinating mechanisms consisting of a profit sharing mechanism in large firms, *shunto*, and the flexible determination of wages of non-regular workers on the basis of the HMFN (Tsuru 1992a; Ebikuza, Uemura and Isogai 1997). In the 1990s,

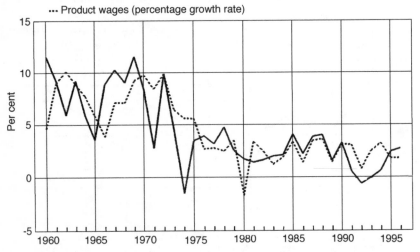

Figure 8.3 Net labour productivity and product wages. Sources: Economic Planning
Agency, *Annual Report on National Accounts* and Management and
Coordination Agency, Statistics Bureau, *The Labour Force Survey*.

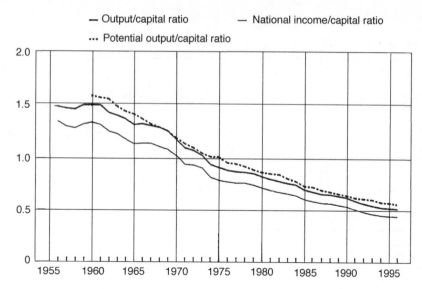

Figure 8.4 The output/capital ratio and capacity utilisation. Sources: Economic
Planning Agency, *Annual Report on National Accounts* and *Gross Capital Stock
of Private Enterprises.*

however, wage shares rose considerably, because labour productivity fell
sharply due to 'labour hoarding' in the severe recession.

Capacity utilisation, *u*, is especially important in investment decisions in the
manufacturing industry (Figure 8.4). It reached a very high level in the
'Izanagi Boom' in the second half of the 1960s, and then started to fall in
1969, which reflected the saturation of domestic demand. After the oil shock,
it fell very sharply, but started to recover soon in 1976. It reached a very high
level again in the 'Bubble Boom' in the late 1980s, but fell sharply in the 1990s.

Potential output–capital ratio, σ, has been decreasing continuously since
the high-growth era (Table 8.1 and Figure 8.4). It was especially remarkable
in the second half of the 1980s, as shall be explained in detail later in the
chapter. Relative prices, *p*, is the ratio of the prices of output (GDP deflator)
to the prices of capital goods (the investment goods deflator) (Table 8.1).
There were large decreases in the relative prices of capital $(1/p)$ in the second
half of the 1960s and the second half of the 1980s, and these pushed up the
profit rate. The changes in price structures seem to have been brought about
by great productivity growth differentials between the investment goods
sector and the consumer goods sector (Uni 1998). Reflecting these changes,
the ratio of output prices to capital prices has been increasing since the high-
growth era, and this has partly offset the effect of decreases in the potential
output–capital ratio.

Table 8.2 Saving function and investment function

(a) Saving function $S = s_0 + s_r\Pi^* + s_w W$

Dependent variable: S Period	s_0	s_r	s_w	$\bar{R}^2$	DW
1963–71	−2181	0.68	0.37	0.99	1.40
	(−5.7)	(9.0)	(7.0)		
1963–73	−1493	0.81	0.28	0.99	1.57
	(−5.2)	(13.0)	(7.5)		
1976–95	3502	0.65	0.28	0.99	0.76
	(1.8)	(10.6)	(8.7)		

(b) Investment function $I/K = g_0 + g_{r-1}\,r^*_{-1} + g_{u-1}u_{-1}$

Dependent variable: I/K Period	g_0	g_{r-1}	g_{u-1}	$\bar{R}^2$	DW
1963–71	−0.56	0.45	0.54	0.63	2.48
	(−2.9)	(2.5)	(2.7)		
1963–73	−0.52	0.23	0.60	0.62	2.28
	(−2.9)	(2.6)	(3.6)		
1976–95	−0.25	0.17	0.34	0.63	0.79
	(−3.3)	(3.2)	(4.2)		

(c) Net export function $NEX_K = nex_0 + nex_{\pi-1}\pi^*_{-1} + nex_{u-1}u_{-1} + nex_{e-1}e_{-1}$

Dependent variable: NEX_K Period	nex_0	$nex_{\pi-1}$	nex_{u-1}	nex_{e-1}	$\bar{R}^2$	DW
1963–71	−0.075	−0.19	0.12		0.30	1.87
	(−3.0)	(−1.0)	(2.0)			
1979–91	−0.187	0.77	−0.039	0.0003	0.65	1.54
	(−2.2)	(3.8)	(−0.7)	(4.5)		

Notes
t values are bracketed.
$\bar{R}^2$ is the adjusted coefficient of determination.
DW is Durbin–Watson coefficient.
S = gross savings.
Π^* = gross profit.
W = wage.
I/K = gross accumulation rate.
r^* = gross profit rate.
u = capacity utilisation.
NEX_K = net export (normalised by $p_k K$).
π^* = gross profit share
u = capacity utilisation
e = exchange rate.

Investment–saving relation and growth patterns

Table 8.2 reveals the results of investigating Japanese patterns of demand formation in relation to income distribution by conducting an econometric test on investment and saving functions, following the studies of structuralist macroeconomic models (Bowles and Boyer, 1995). In the estimation, the coefficients, s_r and s_w, in the saving function are not stable, and there is a structural change in the middle of the 1970s. Therefore, we performed a regression analysis on the data for the period in which the relation is significantly stable.

1963–71: a profit-investment-led growth

During this first period, both saving rates, s_r and s_w, are high, and investment is very sensitive to both the profit rate and capacity utilisation. The high saving rate is very characteristic for the 1960s. In the period 1963–71, the effect of exports was not significant, so it is sufficient to check the sign of $ED_{\pi^*} = -(s_r - s_w - g_r)u\sigma\rho$. According to the estimation, $-(s_r - s_w - g_r)$ $= -(0.68 - 0.37 - 0.45) = 0.14 > 0$. This means the rise in profit share leads to an increase in excess demand because of the high sensitivity of investment to the profit rate. Therefore, the growth pattern was 'profit-led growth' in the sense that an increase in profit share led to an increase in the accumulation rate. However, this result closely reflects the high sensitivity of the accumulation rate to the profit rate. Therefore, there is the estimate on the data for 1963–73 which includes a little more of the downturn in accumulation after the end of high economic growth, $-(s_r - s_w - g_r) = -(0.81 - 0.28 - 0.23) = -0.30 < 0$. This result indicates 'wage-led growth'. Therefore, the growth pattern was 'profit-led' in the high-growth era, but was highly dependent on heavy investment. In other words, it was caused by the high sensitivity of capital accumulation to the profit rate under the condition of the high level of capacity utilisation, because the saving rate from profit incomes was much larger than that from wage incomes. Therefore, more precisely this was 'profit-investment-led growth'.

The institutional arrangements that promoted the high level of investment in the high-growth era can be explained as follows. There was a high availability of capital provided in the form of indirect financing by banks. In particular, big companies enjoyed privileged access to funds by utilising their strong connections with a main bank ('keiretsu financing'). The 'keiretsu financing' was supported by the Bank of Japan that gave equal finance opportunities to each main bank. Furthermore, investment was promoted by fierce competition, and each business group pursued activities in a complete set of industrial spheres (Miyazaki 1985). The high saving propensity was another remarkable feature of the investment–saving relationship. First, the low level of social security benefits made it necessary to save more for one's retirement. The Japanese people did not have sufficient assets and housing facilities, so they were saving a lot in order to obtain the desirable level of assets and a house in future. Second, with unexpected high growth, people were likely to see much higher the ratio of transitory incomes to long-term actual incomes. In addition, the saving rate was usually higher from 'bonus' than other regular incomes. (Shinohara 1982; Yoshikawa 1995).

1976–95: wage-led growth undermined by an export-led growth

In the period 1976–95, both saving rates, s_r and s_w, become a little lower than those in the previous period, and the sensitivity of the accumulation rate to the profit rate decreases to a relatively low level. Accordingly, $-(s_r - s_w -g_r) = -(0.65 - 0.28 - 0.17) = -0.20 < 0$. This means that there was 'wage-led growth', if only investment and savings are taken into account. There was a structural change in the investment–saving relation in the middle of the 1970s. Another important factor in demand formation was the continuous increase in exports. Table 8.2 shows that net export is positively related to profit share. In other words, $\partial(NEX/p_kK)/\partial\pi^*$ is significantly positive, even if the maximum value of $u\sigma\rho$ in the relevant period is used.

$$ED_{\pi^*} = -(s_r - s_w - g_r)u\sigma\rho + \partial(NEX/p_kK)/\partial\pi^*$$
$$= -(0.65 - 0.28 - 0.17) \cdot 0.74 + 0.77 = 0.622 > 0$$

Thus, the pattern of demand formation is 'profit-led', when we take account of the effect of profit share on export. Therefore, the response of export to profit share offsets the 'wage-led' character of demand formation. As the contribution of export to demand formation became greater, the increase in profit share came to promote economic growth through export. In other words, the increasing weight of export undermined the basis of 'wage-led growth' even with the low sensitivity of investment to the profit rate. Later in the chapter the dynamics of the 'export-led growth' in the 1980s, especially based on the analysis of institutional arrangements, are examined in more detail.

Productivity growth and employment

As mentioned above, labour productivity is influenced strongly by capacity utilisation in a business cycle. It fluctuates pro-cyclically, especially in the Japanese economy. Beside this short-term relation, capital accumulation promotes productivity growth through 'dynamic increasing returns to scale', and this also determines the trend of employment growth in the long run. This section investigates the pattern of productivity growth in relation to capital accumulation and employment from a long-term perspective.

In order to obtain a long-term relation, capital stock is adjusted by three-year moving average, and labour productivity is calculated at a full capacity level and also adjusted by this three-year moving average (Figure 8.5).

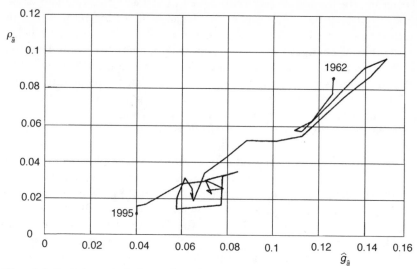

Figure 8.5 Capital accumulation and productivity growth (the economy as a whole).

Notes:

$g_{\hat{a}}$: the growth of capital (adjusted by three-year moving average)

ρ_a: the growth rate of productivity at the full capacity level (adjusted by the three-year moving average)

1962–95 $\hat{\rho}_a = -0.026 + 0.79\,\hat{g}_a$ $\bar{R}^2 = 0.93$
  $\quad\quad\quad (-7.45)\quad (20.7)$

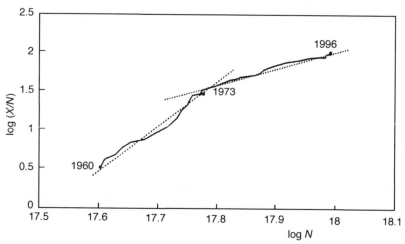

Figure 8.6 Labour productivity and employment.

Notes:

X/N: labour productivity, N: employment (including the self-employed)

1960–72 $\log(X/N) = -92.3 + 5.27\,\log N$ $\bar{R}^2 = 0.96$
  $\quad\quad\quad\quad (-17.9)\quad (18.1)$

1979–96 $\log(X/N) = -33.9 + 1.99\,\log N$ $\bar{R}^2 = 0.97$
  $\quad\quad\quad\quad (-22.7)\quad (23.9)$

Therefore, the long-term relation between capital accumulation and labour productivity can be understood as the dynamic increasing returns to scale. According to the CUSUM test, the relation is structurally stable, and there is no structural change. On close examination, there are some irregular movements and divergences from the trend in the second half of the 1980s, reflecting some increases in private capital stock due to the privatisation of public enterprises, but the relation returns to the long-term trend in the 1990s. In other words, there is no structural change in the relationship between capital accumulation and productivity growth even in the severe 1990s recession.

The relationship between productivity growth and employment growth is shown from a long-term perspective (Figure 8.6). According to the CUSUM test, the relation is not structurally stable in the period, 1960–96. Checking recursive estimates, there is a structural change in the middle of the 1970s, which seems to be brought about by the full establishment of complex coordinating mechanisms to maintain employment, explained in Chapter 2, and the expansion of the service sector. The economy has created jobs with a relatively low level of productivity growth since the 1970s. In the period, 1979–96, the relation is structurally stable, according to the CUSUM test. There appears to be no structural change in the potential ability to create a job at macro level even in the 1990s recession. The problem is the low level of economic growth.

Growth regime after the oil shock

From an institutional perspective, it is important that the HMFN was fully established at the same time as the growth regime underwent a structural change in the 1970s. This section analyses the dynamic logic of capital accumulation, especially in relation to the institutional analysis of the HMFN (Chapter 2).

Dynamic logic of capital accumulation based on institutional arrangements after the 1970s

To present a macroeconomic framework for examining the growth regime that was established after the oil shock, two points are especially important (Figure 8.7). One is the transformation into export-investment-led growth, and the other is the evolution of domestic demand structures.

The transformation of the growth regime in the 1970s has already been examined in the analysis of investment-saving relationships. The causality from exports to GDP, which had not been significant in the period of high economic growth in the 1960s, became also significant in the 1970s (see the Granger test in EPA 1993). More precisely, export came to induce investment with a lag of a few quarters (Table 8.3). Therefore, we can term this growth pattern 'export-investment-led growth'. As for the international environ-

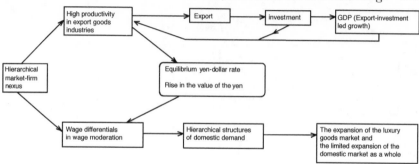

Figure 8.7 Growth regime based on the hierarchical market-firm nexus.

Table 8.3 Factors explaining investment after the late 1970s

Dependent variable: IP								
	C	EXQ_{-1}	EXQ_{-2}	EXQ_{-3}	u_{-1}	SP_{-1}	$\bar{R}^2$	DW
1979:1–	5.56**	0.114*	0.105*	0.106	0.408**	0.203**	0.97	1.23
1984:4	(11.0)	(2.15)	(2.10)	(1.95)	(3.70)	(4.16)		
1985:1–	−2.14*	0.520**	0.531**	0.414**	0.902**	0.248**	0.97	1.49
1990:4	(−2.16)	(3.39)	(3.36)	(2.67)	(3.11)	(8.95)		
1991:1–	0.671	0.341	0.100	0.151	1.12**	0.108	0.76	0.81
1996:4	(0.29)	(1.30)	(0.37)	(1.96)	(5.68)	(1.12)		

Notes
The estimation is done on the logarithms of variables.
Numbers in brackets are t-statistics.
**(*) denotes significance at the 1% (5%) level on a t-test.
$\bar{R}^2$ is the adjusted coefficient of determinations.
DW is Durbin–Watson coefficient.
IP: the investment of private enterprises.
EXQ: export quantity index (1995 = 100).
u: capacity utilisation index (1995 = 100).
SP: stock prices (the Nikkei average).

ment, the appreciation of the dollar caused by Reagan's policies favoured the export-investment-led growth of the Japanese economy in the first half of the 1980s. The depreciation of the yen did not reflect a real productivity growth-differential between the export-goods sector of Japan and that of the US. The trend of the exchange rate was diverging greatly from the purchasing power parity (PPP) of the export goods sector. The cumulative process of economic growth under these conditions can be understood as follows. Workers were highly integrated into firm organisation, and unit labour costs were depressed and responded flexibly to changes in the terms of trade, on the basis of complex coordinating mechanisms in the HMFN. Therefore, high competitiveness in the export goods sector caused companies to take a harsh export offensive to other countries by taking advantage of the depreciation of the yen. The Japanese economy realised dynamic export-led growth with

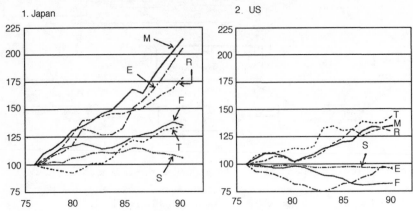

E: Electricity, gas and water service, F: Finance and insurance,
M: Manufacturing, R: Retail, S: Public and personal services,
T: Transportation and telecommunication

Figure 8.8 Productivity growth differentials between sectors: stronger in Japan than in US. Source: Economic Planning Agency, *Economic White Paper*, 1994.

dynamic increasing returns to scale that Figure 8.5 identified in the relationship between capital accumulation and productivity growth. This causal chain in fact constituted a cumulative process of economic growth.

From a more structural point of view, the high accumulation of capital in the export goods industry worked as a mechanism to bring about productivity growth differentials between industries and so-called 'inside-outside price differentials'. The prices of non-export goods priced in dollars became considerably higher than the prices of those in US. In the export-investment-led growth, a high rate of capital accumulation was realised in highly competitive export goods sectors, leading to much higher competitiveness in those industries with dynamic increasing returns to scale. The productivity growth differentials between industries were a key characteristic of the Japanese economy in the 1980s (Figure 8.8). Under these conditions, high productivity growth caused the PPP on export goods to rise continuously, resulting in the appreciation of the yen in the second half of the 1980s. Even in these circumstances, Japanese companies made great efforts to increase productivity by pursuing high levels of investment and innovation. Furthermore, the fully established HMFN sustained export expansion, because it achieved 'structural compatibility' by integrating workers into firm organisations and coordinating wages flexibly responding to changes in the terms of trade. As a result of this cumulative chain of causation, the dollar prices of non-export goods rose continuously.

The appreciation of the yen accelerated very rapidly after the Plaza Accord, so Japan could not depend so much on foreign demand for economic growth, and began to depend more on domestic demand. This was made possible by an extremely loose monetary policy pursued by the Bank of Japan in an attempt to overcome the *yendaka** (high yen) recession. This extreme monetary relaxation caused a rise in asset prices and also promoted a high rate of investment by lowering the cost of finance. Japanese companies focused on both foreign and domestic markets, and targeted increasing consumption. The 'Bubble Boom' promoted this change: the rapid increase in land and stock prices was widening 'assets differentials' between households. Consequently, consumers whose assets were increasing rapidly in value initiated the mass consumption of high-priced goods.

Economic growth appeared to be secured by mass luxury consumption and the rapid increase in investment in the second half of the 1980s. However, this growth pattern could not be sustained in the long run. It should be emphasised that the rapid increase in investment started, not in the 'Bubble Boom', but in the first half of the 1980s. In other words, 'excess capacity', which would not have been sustained by the 'proper' exchange rate, was formed in the special circumstances of the undervalued yen in the first half of the 1980s. Then, during the 'Bubble Boom', this excess capacity was greatly increased. Therefore, the rapid depreciation and scrapping of capital stock in the 1990s can be characterised as the adjustment of capital stock piled up in the Bubble Boom as well as a 'prolonged' adjustment of excess capital accumulated during the period of the undervalued yen before 1985.

The components of the profit rate provide clues about the macroeconomic structure. The profit rate, especially that of corporations, started to fall even during the 'Bubble Boom' in the late 1980s (Figure 8.1). Wage shares were very stable (Figure 8.2), and capacity utilisation was relatively high in the second half of the 1980s. However, the profit rate started to decrease, because a considerable decrease in the potential output–capital ratio was caused by the over-accumulation of capital (Figure 8.4). The decrease in capital stock prices relative to output prices prevented the profit rate from falling rapidly. In this sense, the mechanism to bring about 'the inside-outside price differentials' was also the mechanism to sustain the profit rate. The turning point of the Bubble Boom came in the first quarter of 1991. Capacity utilisation as well as stock prices started to fall just before this, while wage share was quite stable. The fall in capacity utilisation shows that there was an excess accumulation of capital stock at the end of the 1980s.

1990s and 1970s recessions compared

GDP followed very different trends in the post-oil shock recession and in the 1990s recession (Figures 8.9a and 8.9b). Nominal GDP was very stagnant in the early 1990s, while it rose continuously in the 1970s. In the earlier recession, there was a sharp fall in real GDP at first, but the recovery accelerated one and a half years after the turning point. In contrast, stagnation has persisted during the 1990s recession, although the initial decline in real GDP was relatively

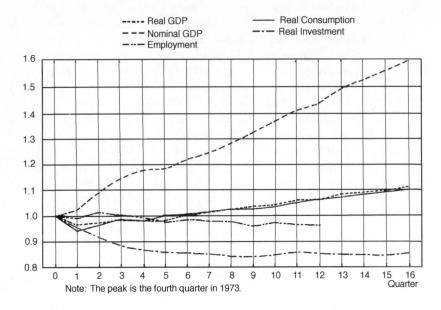

Figure 8.9a Relative changes in macroeconomic variables after the oil shock.

modest. Japan experienced high inflation in the post-oil shock recession, but Japan has experienced a deflationary recession in the 1990s.

Consumption underwent a long-lasting stagnation in this recession. After the oil shock, real consumption dropped sharply, but started to recover one and a half years afterwards. In the 1990s it did not recover markedly even two years after the beginning of the recession, even though the wage share increased considerably. The structural instability of the Japanese economy badly depressed consumers' confidence, and this perhaps shows how hard it is to realise the path of 'wage-led growth' in the 1990s recession.

The decrease in investment in the 1990s recession is much greater than that in the post-oil shock recession, and it took the economy longer to reach the bottom, because of the drastic adjustment of excess capacity created in the 1980s. The long duration of stagnant investment in this recession was caused not only by a usual adjustment process of capital stock but also by the more profound structural factors behind cyclical adjustments. The first is the sequence of financial disturbances in the collapse of the Bubble and the financial burden of the bad loan problem. The second is the transformation of the subcontractor network and its impact on small and medium-size firms.

Employment fell sharply in the post-oil shock recession, because large firms in particular rationalised costs to the new conditions. The decrease has been milder, at least at the macro-economic level, in the first half of the 1990s. This is thanks to the meso-level coordinating mechanisms of employment (see Chapter 2 and later).

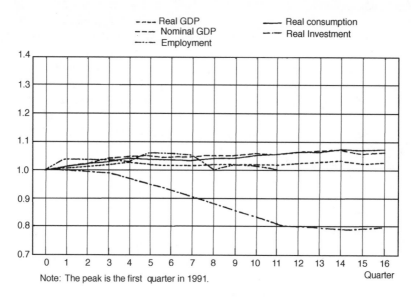

Figure 8.9b Relative changes in macroeconomic variables in the 1990s recession.

To sum up, although the decrease in macroeconomic indicators, except investment, has been rather mild, the economy has experienced persistent stagnation and an inability to recover in the 1990s. In fact, non-manufacturing activities now are not 'recession proof' and have performed very poorly. The discussion of the HMFN (Chapter 2) also reveals the severe problem of small and medium-size firms. Investment in small and medium-size firms has been very stagnant, and there is as yet no indication of recovery in those firms. The increase of foreign direct investment by parent companies, the rise in own plant production and greater standardisation have put a lot of pressure on small and medium-size firms, making a speedy recovery in investment impossible.

Structural changes in the 1990s recession

How did the 1990s recession influence institutional coordinating mechanisms and macroeconomic structures? The answer lies in an analysis of profitability, investment climate, income distribution, and employment.

Profitability of corporations

This has been very low in the 1990s (Figure 8.1 and Table 8.1) due to several factors. First, stagnant demand leads to a low level of capacity utilisation. Second, the potential output–capital ratio fell sharply because of the excess capital caused by 'over-accumulation'. Third, wage shares rise due to a sharp fall in labour productivity with 'labour hoarding'. Furthermore, the bad-loan problem puts great financial pressure on corporate profitability. Although wages are depressed and the employment rate has fallen, it is not likely that profitability will recover quickly under existing institutional conditions. Another important feature is the profitability differential between large firms and small and medium-size ones. In fact, the ordinary profit–total capital ratio has been much lower in small and medium-size firms than large ones, and the differential has been widening since 1994. This may be caused by recent pressure on the subcontractor system, including decreases in both volume of orders and unit prices offered by parent companies pursuing the restructuring of the subcontractor network.

Financial system and investment climate

Instability in the financial system has worsened the investment climate since the bubble burst. Bad loans have imposed a heavy burden on Japanese companies in the financial turmoil, so their business confidence is at a dismal level. Although there are some healthy companies in the export good sector which have abundant cash, the rest of the economy, particularly construction and property companies, is heavily indebted. Without proper oversight and confidence, many investment projects in those companies are in serious trouble. The Japanese financial system is faced with structural changes. The pressure of financial liberalisation has caused difficulties for the main bank system. In the late 1980s, Japanese companies ran up an equity-linked debt to investment, expecting that the economy would grow continuously. In the 1990s, however, the situation is entirely different. There is increasing pressure to make corporate finance more market based. Because the main bank system, a symbol of highly institutionalised corporate finance, is still needed to sustain long-term business confidence and support small and medium-size and rapidly growing firms, a market-oriented change might cause more instability and structural incompatiblity with the institutional arrangements of the rest of the economy.

Income distribution

This has not undergone much change. There is no great change in the employment system, especially the shape of the wage profile, the effect of tenure on wages and retirement pay, and the level of the separation rate (Chapter 2). The incentive mechanism is maintained on the basis of 'the institutionalised job-loss costs', supported by the complementarity of intra-firm and inter-firm institutional factors. What is especially remarkable in the 1990s is the decrease in the accession rate in large firms in the manufacturing sector, which occurs because companies continue to hoard labour. Labour productivity decreases considerably due to labour hoarding, especially in large firms, and this leads to higher levels of wage shares. Under these conditions, nominal wage growth has been depressed by the weakening bargaining position of unions in the spring offensive in the 1990s. This may widen income differentials and aggravate stagnant domestic demand.

Employment

Even in the severe recession, employment is maintained at the aggregate level. This is due to meso-level coordinating mechanisms such as the extensive use of non-regular workers, the transfer of workers from parent companies to subcontractors and the shift of employment from the manufacturing sector to the service sector. Small and medium-size firms and the service sector play the role of employment 'sponge' even in this severe recession. The structural shift in employment from the manufacturing sector to the service sector with stagnant manufacturing output is accelerating 'de-industrialization' in the Japanese economy. In this situation, more structural unemployment might be brought about by coordination failures in the shift in employment.

Concluding remarks

What shall be the future problems related to the structural changes in the Japanese economy and their impact upon: growth potential, income distribution, and the internationalisation of the economy?

In terms of growth potential, there is still high potential for capital accumulation in the export goods sector, especially the automobile and electrical equipment industries, where companies have maintained their competitiveness by inducing an evolutionary adaptation of their subcontractor networks. The structural compatibility of the HMFN is also maintained in those industries, even though the 'increasing fluidity' of the subcontractor network has a strong influence on it. However, corporate finance and inter-firm relations need a proper set of coordinating mechanisms, or mode of *régulation* in order to realise the growth potential of those industries. In this context, the stability of the financial system is crucial. Furthermore, being faced with an ageing society, the saving rate will decrease steadily due to the decrease in working population, but this does not necessarily mean that the real growth path will be determined entirely by the decreasing saving rate. Both growth and profit rates may be sustained under some institutional conditions provided that 'the horse is put before the cart' (Gordon 1995a). Institutional factors such as the financial system, capital-labour relations and the innovation system which have an influence on the investment ('the horse') are the key to achieving strong economic performance. Another likely result of the ageing society is the expansion of the service economy, especially care and health care services for the elderly. Again, a proper set of institutions is needed to guide supply and demand for those services to realise their potential.

Income distribution must also be treated very carefully. Fierce international competition is expected to generate increasing pressure to reduce real unit labour costs in the export goods sector. Wage bargaining will be more decentralised, depending on conditions at a company level. Wage shares will be also depressed at an aggregate level, while employment will be more diversified, or much more segmented. Wage differentials may be widened between different industrial sectors and different sized firms. The previous equalising mechanism of incomes will be weakened by the conflict of interest between different industrial sectors. As Kalecki pointed out, however, wages are a source of demand as well as costs for a company, so this may result in a lower level of domestic demand.

Lastly, the effect of the internationalisation of the economy will grow stronger in the near future. Foreign direct investment in Asian countries is expected to increase rapidly, and the Asia-wide international division of labour will be widened and deepened. This may have an influence on the structural compatibility established on the basis of the HMFN. If no marked change occurs in the structural compatibility even under those conditions, the growth pattern of the Japanese economy may have to remain export-investment-led. Here, there is a serious possibility for vicious circles. The mutually enforcing mechanism between export-led demand formation and productivity growth in the export goods sector may cause large productivity-growth differentials and price differentials between the export goods and non-export goods sectors, and this could in turn cause further appreciation of the yen. As already argued, the general increase in prices in the non-export goods sector in this kind of uneven development is a mechanism to equalise domestic incomes. However, this will aggravate the conflict of interest between the export goods and non-export goods sectors. These structural changes might have a negative influence on incentive mechanisms and the consensus on welfare in the Japanese socioeconomic system.

Data sources and calculations

In Figure 8.1, the profit rate is calculated on the basis of data from Economic Planning Agency, *Annual Report on National Accounts*, and the capital stocks of both corporations and all enterprises are obtained from Economic Planning Agency, *Gross Capital Stock of Private Enterprises*. The profit rate of corporations = (the incomes of private corporations + interest + dividend) / the capital stock of corporations. In constructing the profit rate of all enterprises, the incomes of unincorporated enterprises are formally divided into profits and wages following income distribution in corporations. We obtain the accumulation rate of real capital stock (at the constant prices of 1990), adjusting the data of gross capital stock in order to remove the effects of the privatisation of NTT and Japan Tobacco Industry in 1985, and JNR in 1987 etc.

In Figure 8.2, national incomes, employee incomes, and unincorporated enterprises' incomes are obtained from Economic Planning Agency, *Annual Report on National Accounts*.

In Figure 8.3, net labour productivity is defined as national income divided by the number of employees (including the self-employed), and product wages are defined as employee incomes (including those of the self-employed) divided by GDP deflator and the number of employees (including the self-employed)

In Figure 8.4, capacity utilisation in the manufacturing sector is obtained from Ministry of International Trade and Industry, *Industrial Index*. Capacity utilisation of the economy as a whole is calculated by using the ratio of the real output of the secondary industry to the real output of the economy as a whole. The output–capital ratio is defined as real GDP divided by the real capital stock of private enterprises. The data are obtained from Economic Planning Agency, *Annual Report on National Accounts* and Economic Planning Agency, *Gross Capital of Private Enterprises*. The potential output–capital ratio is defined as the output–capital ratio divided by the capacity utilisation of the economy as a whole.

In Table 8.2, the saving function and the investment function are estimated on the data of gross savings and gross profit including 'depreciation allowance' and the gross accumulation of capital including 'replacement investment' respectively. In the estimation of the saving function, we put a constant, s_0. in order to make it absorb the effect of statistical disturbances (direct and indirect taxes and government transfer payment, etc.) on the level of savings.

9 Beyond the East Asian economic crisis

Yasuo Inoue

Introduction

Contemporary East Asian economies have faced a dual challenge since the mid-1980s. They must not only achieve a regular and sustainable economic growth, but also rapidly introduce and develop a sophisticated system of finance. In fact, to the present day, where industrialisation has been achieved it was in the framework of the nation-state and not followed by financial liberalisation. Contemporary Japanese economic growth is also characterised by a dual system: the industrial and manufacturing sector is open to external competition but the commercial and financial sector is relatively protected by the domestic regulatory system. This seriously affects the present recession in Japan: the crisis is structural, Keynesian demand policy is not a solution, a fundamental restructuring of the economic system is required, especially in how industry and finance interact. Then, for the East Asian economies, there is the additional problem of industrialisation itself, which was so accelerated that the system remains somewhat fragile.

When the Thai monetary crisis began in mid-1987, almost all observers of the Asian economy expected it to be overcome soon and they certainly did not expect it to spread to neighbouring countries. Two years later, on the contrary, the whole region is directly or indirectly contaminated by the monetary crisis. Why does the Asian crisis have such a wide impact in comparison to the Mexican crisis of 1995? And how viable is the export-led growth model in the region? Before the crisis, it was all the rage; now is an opportune time to examine its limitations. Finally this chapter outlines a hypothetical post-crisis scenario.

Why has the crisis been so wide and lasted so long?

Many forms of crisis

First of all, the crisis has attacked almost all the East Asian countries but in diverse forms; monetary crisis, bank crisis but also political and social crisis in certain countries. There are also common factors in these crises: the exchange system based upon the anchorage on the US dollar, the important in- and outflow of short capital, the risk of overproduction in certain key industries like semiconductor and the primacy of export-led growth. However, to build up a likely future scenario, it is necessary to perform concrete analyses of the endogenous characteristics of the Asian crises.

Differences with the Mexican crisis

Like the Latin American crises in the 1980s, the Mexican crisis was characterised by the budget deficit and the deficit of the current trade balance. In these cases, government macro-economic policy was responsible for the crisis. But the Asian crises are different; the private sector was decisive in the economic deterioration caused by an accelerated investment in the capital goods and especially the speculation in the financial and real-estate market (Table 9.1).

The East Asian crisis is both monetary and financial. The former was provoked by the deficit of the current balance, the devaluation of the currency and the outflow of the huge amount of short capital. The latter concerned the breakdown or collapse of the domestic credit system. This is one of the main differences from the Mexican crisis. Despite this evidence, the IMF's saving plan was initially designated to deal with the monetary aspect of the crisis. This plan was certainly suitable for a Mexican-type crisis but in East Asia the IMF's policy aggravated the situation.

Comparing the East Asian crisis to the Mexican crisis highlights a major difference. The Mexican export market was 80–90 per cent US dominated, reinforced by the formation of the NAFTA in 1994. But in 1996, over 50 per cent of the export market of the ASEAN 4 (Indonesia, Thailand, Philippines, and Malaysia) is composed of intra-regional commerce (Japan 20 per cent, Asian NIEs 29 per cent, ASEAN 7 per cent). About 40 per cent of the Asian NIEs export market is also supported by internal Asian commerce (Japan 9 per cent, NIEs 12 per cent, ASEAN 11 per cent).[1] So before the crisis, East Asia was proud of the strong chain of rapid growth during the 1980s. In effect, the high level of growth was spread in the

Table 9.1 Economic situation before the crisis (1996, percentage of the GDP)

	Private saving-private invest.	Budget balance	Current trade balance
Indonesia	−5.9	2.5 *	−3.3
South Korea	−9.6	5.7	−4.9
Thailand	−8.7	0.7	−8.1
Mexico (1994)	−6.9**	−0.7	−6.9

Source: EPA 1998b.

Notes
* Balance of the central government
** Domestic gross saving-domestic gross investment

region from NIEs to ASEAN, China. This rapid economic development was explained mainly as being due to the force of the free-market mechanism.[2] It was not rare for authors to say that a *laissez-faire* market policy would be the way to obtain optimal growth. The change from virtuous to vicious circle happened so suddenly that very few observers had time to diagnose it. The negative conjuncture was reinforced by the long stagnation of Japanese economy from 1991 to the end of 1990s. Unlike the case of the US with Mexico, Japan is unable to absorb the exports of the Asian region.

These differences are tested by certain analyses. For example, the analysis of 'real and effective exchange rate' presents an interesting result. In spite of the high degree of their devaluation, most Asian moneys (except the Indonesian rupee) recover their initial level of exchange rate one year after the crisis. It was exactly the same evolution as the Mexican crisis (EPA 1998c). Nevertheless, the stimulus to export in real or nominal terms in US dollars was not as significant in Asian countries as in Mexico in 1995. In the Mexican case, at the beginning of 1996, domestic production ameliorated the situation so the crisis lasted only one year. In Asian cases, almost all governments now expect that the crisis will last at least a few more years.

Export recovery but domestic stagnation

The reason why recovery is so delayed in East Asia is also explained by the stagnation of domestic production in each country. Even if export recovers very gradually, it does not lead to a production increase. The stagnation is caused by two main factors. Firstly, the austerity of the macroeconomic policy was set up at the IMF's recommendation. Governments have obtained a certain amount of aid but also cooled the domestic economy very suddenly. As seen above, this type of therapy is not appropriate for East Asian countries. Secondly, the credit crunch, caused by the collapse of the bubble economy, makes for a sluggish industrial economy. Financial order was so deeply undermined that it is difficult for the real economy to recover its dynamics. The financial system was not adequately organised and monitored to react quickly and appropriately to the shock of crisis. The financial weakness in the region and the moral hazard of the financial institutions are well known. But financial liberalisation has made the situation far worse. In 1998, the proportion of non-performing assets to GDP was 37 per cent in Thailand, 27 in South Korea, 22 in Malaysia and 19 per cent in Indonesia. And the proportion of non-performing assets to the total loans was 61 per cent in Indonesia, 48 in Thailand, 33 per cent in South Korea and Malaysia. In these countries, many firms face financial crisis.

Reflecting this adverse development, the IMF itself has also gradually changed its macro policy in three stages from December 1997 to July 1998. For example, in South Korea, the IMF initially asked for a return to equilibrium in the budget balance but tolerated 1.75 per cent then 4 per cent of the public budget deficit to the GDP. The IMF also permitted a certain reduction in the interest rate.

Deterioration of the labour market

In spite of this swift economic policy, the crisis now hits the labour market. The unemployment rate rose in South Korea from less than 2 per cent to 9 per cent within one year. In this country, it was largely regular workers who were directly hit by the crisis. Independent workers and daily workers remained untouched by the crisis. Familial enterprises augment workers (EPA, 1998c). The labour market also deteriorated in Thailand, the Philippines and Indonesia. Ordinarily, rural regions absorb unemployment. But when villages are also suffering from the bad economic conjuncture, this type of solution becomes difficult. So unemployment remains in the urban informal sector. This suggests that the solution of unemployment by the free labour market system is no longer efficient for long-term social cohesion. There is an urgent need to establish the social security network in each society in order to ensure social cohesion.

Export-led growth reconsidered

Inequality and welfare in the era of financial liberalisation

What are the consequences of East Asia's economic growth from the point of view of redistribution of national revenue? According to Kuznets's inverted-U hypothesis, the inequality in the redistribution of national revenue increases after economic take-off then becomes stable at a certain stage of development, after which there is less and less inequality. Then the question is whether this inequality is a necessary evil and if it will disappear naturally. Statistics show that there was a degradation of inequality in the 1980s (Table 9.2), and at the same time there was a certain reduction in the poverty rate (Table 9.3).

It is far from certain that all the East Asian countries would be able to realise a Western-style post-war welfare state. Kuznets's hypothesis was based upon Western experiences and may not be valid in a global financial context. It was formulated just when the financial crisis of the welfare State became clear to all governments. The priority with financial liberalisation is to keep the budget balance, and thus it advocates self-reliance over and above the building of a social security system. If the East Asian countries underwent financial liberalisation, the social security system might not be able to provide cover for everyone.

Threat of overproduction

The fragility of the export-led growth model became very clear in the East Asian crisis. This model depends basically upon the evolution of world

Table 9.2 Evolution of income inequality (Gini's coefficient (1980–1989))

	1980	1989
Japan	0.33	0.37
Taiwan	0.26	0.29
South Korea	0.39	0.43
China	0.29	0.32
Philippines	0.45	
Thailand	0.43	0.48
Malaysia	0.46	0.50
Indonesia	0.34	0.36
India	0.34	0.37
Bangladesh	0.36	0.39

Sources: Mizoguchi and Matsuda 1997

demand (Inoue 1992). If the IMF's economic policy recommendations are put into practice, the demand restriction would occur on a world-wide level. A generalised deflation spiral might well be set off: introduction of an austerity policy; level down of demand; competition for export; devaluation of national currency; price competition. Besides, the production over-capacity cumulated in the boom period becomes an acute problem. As long as supply increases are anticipated by the credit money system, there would be no risk of overproduction although current crises indicate that there is a limit to 'ante-validation' by credit money. This very basic aspect of post-1930 economy[3] was totally ignored in the period of the financial bubble, meaning that there was over-lax credit in the boom and an over-hard restriction in the recession.

Social group linked with the bubble boom

The financial bubble led to the emergence of a new social group. For example, in Thailand, the bubble economy and breakdown of the macroeconomic policy are closely linked with the apparition of a new middle class, formed by graduates and MBAs. They demand a new distribution of national revenue. They are professionally mobile and seek a more attractive job

Table 9.3 Evolution of poverty rate (percentage)

	1970–1974	1985–1989
Philippines	43	39
Thailand	39	16
Indonesia	58	17
Sri Lanka	37	27
Pakistan	54	23
India	54	43

Sources: Mizoguchi and Matsuda 1997.

contract with each move. They are less interested in life-long employment and criticise the big-firm administrations that operate as a monopoly rather than in a market economy. They claim that firms should be run by a professional elite, and thus gain foreign direct investment (FDI) by multinationals. But this process was stopped in 1990, as FDI became more sluggish. The Thai economy was challenged by competition with China and Vietnam because of the rising domestic labour cost. To maintain the speed of growth, the government opened BIBF (Bangkok International Banking Facility) in 1993, an easy way to attract short capital that opened and accelerated the way to the bubble economy. The latter offered a big opportunity for those who lost business because of the sluggish FDI in Thailand and the situation bred a group of golden boys who reaped the benefits of deregulation. They were engaged in speculation of the capital, stock and real-estate market in Thailand. The financial crisis was linked with the weak financial system in this country but this social group also played a role. As in Japan, economic growth leading to the bubble supported the new rich, which represent a minority of the active population, about 10–20 per cent.

Price or quality advantage?

On top of the problem of dependence on world demand, the industrial structure may limit the growth of multinationals. As seen above, NIEs and ASEAN countries are directly concerned and face a dilemma as soon as industrialisation accelerates. It is of course necessary to modify the industrial structure, to move on to more sophisticated production techniques, by introducing advanced technology from developed countries and transferring the sector in which they lost the advantage to neighbouring countries. However, if this process does not take place in time, there will be the risk of hollowing out even in the East Asian countries (Inoue 1997). The ASEAN 4 countries, especially, must urgently restructure industry. They are sandwiched between NIEs and China, India, gradually losing their cost advantage in the low-skilled sectors, like textiles and clothing (Table 9.4).

South Korea and Taiwan: contrasting twins

All these problems, however, do not signal the end of the multinationals-led growth model. It worked when internal and external conditions are satisfied, as in East Asia in the 1980s. But we could not say that there is a 'wild goose flying model of growth' (Akamatsu 1961). Even if a diffusion of growth model may exist, the process is no longer linear, but depends basically on local development capacity. This is clearly the case in South Korea, where industrialisation was founded upon the assembly industry and the dynamics of big firms (chaebols). The recurring external trade deficit needs to be financed by introducing short-term capital. The inflow of the latter is assured, as long as there is high growth and the international financial market has

Table 9.4 Evolution of RCA in the textile and clothing sector of Asian countries

	1990	1993	1995	1996
Asian NIEs	3.01	2.51	2.19	2.12
Asian NIEs*	2.43	2.03	1.79	1.73
South Korea	3.46	2.85	2.28	2.19
Taiwan	2.43	2.18	2.24	2.21
Singapore	0.53	0.32	0.20	0.17
Hong Kong	6.35	6.11	6.25	6.59
ASEAN 4	1.90	1.95	1.63	1.54
Malaysia	0.91	0.86	0.76	0.79
Thailand	2.62	2.34	2.03	1.79
Philippines	3.72	3.16	2.54	2.22
Indonesia	1.81	2.58	2.21	2.17
China	4.38	4.58	4.21	4.13
India	4.22	4.23	4.54	n.a.

Source: JETRO 1998

Note:
* except Hong Kong

confidence in the Korean economy. But as soon as there are doubts, the inflow stops. In order to resolve this structural problem, industrial structure needs to be upgraded and oriented towards upstream processes (skilled labour concentrated processes, R&D). An additional factor is the wage increase in the manufacturing sector, which occurred in 1987 with the beginning of democratisation. While from this period the rhythm of the average annual wage increase was 11 per cent in Taiwan and 3 per cent in Japan, it was 16 per cent in South Korea (EPA 1998c).

South Korea and Taiwan reveal two clearly contrasting patterns of export-led growth. The Taiwanese economy is also dominated by the assembly industry, but middle and small firms are highly dynamic and flexible (Inoue 1994). In a sense, South Korea is in a paradoxical situation, where the success of a particular pattern of industrialisation makes a rapid change of the strategy difficult. Finally, external conditions were too bad for South Korea to avoid the crisis: the US dollar was appreciating again, there was the outflow of a critical amount of short capital and the collapse of semiconductor prices in the world market. So South Korea was obliged to accept the economic recovery plan demanded by the IMF. But things are not quite so simple. With the subsidy of 58 billion dollars, this country should satisfy precise requirements. One year after the so-called reform, the capital account shows a large external trade surplus and high unemployment rate. A more appropriate recovery plan, more attuned to local society, is clearly required.

These reflections point to a common conclusion that there are relative limitations in the export-led growth model. There is no longer the miraculous success achieved in East Asia in the 1980s. However, an overly pessimistic view of the post-crisis Asian economy should be avoided. What are the futures open to these countries?

Some lessons from the crisis

According to conventional wisdom, the economic development in East Asia is explained as follows. Policy favoured exports, making the inflow of FDI possible. Foreign exchange was liberalised in the framework of GATT, WTO. There was abundant human capital eager to learn basic techniques. The spill-over effect from one country to another was reinforced by the inflow of FDI. But this virtuous cycle was stopped by the changing international monetary environment, devaluation of the yen and reappreciation of the US dollar since the spring of 1995. With the loss of the price advantage, structural problems, until then concealed, become acute. Firstly, the formation of human capital was lacking. In ASEAN, there are simply not enough engineers for countries to enter a new stage of growth. In Thailand, there is 29 per cent coverage of secondary education in 1990, half that of South Korea at the same level of development (measured in terms of GDP per person).

A yen zone as a remedy for international monetary asymmetry

In the Asian crisis, many authors argued for the formation of a yen zone (Kwan 1994; Yamamoto 1998). The US dollar will always have a potentially disordering macroeconomic effect on Asian money as long as currencies retain a link. From 1985 to 1995, the dollar had a beneficial effect for East Asian countries. But after 1995, they lost the price advantage in the export market, making the formation of a stable exchange system in the region out of the question. But there are serious problems when is comes to implementing such a strategy. Basically, the performance of East Asian financial systems is not comparable to the Anglo-Saxon system, although it is accepted as a 'global standard'. There is an urgent need to establish the autonomy of the Asian financial market so as to overcome the hegemony of the dollar. This is a long-term task that depends on public initiative; the actual privatisation of international finance must be controlled by public intervention to ensure that financial control operates on local, national and supra-national levels.

Fundamentally, what happened in this crisis was textbook predictable. Indeed, for several years, certain authors had been pointing to the fragility of growth in the region (Inoue 1996b). That was one merit of the approach underlining institutional and historical reality. This fragility existed on two sides. The growth of Asian NIEs was based upon one particular type of 'logic of insertion' and 'strategic area'. The so-called 'fourth generation' of industrialisation, (after Great Britain, US, Germany and Japan etc.), appeared with Asian NIEs. But the weak point of their model was that these countries continue to import capital goods from the US and Japan, rapidly accumulating technological dependency. There was a need for public and private initiatives to redesign industrial structures to fabricate more sophisticated products (Aoki, Kim and Okuno-Fujiwara 1997).

The fragility was also due to the privatisation of the international capital cycle. Asymmetry on a world level has a decisive effect. The biggest creditor, Japan, is in recession from 1991 but accumulates foreign exchange surplus. The biggest debtor, the US, in 1999 is still in the boom that started in March 1991 but has a critical amount of current balance deficit. Basically, the 'greenback' gives the privileged position to the US, which can absorb the world's excess savings without respecting external budget and finance discipline. The American federal bond market is occupied more and more by inflow of foreign private capital. In 1997, more than half of foreign capital was occupied by private funds. And in the same year, about a third of Treasury Bonds were purchased by foreign countries (it was a quarter in 1994). This is evidence of the strength of hegemonic currency. Nevertheless this process is supported only by the confidence of creditor countries.

Therefore, creditor countries cannot permanently cope with an overvalued greenback. Inversely, its devaluation would provoke the deflation of the world economy. An autonomous monetary zone in East Asia is evidently necessary, but there are three obstacles to State regulation. Firstly, authoritarian States in Asian NIEs and ASEAN legitimised themselves by pointing to the lifestyle improvement. There exists a social compromise based on the exchange of limited political liberty for steady and rapid growth. Instability of growth could very well lead to challenges to the political regime. In fact, authoritarianism is not 'a necessary evil' to procure development: this point of view may be the result of a period when the cold war dominated international relations, when economic growth was seen as a major way to vanquish socialist countries.

New international division of labour (IDL)

State regulation, challenged because of its eroding internal political legitimacy, is also attacked by the financial liberalisation from the early 1990s. Nowadays, any political regime is assessed by capital markets. The present crisis teaches us to know how to control the private capital movement while reaping the benefits of liberalisation. This does not mean going back to the rather closer system of the 1960s, but it is necessary to avoid introducing global standards in local societies.

A third problem for State regulation is that multinationals develop the production and commerce network beyond frontiers. The tendency, characterised by large transplants, was decisive in East Asia after 1985; there was a wave of transplants from Japan, NIEs and ASEAN. Of course after 1995, FDI becomes more prudent; still, the strategy aiming at the optimal localisation of production in the region was not questioned. In fact, the first turning-point occurred in the mid-1970s when the so-called NICs emerged. Until then, the classical form of IDL, i.e. commerce between industrial products and primary products, had been dominant. But at this moment, the Western multinationals began to follow the strategy of transferring their factories to developing countries, in response to a decline of the Fordist growth regime in industrialised countries. This expansion of the industrial circuit was favourably accepted by developing countries, which were beginning the take-off by supplying the necessary ingredients and conditions for production and intermediate products for the FDI (Lipietz 1985; Ominami 1986). This configuration may be defined as a second IDL; the first IDL remains valid even after this period but is no longer a dominant form.

In the mid-1980s, the IDL changed for the second time, with regional economic integration, although the change in East Asia is less institutionalised than that which occurred in North America and Europe with NAFTA and EU. It is characterised by not only vertical but also horizontal trade supported by the development of intra-industry trade. South Korea and Taiwan developed FDI from the end of the 1980s, reflecting the increase of their labour unit cost, which makes them into an important capital exporter in labour-rich industries. Japanese multinationals develop the production network, and their strategy until now has been based upon regional integration, compared with the decentralised strategy of the American multinationals (Inoue 1997).

Surge of private short capital movement

Actually, the inflow of capital has been very surprising for some years. From 1988 to 1996, GDP and foreign trade of the developing countries and of economies in transition to the market system have increased respectively 120 per cent and 230 per cent (in volume). But the inflow of capital increased more than 1,000 per cent in the same period; there is also a very strong wave of private capital flowing in and out of East Asia (Table 9.5).

Two growth strategies

The first, characterised by the increase of real wage in the manufacturing sector, was linked to OECD countries development and concerns especially South Korea and Taiwan. The 'wage explosion' that occurred in the last two countries in the mid-1980s symbolised this type of growth. It is not the result of a simple market mechanism, but a consequence of social compromise in the wage-labour relation (Boyer 1998).

The other growth strategy is determined by the dynamics of the bubble economy. It relies on financial speculation, stock and real-estate markets. In this model, a new middle class is formed, a professional elite, a tiny fraction of the total population. This type of growth took place in East Asia after financial liberalisation.

Table 9.5 Net inflow of capital in East Asia* (billions of dollars)

	1994	*1995*	*1996*	*1997****
Total net inflow (1 + 2)	47.4	86.3	91.2	25
Inflow of private capital	40.5	83.8	93.8	−6
Direct investment	4.7	4.9	5.8	6.5
Portfolio investment	7.6	11	11.6	−6.8
Bank loan	24	58	58.3	−29.0
Non-bank loan	4.2	9.9	18.1	23.3
Inflow of public capital	7.0	2.5	−2.6	30.9
IMF, World Bank etc.	−0.4	−0.3	−2.0	22.6
Bilateral loan	7.4	2.9	−0.6	8.4

Source: EPA 1998c

Notes
* South Korea, Malaysia, Thailand, the Philippines and Indonesia
** estimation

The question is now to know which is the better of two strategies? The second is very easy to realise in a short period of time but very weak from the point of view of social justice. The first is relatively difficult to realise and needs much more time, but contributes to long-term social cohesion, as proved by the Fordist growth regime in the 1960s.

In terms of industrial structure, the first strategy obviously represents the interests of financial capital and the second the interests of manufacturing capital. The first should begin only after the second model has been well established. The weak financial systems in East Asian countries urgently need reform, for example, to avoid the devastating consequences of the moral hazard inherent in State interventions in domestic financial institutions. The rule of market discipline should be introduced and entrenched in order to abolish such problems. Nevertheless, young industrial entrepreneurs should not be too attracted by the charm of old financiers' industrial strategy, i.e. of cutting down the industrial tree in the bud.

How to get out

So what are the necessary conditions for real recovery in East Asia? Firstly, it will be crucial to build up more autonomous, endogenous industrial structures with a solid supporting industry network. This network is not necessarily limited within the country but is constructed within the East Asian economic integration. Secondly, the development strategy should focus on the dynamic comparative advantage that lies in skill-intensive industries. If the strategy continues to be governed by the static comparative advantage, the countries will not be able to go up the ladder of comparative advantage. Thirdly, on top of the supply-side orientation, main demand should be sought from domestic and regional markets, creating dynamic intra-Asian trade. The crisis could be overcome even without realising these preliminary conditions, if the evolution of the exchange rate is reversed. A Kamikaze scenario (for example devaluation of the dollar) is possible but it would be too easy, the repetition of the past strategy; continued onward escape.

Even if the East Asian economy recovers, there remains one crucial problem to resolve: the ecological crisis (Inoue and Yamada 1995). Given the demographic pyramid (many young people in this region), countries prefer to concentrate on growth rather than environmental control because they need to fight the battle against poverty. This would seem a legitimate strategy but if the wide variety of ecological problems in this region are not dealt with, they may end up driving the whole region into a state of ecological crisis. Any growth regime for the 21st century should take account of the ecological norm in addition to the production and consumption norms. The cost of repairing the damaged natural environment should be included in the price of this growth regime or billed to the Japanese and other multinational firms that, up to now, have always ignored environmental costs.

So how viable is the productivism which led to the mass-production and consumption-growth model? Its validity has been seriously questioned since the 1970s in the developed countries, where it is no longer considered a relevant model in these countries. In East Asia, it would not be realistic to condemn mass-production growth. But society must put firm controls on this kind of growth in order to minimise its social cost. This would be gradually achieved by social consensus formed through social dialogue and negotiation, not imposed by the West or the financial market but as a pragmatic local social strategy. A form of 'neo-liberalism fatigue' has appeared in the 1990s; it is time to seek other means to achieve a more ordered form of market economy.

In addition to the choice between growth models (industrial or financial), and between environmental models (sustainable or productivist), there is the choice of political regime (democratic or authoritarian). One of the main consequences of the East Asian crisis is that authoritarian politics were abandoned in many countries, such as Indonesia, although social balance remains fundamentally unstable. Industrialisation is not in fact incompatible with an authoritarian regime. It can even be argued that the former needs the latter in the sense that political stability is a *sine qua non* for development. The export-led growth model is not properly linked with developmental authoritarianism, but insofar as it promotes FDI, it is clear that local government adopts an economic and social policy that favours multinational firms, with the consequence that political and social rights were and are severely controlled in the developing countries. But after this crisis in countries that have experienced two or three decades of control of civil rights, it is clear that social hegemony would be founded upon the interests of a large number of people, no longer the rich groups and the reigning elite. The history of capitalism shows that the democratisation process does not necessarily take place in parallel with industrialisation.

Finally, internal social hegemony requires international political stability in the region, which depends largely on political initiatives to promote economic integration. It does not simply depend on market mechanisms, because they operate in the institutionally determined context. If this were not so, excessive competition could drive the economy into a major crisis. The political consensus should always be sought at the regional level, at least on main topics such as social rights, ecological rights and monetary stability.

Conclusion

This brief analysis has made clear that the East Asian crisis provoked by monetary disorder with devaluation of Asian currencies is a structural crisis in the sense that it concerns not only the nature of the growth regime but also the mode of *régulation* itself. In other words, the external monetary shock revealed internal contradictions previously concealed by the virtuous cycle. The present crisis teaches us about both the merits and weaknesses of export-led growth. In terms of the mode of regulation, the present crisis is similar to that of 1930, when financial deregulation led to the historic boom in stock, capital and real-estate markets. Certainly, nowadays a solid safety net exists where there was none before. But, this does not mean that any crisis or problem is easily solved within a credit economy system: the 'nominal world' cannot live independently of the 'real world'. The solution depends on formation of social hegemony; a society is usually more stable when the greater number of people agree. Beyond the problem of the interactions between industry and finance, this analysis points to several patterns and configurations between democracy and economic development in East Asia. The relation is complex and non-linear. Given the different levels of democratic maturity and different historical backgrounds, the end of the crisis will also be different from society to society, and not uniform throughout East Asia.

10 Some limitations to Japanese competitiveness[1]

Benjamin Coriat, Patrice Geoffron and Marianne Rubinstein

Introduction

At a time when the Japanese economy is increasingly being questioned, the purpose of this chapter is to contribute to earlier studies regarding its so-called limits. The present study is based on two sources: (a) it develops and updates the first analyses of the Japanese crisis as they appeared in *Made in Japan* (1994), and already interpreted and classified by Benjamin Coriat (1998); (b) it uses and updates Geoffron and Rubinstein (1996), their approaches being complementary or convergent on several key aspects.

More precisely, we examine the extent to which the difficulties that Japan faces today may correspond to the fading out of its competitiveness. If such is the case, the various signs of Japan's crisis might indicate the limits reached by some of the basic and structural elements, which, until the 1970s, made the amazing growth rate and the competitiveness of the Japanese economy possible.

In the process of the analysis, it is indispensable first to re-examine and give a definition to the notions of competitiveness and crisis, in order to indicate the nature and limits of the exercise undertaken. This chapter later examines three of the 'pillars' traditionally seen as fundamental to Japanese competitiveness, to assess to what extent today's noticeable changes foretell the fading out of its dynamic principles. The three pillars considered here are the corporate governance organisation (and to the relationship between banks and industry), the employment and the national innovation systems. The changes currently under way that are mentioned here are selected because they have a bearing on Japanese competitiveness.

Competitiveness: in search of definitions

There are three main approaches to this notion:

1. The most widely accepted way to assess a nation's competitiveness is through a series of indicators measuring the development of the external performance of a given economy, frequently captured by the relative

wage cost. It is often used (if not over-used) in OECD studies. This indicator implies that the overall competitiveness of different economies is cost related, and more particularly wage-cost related. It is admitted that competitiveness and wage cost are directly related, and that they vary in opposite directions. A variant of this model consists of a price-related approach to competitiveness, which takes into account the influence of relative exchange rates based on different indices of purchasing-power parity. Various econometric tests (Kaldor 1978a; Fagerberg 1988; and more recently Lafay and Herzog 1989; Lafay *et al.* 1991; or Asensio and Mazier 1991), have been performed over long periods of time (usually decades), and this reverse correlation was not verified. Conversely, Japan has posted a simultaneous increase of its relative individual wage costs and of its relative market shares. Hence the assumptions about the role of non-cost-related competitiveness in global competition have gathered momentum, although this has not yet been assessed.

2. The notion of competitiveness has also been approached by taking into account other indicators of 'well-being' in the national economy, such as the evolution of the employment level, time spent at work, purchasing power, and access to health and educational services. To quote the American Council of Competitiveness in 1992, it is 'the ability to produce goods and services corresponding to the needs of international markets, while enabling American citizens to enjoy an improving and durable standard of living'. The various studies out in the successive 'Made in' series (*Made in America* 1989; *Made in France* 1993; *Made in Japan* 1994), as well as in the EU (Coriat, Adreassen *et al.* 1995), have all taken this indicator into account.

3. This chapter takes a step in the same direction, and proposes a synthetic definition of competitiveness that combines the narrow and more comprehensive definitions. A nation is competitive if it can, through its exports, pay for the imports necessary for growth and to increase its standard of living, without running the risks of major imbalances or of coming to a complete standstill.

By introducing the ideas of preservation and standards of living in the evaluation of competitiveness, the above definition avoids the dangerous[2] and narrow idea that competitiveness is merely competition for market shares, and could be measured only in terms of trade balance, whatever the effects or consequences of those external performances on domestic growth. Because this notion involves intricate links between domestic growth and external performances, it emphasises the key role played in a nation's competitiveness by its degree of independence in managing its domestic policy, while overcoming external pressure.

Japanese financial system under strain

The financial system has always been one of the major assets of the Japanese model, and has contributed a considerable amount to its competitiveness. Very close links between banking institutions and industry have improved the long-term coherence of industrial organisation. There is of course an advantage too in terms of capital cost, which could favour, combined with a low yen, cost-competitiveness for Japanese companies. Yet, financial links should also be examined from a 'qualitative' standpoint. Financing has helped stabilise profits (by undoubtedly reducing them), made long-term industrial strategies possible, and perpetuated wage agreements. However, the industrial environment has gradually been changing with the financial deregulation initiated in the late 1970s. Deregulation has unquestionably altered the financial organisation of the Japanese model, introducing disruptions that started the financial crisis in 1989, which has not yet reached its end (see Chapters 4 and 6).

Main bank system (MBS) was at the heart of the Japanese model

The MBS, as an institution, has allowed remarkable financial relationships to develop. The origin of this system dates back to the 1950s, when credit started to be rationed and many firms, faced with a shortage of liquid capital, had to ask for the banks' help. Banks were then in a strong position to interfere with the firms' management,[3] and these relationships allowed a channelling of credit. The Ministry of Finance (MOF) controls bank loans, and the Ministry of International Trade and Industry (MITI) identifies priority sectors. When the firm is in difficulty the true nature of the main bank system (MBS) reveals itself. The main bank enjoys the strategic position of being main lender, main financial shareholder, and fund manager. It can then organise financial adjustments and offer various services, ranging from management skills to the search for new outlets. This system means that a firm may be more rapidly rescued than if it is left to market forces, thus reducing the risks of bankruptcy.[4] The industrial effects of the MBS have often been discussed, the main argument being that such links facilitate the adoption of long-term strategies that have major consequences on firms' investment decisions. For example, firms that can rely on the MBS maintain a higher level of activity than those that are independent, after a period of financial difficulties, both in terms of sales and investment (Hoshi *et al.* 1990). Firms with financial shareholders go through less frequent and less serious critical periods than others (Lichtenberg and Pushner 1992).

Endogenous or exogenous origin of financial deregulation

How did such a complex and efficient institutional construction – based on incentive more than on compelling measures, unlike the Korean example –

come to be deregulated? External pressure was a decisive element, notably the law on exchange controls, voted in 1947, and revised in 1980 to comply with US wishes. Similarly, the 1984 yen-dollar agreement made the Japanese financial market more accessible to foreign investors. Such pressures led to an increased flow of capital held in yen, thus reducing the possibilities of under valuing the Japanese currency.

Yet, this 'exogenous' interpretation of the origin of deregulation excludes some major domestic factors. First, slower growth in the 1970s produced a surplus of liquid capital. Japanese firms wanted to adopt more efficient financial strategies. More generally, the macro-economic environment led to increased awareness, among economic actors, of the cost of financial resources and of capital yield. The public deficit due to the first oil crisis led the government, from 1975 onward, to issue deficit bonds, and simultaneously to look for an increased liquidity of treasury bonds by gradually making it easier for banks to have access to the secondary market. The first stages of financial deregulation also testify to the end of the financial institutions' attachment to the traditional pattern. The city banks, faced with a fall in the amount of deposits and the preference of big firms for euro-markets, asked for a reform of the fixing of interest rates and to be allowed to deal with other financial activities, such as security trading (see Chapter 6).

There are also some specific costs inherent in the MBS. The firms that were closely linked to a bank put up with inferior results in terms of profitability and growth rate, to make up for the guarantee that such a system brought them (Nakatani 1984; Weinstein and Yafeh 1994). After 1985, an increasing number of firms no longer wished to bear the MBS cost, since it had lost much of its interest for them. This may be one explanation for the massive issue of convertible bonds; the most profitable firms wanted to save on the cost of bank monitoring, while the less successful ones tried to escape this monitoring system via more open financial markets (Horiuchi 1995; Hoshi 1994).

Effects of deregulation in industrial financing

It cannot be denied that the fading out of the competitiveness of the Japanese model was partly due to the financial crisis. This crisis was channelled from the financial world to the industrial one via real assets markets and the banking system.

Some temporary effects linked to the financial crisis ...

Japanese corporations were first hit by the difficulties of converting bonds into shares, and by the deterioration of their capital or property portfolios, hence a negative effect on their wealth. Moreover, they suddenly had to deal with financial institutions deeply concerned with wiping out their bad loans, and consequently unable to meet their clients' growing demand for credit. Financial institutions can hold a lot of information on their clients, but in today's environment, this is no longer sufficient to assess the degree of risk involved, which has led banks to ration credit.

Thus, main banks increasingly tend to bring conditional financial support to their clients. Some conflicts that end up in court occur between financial institutions and industrial firms, or even worse, among financial institutions themselves, when they disagree on the way to share losses between the main bank and the banks of the syndicate. It is the corporate shareholders' duty to help rescue failing financial institutions, according to the contract binding the members of the same *keiretsu*.

... combined with structural effects

The structural effects of deregulation on the relationship between banks and industry are partly concealed by the economic crisis. The low level of applications for credit since 1992 and the banking system strangulation make for a highly unusual situation. It is thus difficult to extrapolate the reorganisation of financial relationships from recent analyses. This reorganisation depends on the achievement of reforms that have been announced for the end of the 1990s.

- Basically, the deregulation process has enabled corporations to use alternative sources of financing (such as the capital market or non-banking financial institutions), as well as furnishing a possibility of arbitrage between financial and industrial profits. They have reoriented their objective-function since 1985, thus contributing to the formation of the speculative bubble, and they have abandoned the virtuous circle that since the Second World War had linked financial and industrial worlds.
- The deregulation process could also lead to a relative deterioration of capital costs. Several studies have pointed to the advantage Japanese corporations have over their American counterparts, estimated to vary between 2 per cent and 6 per cent in the years 1961–86. This advantage was due to a certain number of elements that it will no longer be possible to combine, such as the low returns for shareholders who have become much more demanding.
- Moreover, foreign investors could also play a role in the relationships between banks and industry. The fading out of the MBS, along with discord among Japanese financial institutions or with their supervisory authorities, show us that the financial system can no longer be considered as a monolithic organisation. The achievement of the big bang planned over the years 1997–2002 will contribute to the opening of the Japanese financial market, as can already be seen in the sector of security houses.

All in all, it is most likely that the banks' share in corporate financing will be reduced and compensated for by the arrival of new foreign or non-banking investors, as well as by a larger access to financial markets, once the economic crisis is over. One of the consequences would be the introduction of set standard prices for financial services to firms, a much more dynamic activity than the mere supply of capital, following the OECD trend (Campbell 1994). Within such a framework, it is unlikely that a MBS with a central monitoring function should reappear. By holding industrial equity, banks still play a strategic role. Yet, since the logic of the MBS consists in lending money, they naturally feel the need to strengthen their monitoring role and to share it amongst themselves at lower cost. Without this function, banks are deprived not only of some information that is a real tool for *ex ante* monitoring (project analysis prior to the setting up of loans), but also of some profits (rent collection). Since cooperation between banks has been made more difficult by a deregulated financial environment, the MBS will now inevitably become increasingly fragile.

Lost harmony between finance and production

Production principles are no longer in harmony with financial methods, and need to be adapted to suit the new deregulated financial environment if this maladjustment is to be redressed. To quote Aoki: 'A core of employment and financial agreements is more efficient if those agreements all belong to the J or A category' (1988: 359). Indeed, the changes taking place in the J (for Japanese) financial organisation may be interpreted as a shift towards financial agreements belonging to the A (for American) category. This shift also indicates a reconsideration of the role of financing in the competitiveness of the model.

Short-term orientation

The appearance of finance-led strategies in the 1980s clearly involved a risk of limiting Japanese firms' horizons. Even if there is nothing to tell that this development was more marked in Japan than in other OECD countries, notably in America, it certainly represented a striking contrast with previous Japanese economic practice. Latent short-termism does not so much represent the danger of a speculative drift – which might lead firms to favour short-term financial profits – as the development of financial relationships based on short-term indicators.

Basically, it all depends on the way things are handled between managers and shareholders, and there are two main, but conflicting, approaches. The first one consists of adopting the same goals for shareholders and managers, by assessing the latter's performance through the evolution of the market value of assets. The advantage of this approach is to divert managers from projects that would not meet the shareholders' interests, but its drawback is that it introduces a short-termist bias. On the contrary, according to Japanese tradition, the manager is almost fully employed within his firm and thus has no incentive to favour short-term projects, since his performance is assessed over the long term. Moreover, he participates in the accumulation of human capital specific to the firm. Asymmetry of information is reduced through main bank control, which is in a better position than the capital suppliers present on the market to check the earmarking of funds, so that firms are not submitted to a risk of liquidity crisis and can undertake long-term commitments (Hoshi *et al.* 1990; 1991). Furthermore, the cross-shareholding system does not penalise long-term projects, joint ventures remain stable and their development is not linked to the short-term variations of asset prices. This is important because if it were not for the common interests shared by all the actors of the cross-shareholding organisation, the main bank might adopt opportunist behaviour. Indeed, by taking advantage of the secret information it holds on the firm, it might feel tempted to pocket excessive profits beyond the collection of an insurance premium in return for its intermediation (Chen 1994). The system of financial intermediation also allows for the compensation of losses on inefficient long-term projects by profits on long-term efficient ones. It finances both inefficient and efficient projects, whereas a market system is not propitious to the refinancing of inefficient investment schemes. Unfortunately, the market tends to avert long-term projects, including efficient ones (Amable and Chatelain 1995).

Financial hybridisation versus production hybridisation

The analysis of Japanese trends provides an example of the financial hybridisation of a production system. The last decade has seen the spread of innovative Japanese production methods throughout Western Europe, notably Toyotism. The reasons for production hybridisation are well known. The Fordist organisation, based on economies of scale, came to appear too rigid to meet an increasingly diversified demand hence Toyotism, more adapted to the scope of economic achievement (Boyer *et al.* 1998). Today's shift of the Japanese model is more akin to a financial hybridisation process linked to adopting financial principles – or of organisation of the financial environment – from the Anglo-Saxon model, i.e. bank-industry relationships in which the insurance role of the main bank is restricted, and shareholding relationships with increased profitability constraints.

It is nevertheless difficult to put both processes – production hybridisation and financial hybridisation – on the same level since the Japanese model has not only been endowed with different financial functions, but has also been the victim of considerable disruption. Rather than a mere international convergence of industrial finance, some think there is a risk of bringing instability to the most idiosyncratic finance systems, threatening the viability of the industrial models that are linked to them: 'the economies whose production model is lagging behind, and which are under the spell of a "return to the market" are ahead of those sticking to organised capitalism systems. [...] If the global economy's current trends were to go on, the bad regulations might replace the good ones, and in the long term stagnation and/ or instability might prevail over the model that took shape between the First and the Second World Wars' (Boyer and Saillard 1995: 376).

A purely financial interpretation of the shift of the Japanese model, particularly of the changes in the Japanese Employment System (JES), should be treated carefully. Nevertheless, in the current crisis, the financial component of the model, instead of accompanying the shifts and adaptations, as it did in the 1970s, introduces disruptions that weaken the coherence of the JES and give birth to changes in the production environment. The duration of today's crisis must be seen as the result of a major disruption of the financial environment, combined with the fatigue of certain elements of the industrial model.

Shifts in the employment system: the 'desanctification' of the treasures

The JES, operating with basic 'sacred tenets', has contributed to the competitiveness of national firms by allowing them to take advantage of both internal and external assets. But as these 'sacred cows' have recently become increasingly fragile, one observes significant shifts in the employment system, in the search for a higher competitiveness.

A brief look back at the 'sacred cows'

The JES, as defined after the Second World War, has three pillars: lifetime employment, seniority in wage systems and enterprise union. These three features have created long-lasting, cooperative relationships between labour and management, and contributed to a stable corporate development.

- *Lifetime employment* has no legal basis, and it is difficult to estimate its share in total employment. Yet, in the 1970s it represented probably 30 per cent to 40 per cent of the total number of wage earners. By contrast, workers in medium and small-sized firms, women and younger people change status (periods of inactivity, interfirm mobility) more often than male workers in big firms. Overall, in these big firms the division also exists in the labour market between permanent and unionised workers on one hand, and part-time or seasonal ones on the other (see Chapter 2).
- *Seniority* constitutes a major factor in the setting up of wages, as several studies have pointed out, mainly when compared to the situation in the US (Mincer and Higuchi 1988). If in the US mobility often represents a means to improve wages, when Japanese workers have acquired their skills in a different company, they are often poorly paid, so that the seniority system offers few alternatives.
- *Trade unions* have largely contributed to the stability of relationships between labour and management. The stereotyped image of an 'in-

house' union has undoubtedly led to a wrong perception of its real function in the model. Modern trade unions, peaceful negotiators, do not date back to the post-war period. Remember the very severe strikes of the years 1950–60, that only lost their impact after the first oil crisis, when unionisation lost much of its clout due to the decline of traditional manufacturing industries and to the more and more frequent hiring of temporary, non-unionised workers. This is how the union came to be considered as the embodiment of the mutual interests of labour and management, while being the guarantor of lifetime employment.

This employment pattern has strengthened the competitiveness of Japanese firms, by allowing them to take advantage of both internal and external flexibility. On the one hand, the firm can set up long-term employment relationships with its workers who benefit from these privileges. These permanent workers are encouraged to upgrade their skills in order to move up the hierarchy. Thus the firm has a dedicated and widely skilled workforce at its disposal, which ensures the advantages of internal flexibility and strengthens the quality-competitiveness of its products. Stable labour-management relationships might lead to serious constraints on the firm in difficult periods, and thus affect its price-competitiveness. That is why the other components of the labour-management relationship are conceived in such a way as to give the firm external flexibility.

Traditional adjustment mechanisms have helped to cope with the 1990s

The bursting of the bubbles on the real assets markets from 1989 onwards and the start of the Japanese recession as early as 1991, led economists to ask whether the JES was compatible with the new demands on industry. Does it still contribute to the coherence of the Japanese model? Is it compatible with new demands of Japanese actors? Is its scope being restricted?

Even if the unemployment rate reached a record 4.8 per cent in March 1999, it still remains far inferior to average rates in OECD countries. On the one hand, it corresponds to historically high levels that have never been reached since 1955, and on the other hand, it is considered as notably under-estimated compared to Western countries' rates.[5] The years after 1991 saw a significant rise in the unemployment rate, even though it was still contained by the traditional adjustment mechanisms inherent in internal flexibility.

- In order to come to terms with overmanning, firms have curtailed their hiring of young graduates, shifted staff members towards other positions or other production units (which is part of their discretionary powers), launched early retirement schemes and laid off non-permanent workers.
- As from 1991, the variable components of wages have hardly varied at all, so that the payroll has remained under control. In 1998, wages increased

by a monthly average of 2.3 per cent, which is the lowest ever rate observed since this statistic was first collected in 1969.

- Lastly, working hours have been significantly reduced, thanks to a limited recourse to overtime, to the extension of the 40-hour week, and to the increase of paid holidays.

The system becomes fragile

Nevertheless, recourse to these traditional adjustment mechanisms appears insufficient today. The prospect of the decline of lifetime employment, though frequently mentioned, is generally ill-documented, probably because of the absence of jurisdiction on this point. Its scope may be controlled by increasing the hiring of part-time or casual workers (Figure 10.1), which allows management to maintain the permanent workers' status, because casual ones get lower hourly wages and do not enjoy the same benefits (wages linked to seniority and to the firm's results, health insurance, pensions, etc.).

Beyond the issue of lifetime employment, the weight of seniority is now questioned, people increasingly favouring performance-related criteria. In 1998, 80 per cent of listed corporations planned to launch systems that would allow them to individualise wage costs. Several factors account for such moves. First of all, it has become more essential today to stimulate each worker's creativity, than to maintain his attachment to the firm's culture. In such a framework, wages based on individual performance seem better adapted to the new rules of competitiveness, thus making it possible to bypass the hierarchical wage scale, based on position and seniority.

Furthermore, taking into account the fact that many firms have slowed down their hiring of young graduates and accelerated their retirement policies in order to maintain lifetime employment, the number of middle-aged

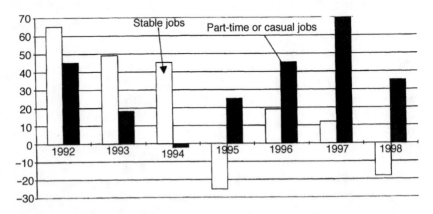

Figure 10.1 The erosion of stable jobs (annual variation of employment × 10,000).
Source: Ministry of Labour, *White Paper of Labour* (1998a).

workers has automatically increased, where they already used to represent a big share of the workforce, which had led their employers to create management positions without any real responsibilities attached to them. Within the seniority system framework, wages rapidly increase after 40, to culminate at about 55, which adds a burden to the payroll. Honda, for instance, introduced in 1994 the new rule of 'reversed promotion' in order to overcome this deadlock. It means that when top managers reach a certain age without any promotion, they are asked to take an early retirement or demoted in the firm hierarchy, with a lower salary (Garanto 1994).

The third reason is that some wage claims contribute to the fatigue of the seniority system, which appears as less and less adapted to a worker's financial needs over the course of his life cycle. The 1993 wage reform at Toyota is an illustration of this new trend. Before the reform, workers between the ages of 25 and 40 used to complain about the slow increase of their salaries at the beginning of their careers. The standard wage curve would in fact slightly rise until the age of 40, corresponding to a change of direction. In order to meet wage claims, the reform led the firm to accelerate pay rises along the first period and to reduce them later, after 50 (Shimizu 1994; 1999). This reform may attempt to reallocate the seniority effects that have more importance in the first part of a worker's career. It also points to (similarly to the approach of Sony and NTT) the necessity of finding new wage systems, in order to eradicate the contradictions inherent in the present system (see Chapter 7).

Lastly, the enterprise union's strategy, which used to be confined to protecting permanent workers and ensuring they moved upward in the hierarchy, is no longer adequate for the changes in in-house promotion mechanisms that occurred as a result of the double effect of economic stagnation and the demographic burden represented by baby boomers. It is a sign of the times to see more and more top managers join trade unions, and in 1998, there were more than 70 unions where executives could enrol individually.

Three structural shifts challenge the employment system

Other major changes, external to labour, foretell a structural transformation of the JES.

Financial deregulation and the erosion of incentives linked to the employment system

Beyond the financial crisis and its economic consequences on the employment situation (via a possible credit crunch, the negative effect of wealth for firms, etc.), the new modes of industrial financing linked to financial deregulation lead to a loss of coherence in the incentive system that used to characterise labour relationships. Indeed, the relationships between banks and industry that existed prior to deregulation allowed them to strengthen and to complete the intra-company incentive system. It may be necessary to look back on the financial logic of the J firm to understand this (Aoki 1990; 1994).

In the J firm, the production organisation directly depends on bank control. The internal organisation of the firm is characterised by the combination of a non-hierarchical coordination of operational units and a hierarchical incentive system (Aoki 1990). Production is based on collective knowledge, teamwork, and requires long-term employment relationships combined with an ambitious training policy which allow for this unique accumulation of knowledge and contractual conventions inherent in a decentralised coordination. The incentive method is based on rank hierarchy, a continuous promotion system within the internal labour market linked to specific skills acquired through training sessions. Yet the incentive effects of rank hierarchy may fail to meet the problems posed by workers who act alone in a teamwork environment. Moreover, in the absence of external control, insiders (management and labour) might appropriate the firm revenues, which would lead would-be creditors to refuse to finance. The J financial contract – the characteristics of which are defined in the MBS framework – completes the internal incentive system and allows the firm to get external finance. Bank monitoring means that insiders make a minimum effort to pay back loans, and thus to avoid the main bank's interference. This possibility of intervention, as well as acting against bankruptcy risks, makes it possible to reach long-term employment agreements and to capitalise on the accumulated collective know-how. As a corollary, the MBS allows firms to invest in human capital, unlike financial markets that offer few incentives to managers in favour of this kind of investment (Sheard 1994a).

The new statutory environment is less favourable to the working of this incentive system. The erosion of the insurance and control functions of the MBS is thus likely to disrupt the production organisation and the previous wage arrangements, all the more so since an increased recourse to market financing might reduce the share of investment in human capital.

Demographic evolution and increased external mobility

As from the year 2000, the labour market should face a shortage of young, skilled workers, corresponding to the arrival on the labour market of the lean generations of the 1980s. Such a situation might lead firms to hire middle-aged workers (Jaussaud 1996; Ebizuka, Uemura and Isogai 1996). Yet, even though permanent middle-aged workers already feel the pressure to change employers (because of deadlock situations in their own firms and of increased take-over risks), they have so far not exhibited interest in leaving their company in mid-career because it would mean a substantial loss of their capitalised pension (Chapter 5) and it would also put a halt to their wage increases (Chapters 2 and 8). If external mobility is to be encouraged, separation costs must be substantially reduced. Although no reform at the moment allows for the transfer of pension rights from one firm to another, the Tokyo Mitsubishi Bank announced to its personnel in 1998 that they would not be allowed to join the company pension scheme in exchange for a share of the profits. Indeed, in a situation of almost full employment, these separation costs play the same role as the risk of being unemployed in a 'shirking' model (Shapiro and Stiglitz 1984) by leading workers to make the minimum efforts to keep their permanent employment (Ebizuka, Uemura and Isogai 1996). Similarly to financial deregulation, the demographic trend might very well upset the incentive system prevailing in wage relations and increase the need for a structural change of the employment system.

Tertiarisation and the pursuit of industrial relocations

The tertiarisation of the Japanese economy also contributes to making the employment system, until now very dominated by industry, more fragile. Indeed, the optimal employment system in the service sector is different from the optimum for the manufacturing sector, which confirms the trend of the service sector to develop temporary or part-time jobs. The evolution of the employment system would then also proceed from a 'structural effect' linked to the rise of the service sector, whose influence is likely to be reinforced by the acceleration of industrial relocations in Asia since 1993.

Furthermore, the pursuing of these industrial relocations should contribute to making the employment system, originally set up for manufacturing, even more limited or fragile, by accelerating the tertiarisation process of the economy. If the hypothesis of a structural shift is verified, it is likely to have a negative effect on Japanese competitiveness in a transition period, partly because the search for new coherence is a costly and lengthy process. But in the long run, improved wage relations may make an positive contribution to Japanese competitiveness, better adapted to the new production requirements and social demands.

National innovation system: limits of a market-driven innovation system

While Japan was making an extraordinary breakthrough on the world economic stage in the 1980s, close attention was being paid to the analysis of national innovation characteristics. Clark and Fujimoto's study (1989) and Womack, Jones and Roos (1990) spread the idea that, in the field of design and development, Japan has a considerable advantage since it can rapidly design better-quality, cheaper products, thus always appearing as a 'first mover'. Some other studies from the same period are more balanced. Without denying Japan's ability for designing and developing new, quality products, they also point out a certain number of limits (Odagiri and Goto 1993; Aoki 1988).

The Japanese R&D system should also be envisaged as having reached some of its limits (Yoshikawa 1994), which is confirmed by the recent performances of Japanese exports, notably on the international market of domestic information technology products. There is also another question to pose: why is it that some of the traditional virtues of the system have reached their limits and are now in a position where they might contribute to the decline of the nation's competitiveness?

Traditional virtues

The description of the Japanese innovation system presented here is not exhaustive, but includes some of its main features.

- Notwithstanding the fact that, in the long term, Japan has invested large amounts of money in its R&D, the virtue of the system lies actually in the firms' own investment effort in R&D, which appears to be considerably higher than in other industrial countries. Firms account for more than 70 per cent of the total investment in R&D vs. 50 per cent in the US or in Europe (European Commission 1994). R&D in Japan is deeply rooted in firms and industrial groups, close to their concerns and to the market.
- In Japanese companies, research activities are carried out far less individually and selfishly than in the US or in Europe (Odagiri and Goto 1993). Chandler's 'M' pattern is also less felt in Japanese companies, which contributes to a better circulation of knowledge.
- Some comparative studies note that in many large corporations (Toshiba for instance), a real career is offered to R&D personnel, not only in the specific area of research, but also in management areas.

These characteristics contribute to the representation of the Japanese corporation as a place where R&D production-marketing relationships are efficient, in compliance with Kline and Rosenberg's definition (1986) of the efficient condition of an innovative production. Indeed, they both insisted on the fact that the 'short loops' making repeated cooperation possible between research, production and market, really existed within Japanese corporations. This system offers other advantages in terms of industrial organisation.

- The first of these arguments is that the nature of the relationships between contractors and suppliers is propitious to the generation and dissemination of innovations: long-term contracts, incentives to innovate through profit-sharing schemes, etc. (Asanuma 1989; Coriat 1991).
- The other aspect of the Japanese industrial organisation is related to the forms of competition. The Japanese economy long remained protected from international competition and thus developed its own competition pattern, characterised by the fact that among all existing companies, only a few undoubtedly act as leaders. These leaders are in a position to impose

their prices on their rivals, whose only means to survive is through innovation. Competition thus develops itself at prices almost exclusively depending on the market shares that are secured thanks to differentiation. Stackelberg's competition pattern is a powerful and permanent innovation factor.

All these different elements represent an extraordinarily efficient machine which combines cost-advantages (various savings linked to the lean-production system), and non-cost ones (strong tendency to innovate and differentiate production). Nevertheless, the problems that have appeared in the 1990s on several markets lead to a complete reappraisal of these characteristics, so as to highlight the limits, and not the virtues, of such an innovation system. It is then possible to envisage two different categories of problems.

Excessive product differentiation

Actually, there is a R&D non-profit-making paradox, since increased R&D expenditures have not lately shown better economic results. There are multiple reasons for this paradox.

- The previously reviewed characteristics of the Japanese industrial organisation and its competition pattern have finally led to a situation of excessive competition, in which excess costs due to differentiation (for products as well as for their components) have become too high, thus leading to a considerable waste of resources.
- The emphasis is then laid on the 'fat design' of the easy-growth years and of the bubble economy. The race for innovation has reached such levels that the process has become largely counterproductive. It is necessary then to decrease the number of variants for each product and to slow down the launch pace of new products in order to lower the fierceness of competition and reduce the excessive consumption of resources, especially R&D.
- With the yen appreciating, final assemblers have asked their suppliers for significant discounts (e.g. 10 per cent to 15 per cent on average over three-year periods in the automobile industry). Engagements like this can be kept only if less diversity is required, so that it is indispensable today to ease off on this pressure that has become unbearable for a good many firms. In doing this, the system undoubtedly deprives itself of one of the traditional non-cost advantages it used to enjoy when able to offer a wide range of products for each basic model and renew them at a fast pace in order to remain a first mover. It seems today that the monopolistic rent has lost its stamina because of the excessive design and production costs.

Basic research lacking in scope

The second series of reasons supporting the idea of limits to Japan's competitiveness is as follows:

- The argument is that as long as Japan was in a catching-up process (that ended in the 1980s), it could ensure its own steady economic growth by developing rent-collecting innovations of numerous products, thanks to a generous use of international patents and its own dynamic innovation system. As a leader country, if today's Japan is to go on developing and strengthening its position it will be hindered by the lack of scope of its basic research activities.

- The US accounts for approximately 50 per cent of the world's basic research, versus about 40 per cent for Europe and only 10 per cent for Japan (Amable and Boyer 1994). If such a situation is not a major handicap in a catching-up process, it can become heavily penalising once the process is over and as Japan, in turn, must contribute to 'invent the future'. Furthermore, the importance of private R&D may appear as a structural weakness of the system. Publicly funded research is insufficient, when it is the only one to be able to pursue the kind of basic research whose returns in terms of profitability cannot be anticipated.

- Since the technological race has accelerated in the R&D intensive industries, the traditional Japanese advantage (that used to lie with 'D' and manufacturing) may no longer be enough. This seems to be the case with some information technology products. The paradox of the situation lies in the fact that Japanese firms seem to be caught in their own trap: that of an accelerated differentiation in a sector in which the weakness of the nation's basic research prevents them from reacting vigorously.

- Under such conditions, one may question the patent system and the protection of intellectual property which prevail in Japan. The Japanese system is different from the American one insofar as it is easier to get a patent, but the rights attached to the patent are not well protected. Even if such a system is considered as being favourable to 'incremental' innovation, since each company can, at low costs (or risks) take advantage of its rivals' breakthroughs to contribute to the improvement of the state of the art (in perfect accordance with the 'continuous improvement' theory commonly followed by those same firms), one is puzzled by the weak incentives of this system when it comes to promoting basic research.

Conclusion: a major crisis

Does all this mean that Japan is doomed? Certainly not, but adding up the evidence of fatigue in the innovation system, the slow but visible failing of the employment system, and the real threats to the banking and financing system, one is forced to acknowledge that the Japanese economy has reached a stage where the economic aspects of the crisis are the symptoms of structural problems. The prolonged recession hides, then, a major crisis, insofar as the structural reforms that made Japan's success possible in the past decades have now reached their limits.

According to this interpretation, the return to economic growth and well-being depends on far-reaching restructuring and reorganisation measures. Today's uncertainties do not really concern Japan's ability to achieve a new coherence, but rather its capacity to preserve, or conceive, such unique mechanisms as those devised in the past in order to build on its prosperity and ensure its economic development.

Conclusion

An epochal change ... but uncertain futures

Robert Boyer and Toshio Yamada

This book opened with a series of dilemmas: is Japan totally exceptional or is it a typical market economy? Does the archaism of Japanese institutions explain the poor macroeconomic performances of the 1990s or are the short-term monetary and budgetary policies only to be blamed? Is the Japanese manufacturing system extremely efficient or does the bursting out of the bubble show all its structural weaknesses? Should Japanese authorities preserve the totality of the post-Second World War economic institutions or should they definitely import typical market-led capitalism?

This book argues that a third way can be traced between these extremes and that it delivers two benefits, namely, a new understanding of Japanese long-term development, and a generalisation of the *régulation* theory, which was initially elaborated by Western scholars in order to understand the long-term dynamics of the American and European economies after the Second War War.

Success leads to a major crisis

The preceding chapters have developed this paradoxical and general statement for various institutional forms and their joint evolution. This conclusion proposes a synthesis, based upon the mutual relationship between the growth regime and the organisation of banking and finance.

Growth slow-down and internationalisation destabilise the financial regime

Basically, many problems of contemporary Japanese economy originate in the 1970s, when at least three intertwined factors caused a drastic slow-down in the growth rate. First the two oil shocks destabilised the international economy and spread the American productivity slow-down to all other developed countries, including Japan, a country where deceleration is the most spectacular (Boyer 1999b). Second, the inner logic of a period of catching-up of international production norms is to follow the equivalent of a logistic curve, i.e. to decelerate when the economy matures. Last but not least, the shift from an investment-led growth to the rapid surge of mass consumption, and then an export-led regime (Chapter 8) introduced strong and new pressures into the Japanese economy (Figure C.1).

Slow-down induces significant changes in the behaviour and financial strategy of the main actors. The private investment growth rate decelerates, whereas R&D expenditures increase in order to provide a new basis for Japanese competitiveness. Consequently, even if the mark-up is declining, external financing by large firms is decreasing. The public budget, which used to be nearly balanced over a whole cycle, experiences a structural deficit; the tax basis is growing at a lower rate than the public spending associated with past institutional compromises, even taking into account that universal welfare is limited (see Chapter 5). Thus, in close parallel with the evolution of many OECD countries, the Japanese government issues an unprecedented volume of public bonds, which, in turn, requires a significant reappraisal of banking and financial regulations (see Chapter 6). Given this new context, private firms shift from credit banking to direct finance and the Japanese regime therefore undergoes a structural transformation, long unnoticed but far-reaching, as the evolution of the 1990s has finally shown.

These two domestic structural transformations move the Japanese financial system towards less banking credit and more direct finance for large firms, but the progressive insertion of the Japanese economy into the international system puts strong pressures on this shift. The large and recurrent external trade surplus derives from the fact that the household savings rate has declined less than the corporate investment rate during the 1980s and the 1990s (Chapters 3 and 8). Therefore, Japanese financial institutions are induced to buy foreign productive and financial assets and this precipitates a redesigning of domestic financial regulations which used to prevent such a portfolio approach to asset management. Symmetrically, American (and European) firms and banks ask for a liberalisation of the Japanese product and financial markets. The governments finally yield to these converging domestic and international pressures, and financial liberalisation takes place.

All these forces and factors converge to destabilise the Japanese financial regime which shifts from a MBS towards a more hybrid system with significant direct finance (Chapter 10). In a sense, the very success of the high-speed-growth period leads to major structural changes and a slow-down, that induces various financial reforms. Finally, one of the main pillars of the Japanese growth regime has been challenged, and this becomes evident with the quasi-stagnation and major uncertainties of the 1990s.

Destabilisation of finance reinforces the crisis of the growth regime

Conversely, the lost coherence of the financial regime triggers a series of institutional transformations, that directly or indirectly affect the inner dynamism of the growth regime. Closer integration into the world economy means that finance again dominates productive capital back into the idiosyncratic Japanese institutional architecture. Therefore, companysim the

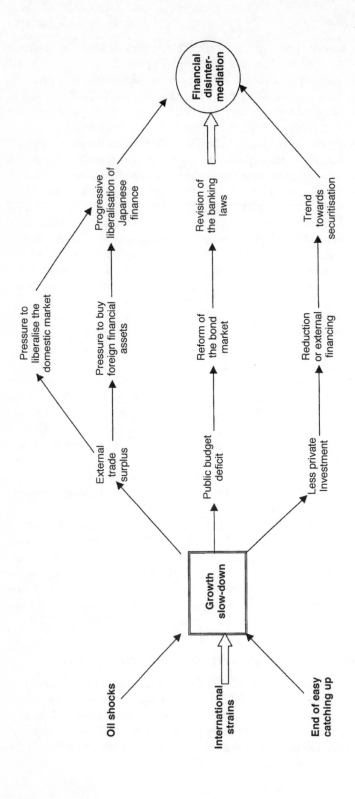

Figure C.1 From growth slow-down to destabilisation of the financial regime: the 1970s and 1980s.

compatibility of institutional forms and the clear hierarchy that previously formed a virtuous macroeconomic circle – is challenged, first mildly and then more and more drastically, thus introducing and exacerbating an unprecedented vicious circle (Figure C.2).

The pressures of international financial markets and the strategy of *keiretsu* to restore adequate profitability ratios and financial stability directly affect the governance mode of most manufacturing firms. Given the legacy of over-accumulation during the bubble years and the unexpected sluggishness of domestic demand, the competition on product markets become more severe than ever and triggers deflationary pressures, i.e. absolute fall of producer prices and even consumer prices. A large fraction of the employment adjustment burden is shifted onto subcontractors, which are no longer able to accommodate it with their conventional counter-cyclical approach (Chapter 4).

Furthermore, the large manufacturing firms force strong costs reductions on their subcontractors, the antithesis of transferring excess labour to them. Similarly, the period of over-evaluation of the yen triggers the transfer of many manufacturing operations to a low-wage area, a trend that might, in the long run, destabilise the complex process of product innovation, which previously bound the large firm and its subcontractors, through very localised interactions within the domestic territory. During the 1990s, the piling of bad debts within the banking sector reverses the old pattern of risk management. Whereas previously, public authorities assumed responsibility, now it is up to each individual bank. Thus, small and medium-size firms are undergoing a severe credit crunch, which has an adverse influence upon hiring and investment decisions. More generally, structural uncertainty about the way out of the banking crisis makes investment behaviour quite risk averse. Such a reappraisal stalls this component of demand, and ultimately the growth regime itself.

Actually, the financial crisis has a strong influence upon household consumption. Losses incurred by many firms jeopardise the previous capital labour compromise on employment stability. When the Japanese economy was able to bounce quickly out of short recession into a new boom, the capital labour compromise made sense but after a decade of quasi stagnation it began to have a negative impact on profitability. Wage-earners clearly perceive this antagonism and fear losing their jobs. During the 1990s, the bankruptcy rate has reached an unprecedented level and numerous workers did indeed lose jobs. The recurrence of deflationary episodes also changes household behaviour: people postpone the consumption of consumer durables, because they expect that quality and price will be better next year. Housing expenditures were initially stimulated when the bubble burst and long-term interest rates decreased but after 1997 the uncertainty about employment, life-cycle income and the solution to the banking crisis reverses this trend.

Finally, the evolution of the exchange rate perturbs the adjustment of external trade and the export-investment-led growth regime. It becomes more

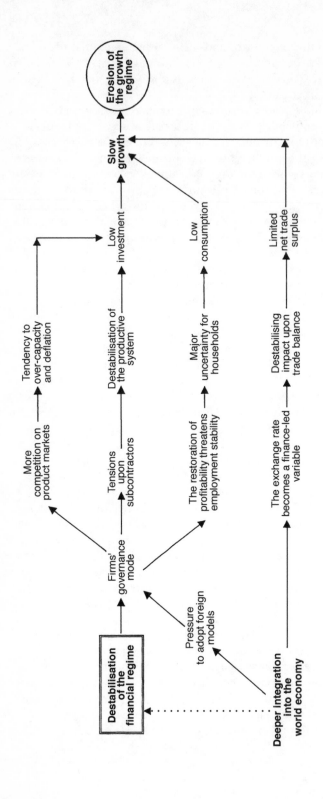

Figure C.2 From destabilisation of the financial regime to erosion of the growth regime: the 1990s.

and more difficult for Japanese exporters to compensate the sluggishness of the domestic demand, which still declines in 1998. Of course, world markets are even less reliable after the 1997 Asian crisis. Consequently, the large openness of the Japanese economy shifts from an asset to a liability for the stability of the companyist *régulation*. Furthermore, international financial markets tend to assess the viability of Japanese economic and social institutions while thinking that market-led capitalism, American or British style, is better fitted to respond to the challenge of financial and economic globalisation. The Japanese elite seems somehow lost in many areas: most discussions put the typical Japanese model up against one form or another of Americanisation (Gibney 1998), and all too rarely assess alternative reform programmes.

An unprecedented crisis of the *régulation* mode and growth regime

Three sets of evidence support the conclusion that the Japanese economy has entered into a new phase, with major disequilibria in the adjustments of economic activity, a clear destabilisation of most institutional forms and long-lasting structural incompatibilities between these forms.

The 1990s: the lost decade for Japan?

All macroeconomic variables point out that development after the bursting of the bubble does not at all resemble the previous business cycles. The rate of growth is not recovering its previous trends, unemployment is rising to unprecedented levels, the decline in consumer prices is no more exceptional, the public deficit is no more self-equilibrating, and a significant external surplus is still observed, whatever the contrasted evolutions of the exchange rate and the Japanese and US cycles. Such a configuration has never been observed before and is not at all the typical outcome of the *régulation* mode that was in place until the mid-1980s. To some extent, if the 1980s have been the lost decade for Latin-America, the 1990s may well deliver the same painful experience to Japan. This is the first evidence for a major crisis. But there is a second criterion for detecting such an episode.

All the institutional forms are under stress

Basically, a *régulation* mode enters into crisis when existing institutional forms put forward economic adjustments that threaten their stability and viability. This is precisely the process which the Japanese economy has been undergoing since the early 1990s (Table C.1).

The JWLN is unable to deliver a dynamic recovery of the profitability of the firms, nor does it seem viable in the long term to an increasing number of firms and wage earners. The discussions of the 'end of life-time employment',

Table C.1 From the Japanese miracle to structural crisis

Components	Basic strength 1960s–70s	Inner destabilisation sources 1980s	Nature of the crisis 1990s
Wage labour nexus	Employment stability and the cost of job loss generate commitment and polyvalence of employees within large firms.	Stress at work, labour scarcity for manufacturing, different expectations of young generations.	Open conflict between profit restoration and employment stability. Small- medium-sized firms can no longer play the role of shock-absorber.
Forms of competition between *keiretsu* with subcontractors	Active domestic competition. Organised complementarity.	Trend towards over capacity for manufacturing and exporting sectors. High costs trigger a move towards Asia and low-wage countries.	Recurring financial losses call for restructuring, mergers and alliances. A credit crunch severely affects subcontractors. Few risk capital for 'start up' in high tech.
State	A catalyst for companyism: supply of basic infrastructures, information sharing, coordination of strategies.	Loss of control over private actors, specially finance. Structural changes, end of catching up.	Loss of efficiency of most economic policy tools. Inability to work out new political compromises.
Monetary regime	Active role in the promotion of growth (low real interest rate, selective credit).	Exchange rate variability destabilises industrial strategies. The bad loans hinder the autonomy of monetary policy.	A liquidity trap. A debt deflation depression recurrently threatens macroeconomic stability.
Insertion into the international regime	Strong filters between Japan and foreign economies.	Stronger dependency with respect to world trade, high-tech innovations and finance.	Open conflict between the 'Japanese way' and 'the market-led model' promoted by international finance.
Régulation mode	Companyist compromise.	Strains brought by the bubble years (over investment, asset inflation).	Inability to maintain previous institutionalised compromises.
Growth regime	From profit-led regime …	… to export-investment-led regime.	Discrepancy between the Japanese governance mode and the evolving financial international regime.

the incompatibility of seniority wage with a slow-growth economy or the inability of large corporations to nurture the talents required by the information-led production paradigm, point out these limitations. Even if the macroeconomic aggregates do not exhibit any structural shift before the mid-1990s (Chapter 7), these concerns must be taken seriously.

The clear discontinuity between domestic and international price formation, which was so crucial for the evolution of profitability (Chapter 8), is changed by a new configuration for the form of competition. On the one hand, pressures from North America and Europe, as well as from the World Trade Organisation, make domestic price more sensitive to the impact of foreign competition, especially since the over-capacity inherited from the bubble years is still present at the end of the 1990s. On the other hand, many manufacturing and financial firms going through hard times financially go into various alliances and mergers, not only on a domestic level but also joint ventures with foreign multinationals. Clearly, the post-Second World War configuration for productive and financial capital is eroded, more or less irreversibly, which does not mean that typical American-style regulation of competition is necessarily the solution.

The links between the State and the economy contributed to the growth regimes observed since the end of the 1950s. Typically, civil servants coordinated long-term expectations, providing administrative guidance for each sector and the State financed collective infrastructures (transport, education, urban infrastructures, etc.) that were not easily provided by the *keiretsu*, even if they acted jointly. The 1990s scenario is completely different. First of all, the situations of the manufacturing firms belonging to the same sector are so diverse that it is difficult to provide uniform regulation, and conversely financial and banking losses are so widespread that conventional mergers of wealthy entities with bankrupt ones are no longer a sufficient solution. Second, given the near complete urbanisation of Japan, the spending plans built upon public infrastructures no longer have the large multiplier effects they used to exert, whereas the public debt is increasing and challenging, in the long run, the quality of Japanese public bonds. Newer instruments, such as consumer vouchers, have not overcome the gloomy prospects for the future of household income and employment. There is a strong discrepancy between the tools of the MOF inherited from the past and the productive and social structures of contemporary Japan. Third, as mentioned previously, it is especially difficult for the various public bodies, MOF, BOJ, MITI, EPA to reach a consensus on the future of Japan.

The monetary regime itself undergoes some major transformations, not really in terms of objectives, because promoting growth and stabilising the cycle are still pursued at the end of the 1990s, but rather in terms of implementation. A record low short-term interest rate maintained from 1995 to 1999 has not promoted the expected recovery in productive investment, and consumer durables. Quite on the contrary, the easy refinancing of banks has been associated with an unprecedented credit squeeze, in response to a drastic re-assessment of business risk. Therefore, demand and consumption have levelled off, quite a paradoxical result by comparison with the Keynesian multipliers observed during the 1960s and 1970s. Basically, fine tuning by monetary tools becomes nearly impossible when financial institutions are nearly bankrupt and the perception of a systemic risk stifles expectations. Furthermore, the impact of this low interest rate upon financial flows and exchange rates challenges the previous monetary regime, another outcome of the internationalisation of the Japanese economy.

Finally, the integration into the international scene progressively erodes the clear and efficient frontiers that used to separate domestic and world economies. From a pure economic standpoint, price formation at home is influenced by importers and foreign firms, and the price of Japanese exports has to take into account the emerging specialisation of newly industrialised countries. As far as finance is concerned, Japanese savers have interest in investing abroad and getting higher rates of return, especially when the yen declines with respect to the dollar. But, on the other side, banks and financial firms need to call back their foreign investments in order to get satisfactory reported financial results. In any case, the Japanese financial market is no longer isolated and the bursting of the bubble calls for the risk-management and prudential ratio, that have proved crucial in North America and the UK. Finally, internationalisation involves competition among alternative brands of capitalism, and Japanese companyism is under close scrutiny: its limits become evident, and the charm of market-led capitalism seems irresistible to many, particularly because the more depressed the Japanese domestic market, the more buoyant the American mood.

Rising systemic incompatibilities

So every institutional form has been altered, in a way that has taken them far away from the structural stability that prevailed during the previous decades. Moreover, the *régulation* mode that emerges from the conjunction of these institutional forms has become self-contradictory. This is the central message of all the chapters of this book. This crisis of the *régulation* mode is associated with the exhaustion of the growth regime built upon the stimulation of investment by exports. It means that the crisis is quite different from the cyclical down-turns previously observed and much more severe than the crises associated with the oil shocks and the *yendaka**. The mechanisms that were previously at the origin of Japan's good macroeconomic performances are in jeopardy, past certainties are vanishing and the structural compatibility of the five institutional forms is in the balance. For instance, a pure market-led financial system is probably incompatible with the companyist WLN, the permanent nature of previous public interventions is not appropriate to deal with the emerging and recurring financial imbalances, and oligopolistic competition at the domestic level is no longer allowed by new rules of the game put forward by international organisations such as WTO, OECD and IMF.

Key case study for generalising *régulation* theory

This approach delivers a fresh diagnosis about the evolution of Japanese capitalism. It suffers neither from too little Keynesianism (Krugman 1998), nor from too little market-led philosophy, still less from being different from the American economy (Dornbusch 1998). On the contrary, the 1990s have seen the painful unfolding of a crisis that actually originated in the success of an original companyist *régulation* mode and export-investment-led growth regime. The Japanese case confirms previous results obtained for the US and European countries, provides fresh conclusions, and calls for new extensions of *régulation* theory.

From complementarity to hierarchy of institutional forms

A study of American and French capitalism first explained the emergence of the Fordist growth regime as the result of a rather miraculous fit between disparate reforms defining new institutional forms (Lipietz 1979). But the explanation has turned to be quite partial, since it plays down the major role of the inter-war great crisis and Second World War in the synchronisation of a series of reforms that were intended to correct the structural instabilities associated with the domination of a competitive regulation (Chartres 1995). In some respects, the complete redesign of most Japanese economic institutions after 1945 provides another example of such a process of synchronisation.

The Japanese case brings a novel understanding of the cohesion of a *régulation* mode: the companyist compromise, as well as the hierarchical market-firm nexus permeate all other institutions, from the political sphere to the inner family circle. Therefore the chapters of the present book give many examples of the structural complementarity of Japanese institutions. Considered in isolation there seem to be as many departures from pure market mechanisms and external flexibility but analysed simultaneously they exhibit a remarkable structural fit, far away from a pure evolutionary process of trial and error. Such a process may govern the selection of techniques and the emergence of a production paradigm, but it is not sufficient to shape institutional forms, since power relations are crucial to their emergence and stability over a given period of time.

The transition from the 1980s to the 1990s forces the analysis to take into account the hierarchy among institutions and its shift from one historical period to another. In the 1960s, the compromise set between managers and workers on one side, manufacturing and finance on the other side, permeated the whole social, political and institutional architecture. But when the more vibrant innovations concern information technologies and the opening to sophisticated financial instruments, the previous hierarchy is destabilised and the market forces governing finance tend to impose their logic on the rest of the system and challenge the Japanese employment system, as well as the role of the main bank. Thus the Japanese trajectory makes quite clear another conclusion already derived from international comparisons (Amable, Barré and Boyer 1997), the diversity in institutional hierarchy.

The variety of régulation *mode: Japan is not a minor variant of America*

Much contemporary research in New Institutional Economics (NIE) extends rational choice theory to the analysis of institutions or organisations and, implicitly at least, looks for an optimal configuration, a benchmark against which to compare existing institutional economies. The Walrasian general equilibrium is the natural reference, in such a way that the better economic system should in fact totally and exclusively be governed by market mechanisms. Within this vision, it is not a real surprise if the Japanese economy seems quite odd to many foreign scholars. This book promotes a totally different interpretation: a series of more or less radical exceptions to typical competitive markets may actually define a quite coherent system, provided they display an institutional complementarity (Table C.2).

Often, economists and social scientists compare the US and Japan and oppose the US external market flexibility to the Japanese employment stability. It seems more enlightening to check how apparent imperfections in pure market logic complement one another in order to define a coherent and even more efficient system. When Table C.2 is read horizontally, Japan becomes quite mysterious, whereas when read vertically, the coherence of the institutional arrangements tend to appear quite clearly (remember, for example, Table 1.1, Figure 2.1, Figure 6.1, Figure 7.1). The fact that the Japanese *régulation* mode is so different from the American one helps social scientists in understanding the very significance of institutional complementarity and hierarchy.

The rational choice theorist will object: one only of the two configurations delivers superior results, thus one will overcome the other and consequently should be used as a reference. Numerous international comparative studies show recurrently that each *régulation* mode is to be assessed according to its own performance criteria, each configuration has therefore pros and cons and it is quite impossible for private and public decision makers consciously to select a preferred *régulation* mode, since it is mostly the unintended outcome of strategic interactions however rational may have been the selection of his/her strategy by each individual collective actor.

Empirical analyses confirm the long-run coexistence, at least until the 1980s of contrasted principles for organising economic and social activity. A market-led configuration is only one among the four currently observed among developed countries (Table C.3). The companyist architecture is not the only exception, since other economies are run according to social democratic principles or alternatively, they are largely state-led. Each single configuration benefits from clear superiority for some domains or criteria, whereas it turns out quite inferior for others.

Table C.2 The differerence between Japan and the US: two opposite *régulation* modes

Institutional forms	Companyist capitalism		Market-led capitalism
Wage labour nexus			
	Stability of employment (companyism)	⟷	Stability of nominal (or real) wage formation (Fordism)
	Internal flexibility of jobs	⟷	Strictly enforced job content and rules
	Firm-specific skills	⟷	Transferable skills
Forms of competition			
• Products	Mild enforcement of fair competition	⟷	Strong rhetoric of fair trade
• Finance	Cross-holding within *keiretsu*: stable governance	⟷	A market for governance of corporations
• Credit	Bank-centred system	⟷	High liquidity of equity market
State			
	Role in collective infrastructure supply	⟷	Low supply of public infrastructures and services
	Coordination of the strategic issues not adequately dealt with in the *keiretsu*	⟷	Enforcement of property and constitutional rights
Monetary regime and budget			
	Close links between Bank of Japan and Ministry of Finance	⟷	Search for policy mix between fiscal authorities and central bank
	From surplus to larger and larger public deficit	⟷	From three decades of deficit, to a surplus (1999)
Insertion into the international economy			
	Organised relations with the rest of the world	⟷	Open domestic market but strong anti-dumping tools
	Structural trade surplus	⟷	Structural trade deficit
	'Saver of last resort'	⟷	'Consumer of last resort'

Table C.3 The contribution of the Japanese case to a general taxonomy of capitalism brands

Component	Brand of capitalism			
	Market led	Companyist	Social democratic	State led
General principle.	**Coordination by the creation of markets controlled by several independent public authorities.**	**Shaping of economic activity and social life by the large corporation.**	**Bargaining and negotiation of institutionalised compromises between social partners.**	**Direct or indirect intervention of public authority in the structuring of institutional forms.**
Leading institutional form.	In contemporary economies, the financial regime.	In the golden age, form of competition.	The wage labour nexus and its institutionalisation by State.	The State/Citizen relationship.
Subordinate institutional forms.	The wage labour nexus, the form of competition and to some extent the State/Citizen relationship.	The wage labour nexus, the financial regime, the State/Citizen relationship.	The financial regime. Generally, the form of competition is set by insertion into the international system.	All other institutional forms: form of competition, wage labour nexus, financial and monetary regime, insertion into the international system.
Properties of the *régulation* mode • Strength	• Fast adjustment to shocks and disturbances. • Ability to generate radical innovations and breakthroughs. • Excellence in finance and related innovations.	• Medium– long-term economic and social stability. • Easy catching-up of state of the art technology and incremental innovations.	• Compatibility between domestic solidarity and external competitiveness. • Ability to generate innovations related to the Welfare State and the preservation of environment.	Compatibility between citizenship and the acceptance of capitalist logic. • Easy catching-up of mass production techniques.

	US–UK	Japan	Sweden–Austria	France
• Weakness	• Marked tendency towards speculation and financial instability. • Rising inequalities in terms of income, assets and access to political power.	• Sluggish reaction to unexpected shocks and radical innovations. • Heterogeneity of wage contracts and productive status (including gender).	• Large public intervention is required in order to implement social compromises. • Possible incompatibility with the trends of the world economy and finance.	• Mixing of polity and economy, as a permanent phenomenon. Difficulty in reforming institutional forms, when a *régulation* mode crisis takes place.
• Nature of structural crisis	• Increasing financial instability. • Inability to overcome stagnation of productivity, due to excessive wage flexibility.	• Inability to cope with large international fluctuations and shocks. • Difficulty in reforming previously successful institutions.	• Inflation as a solution to conflicts upon income distribution. • Impact of financial deregulation upon the viability of domestic productive compromises.	• Incompatibility with the constraints and opportunities brought by the internationalisation. • Difficulty in coping with emerging productive paradigm.
Typical examples	US–UK	Japan	Sweden–Austria	France

Each society has the crises of its socio-economic structure: the 1990s in Japan

For most economic historians, the observation of past major crises is supposed to exhibit a series of regularities, that can be used in order to analyse contemporary crises and forecast their unfolding. Analysts of business cycles, experts in Kondratief waves or neo-Schumpeterian economists tend to share this view. Therefore when the Nikkei index collapsed, many financial analysts made comparisons and saw similarities between the Japanese situation and that of Wall Street after the Black Friday crash of 1929. In spite of some similarities about the initial shocks, the two situations turn out to be largely different (Okina 1999), and it is not a surprise since the interwar *régulation* mode in the US and the contemporary *régulation* mode in Japan are not at all the same. Furthermore, the institutional reforms, regulatory system, and economic policy tools that have prevented the repetition of a cumulative and deflationary depression, usually trigger a totally different form for the next structural crisis, for instance, stagflation after 1967 and 1973.

Again, contemporary Japan gives a new confirmation to this main finding of regulationist research. Furthermore, this vision shifts the debate on economic policy recommendation from the mere importation of the policy mix of the most successful countries, i.e. currently the US, to an original analysis of the roots of each domestic crisis and its possible remedies. Some common features may or may not emerge afterwards from a careful comparison. But in general the therapy has to be rather specific, given the heterogeneity in the *régulation* modes operating on both sides of the Pacific Ocean.

Against economic determinism: the crucial role of political processes

Finally, the present book brings a last but important result: since the process of structural crisis is totally different from the usual business cycles or reproductive cycles, the way to overcome such a turmoil is not at all ruled by economic determinism but is largely open on the very intricacy of each national political process. This result came out clearly from the great transformation of former Soviet-type economies. Apparently small differences in the implementation of democratic institutions turned out to have a major impact upon the strategy adapted by governments and thus the speed and direction of institutional transformations (Chavance 1998). The ways the East Asian economies have reacted to the 1997 financial crisis are very diverse (Chapter 9) and largely dependent on the interactions between past specialisation and financial organisation (Contamin and Lacu 1998) and the evolution of political coalitions (Godement 1999).

Why is the way out of the 1990s crisis so long and uncertain in Japan? First, because the quality and the coherence of the companyist *régulation* are smoothing the reaction to the financial and economic crisis and making less urgent radical decisions from the government. Second, contrary to the intense social struggles that launched the emergence of companyist compromise back in the 1950s, the 1990s have experienced a loss of confidence of Japanese citizens with respect to their government, and thus a quasi-absence of society-wide political demands. Last but not least, the political institutions themselves entered into a crisis with the apparent breaking down of the party system that has ruled Japan for half a century. The quasi-paralysis of the government played a major role in the long duration of the banking and financial crisis, that have been sorted out in the US and other developed countries within less than one year, since the political constituency allowed a quick rescue of ailing financial institutions with subsidies from public budget, or even nationalisation.

By contrast it took nearly a decade for the Japanese government to pass such a financial law. This was the result of the reluctance of the political groups supporting the ruling coalition to adopt such an unpopular bill in spite of an unprecedented piling-up of bad debts in the financial sector. Such a discrepancy with respect to other countries cannot be explained without reference to the inner functioning of the government, the administration, the parties and their links with public opinion (Gibney 1998). Thus it is easy to find an interpretation for one of the major paradoxes of the Japanese crisis. A vast majority of analysts think that the issue is quasi-exclusively economic, i.e. related to the adoption of a good policy-mix between monetary and budgetary instruments. But a closer look should convince the reader that financial fragility is mainly responsible for the loss of efficiency of public management and that the radical uncertainty thus generated is paralysing most of the decisions related to the long term. A still deeper look leads to the conclusion that the inability of successive governments to pass quickly a law in order to bail out the nearly bankrupt financial system is at the root of this paralysis and the slow but steady erosion of the companyist compromise. This bill finally went through during autumn 1998 and began to be implemented in 1999 but still other structural reforms are to be decided. The future of the Japanese economy is therefore debatable and depends upon some possible strategic political choices. This teaching is quite general, since it recurrently emerges from the most recent research about economic policy formation and the role of the State in the way out of structural crises (Théret 1999; Palombarini 1999; Lordon 1999, Boyer 1999a).

Three scenarios for the next decades

These findings help in mapping out some possible future scenarios for Japan, however difficult it might be to anticipate largely open domestic strategic choices interacting with rather uncertain evolutions of the international system. Whereas the conventional debate is about the opposition between a specific Japanese trajectory and the adoption of typical market-led institutions, a third way is much more likely and deserves some analysis (Table C.4).

Table C.4 Some scenarios for the Japanese economy

Features	Scenarios		
	Sticking to Japanese 'companyism'	*Muddling through by hybridisation*	*Full Americanisation, i.e. convergence towards a market-led capitalism*
Leading force	**Embeddedness of institutions and practices leads to path dependency and inertia.**	**Consciousness by Japanese actors of the need to cope with the new economic and technological paradigm while sticking to Japanese style.**	**Severity of the financial troubles, strong external pressures, lack of clear alternative.**
Financial regime	Marginal adjustment of the Main Bank system.	Hybridisation of the main bank system with financial markets in charge of assessing the management of each subsidiary or parent company.	Complete redesign of the financial system, along international standards.
Insertion into the international regime	Defence of the distinctiveness of the Japanese territory: strong control about inflows.	Careful and selective opening: reconcile external pressures with new domestic modernising coalitions.	Complete erosion of Japanese asymmetric international relations: the end of Japanese exceptionalism.
Forms of competition	Still organised by *keiretsu* and significant public monitoring.	More open competition but still organised in order to minimise the social disruption associated with modernisation, specially in the service sector.	The new governance of firms calls for a more externally enforced competition: importation of American or British legislation.
Wage labour nexus	Rationalisation of the present Japanese employment system: it is restricted to core competencies, but lasting.	A series of piecemeal reforms (merit wage, hiring, training, …) finally end up into a new wage labour nexus adapted to the new macroeconomic context.	External labour mobility becomes the rule, professional markets replace internal market, diversity and flexibility of labour contracts.

State	Still the catalyst of 'companyist *régulation*'.	Still the major mediation within Japanese society, but a shift in objectives and tools.	Largely replaced by independent regulatory agencies. Drastic slim down of 'bureaucracy'.
Degree of change in the *régulation* mode	**Updating of the corporate-led *régulation*, without any significant structural change.**	**By a series of reforms, the *régulation* mode is progressively transformed into a qualitatively new one, a complex hybrid between corporate led and market led.**	**Radically new for Japan: unprecedented structural transformations affecting society, polity and economy lead to a brand of market-led *régulation*.**
Nature of the political process	**Structural blocking of modernising coalitions, marginal shifts in sectoral arrangements.**	**Past compromises along with some political *aggiornamento* allow the emergence of a new institutional architecture.**	**Full coalescence into new political alliances.**

First scenario: the embeddedness of institutions preserves the companyist régulation

Many features of the Japanese configuration seemingly argue in favour of such an evolution. The strong complementarity between industrial relations, the organisation of the financial system, the companyist governance mode and even the style for public interventions, continues to make quite difficult any radical reform of any part of this complex institutional architecture. The inertia of the political institution reinforces the likelihood of this scenario, that furthermore assumes that some kind of reform of the international financial and trade system would allow a fast and rather stable growth for the markets of Japanese manufacturers.

Under these quite optimistic hypotheses, the basic institutional forms are only marginally redesigned and they preserve most of their 'Japaneseness'. The Japanese employment system is rationalised and limited to the workers bringing the core competencies to the large corporation, competition continues to be oligopolistic and domestically organised, the main bank is again the key mechanism in the allocation of capital. Last but not least, the State is still carefully organising relations with the world economy in order to preserve basically the same social and political compromises. Even the burden of an ageing population, frequently presented as a threat for the 21st century, could be easily financed given the recovery of growth and productivity and possibly a continuous rise in female activity rate, the insertion of women into the Japanese work force providing the new talents required by the firms (Yokoyama 1999).

The success of such a scenario is not at all evident. First it is built upon the conjunction of quite optimistic hypotheses: a soft way out of the Japanese financial crisis, the dynamism of world trade, a quick recovery of Asian countries, a continuous prosperity of North America and/or the EU and the absence of a global financial melting down. Second, this scenario drastically underestimates the structural changes, largely irreversible that take place at the international level: a shift of productive paradigm under the pressure of information technologies, the emerging power of financial capital over the governance mode of firms and the economic policy of governments, not to mention demographic problems both within developed countries and in the developing world or the rise of environmental problems. Third, the tight cohesiveness and complementarity of economic and political institutions may well postpone long-needed restructuring but not prevent it from happening. The surprising collapse of Soviet-type regimes should warn Japanese decision-makers about the dangers of such a conservative attitude toward rising economic imbalances. The later the economic reforms, the more severe the structural crisis that may totally destroy the past institutional order (Sapir 1998; Boyer 1995b).

Second scenario: a major crisis urges the adoption of a typical market-led capitalism

Such a radical crisis could open the way for this second scenario. As with many other East Asian countries, the failure of the so-called 'Asian development model' would facilitate the direct importation of reforms from Western industrialised countries (Godement 1999: 202). But, even in the absence of such a dramatic episode, this scenario can be reached too by a possible re-composition of domestic political coalitions, if for instance, highly internationalised Japanese corporations and a new generation of politicians ally in order to promote a third opening of Japan to the world economy. By lack of any relevant alternative or by necessity, Japan would import typical market-led institutions, under the aegis of American expertise and direct pressures for 'levelling off the playing field', i.e. for adopting most American regulations or practice in terms of fair competition, financial supervision, external labour market flexibility, intellectual property rights, governance mode, economic policy and even life-style.

The 'big bang' already decided for financial markets would be extended to any other economic institutions. The vanishing of the MBS would imply that Japanese firms would aim at maximising profitability, if not shareholder values. Therefore the companyist compromise would concern a declining and very small fraction of workers, since a high labour mobility would necessarily complement the objective of stabilising the financial rate of returns of large firms. The companyist welfare should be replaced by a limited but universal unemployment coverage, to replace the previous subsidies to preserve employment in crisis sectors. The constant pressures of WTO would progressively remove the asymmetry between domestic producers and foreign competitors, with a significant impact upon consumer price formation. State organisation would change drastically in order to comply with the requirement of world financial markets. The BOJ would become more and more independent, the MOF would be split into separate entities and new independent agencies would be created in order to monitor finance, labour, technical norms, welfare and environment.

Clearly this would be the end of 'Japanese exceptionalism' and a form of convergence towards a typical market-led capitalism. Thus, the realism of such a scenario has to be assessed carefully. First, it would be emulated by the observation of the American long boom of the 1990s and the perception that the so-called 'New Economy' has succeeded in promoting an unprecedented *régulation* mode led by financial innovations. But the long-run viability of such a regime is still under scrutiny (*The Economist* 1999a; Boyer 1999a). Is it really recession proof and immune from speculative bubbles and macroeconomic instability? Second, the economic performances of the US are related to its position in the world economy and specially its role in financial intermediation, scientific advances and technological innovations but cultural values as well, and not only to the domination of a pure market logic. Importing the former would not imply getting the rewards of the latter. But the major objection is about the ability of public authorities to manufacture such a silent revolution, against most of the past institutionalised compromises. The adoption of an American model would imply an unprecedented rise in unemployment, temporary or long lasting, and a complete redesign of the basic compromise between managers and wage earners, as well as the building of a fully fledged welfare system, at odds with the segmented, large corporation-based present configuration. Such an achievement is not impossible, but not very likely. Furthermore, it contradicts one of the century-long features of Japanese society: the ability to import foreign technologies and practices and convert them into quite original organisations and institutions.

Third scenario: muddling through and reforming Japanese institutions by hybridisation

Therefore, a rather likely scenario takes into account the contradictory influence of new external pressures and domestic institutions' inertia, the two factors at the origin of the previous Japanese scenarios. On one side, the post-Second World War institutional configuration cannot be prolonged unchanged into the 21st century, because most, if not all, economic and political actors become convinced that the old system has reached its structural limits and has to be somehow reformed and the present system delivers poorer and poorer results. On the other side, a pure market-led configuration cannot be implemented directly into Japanese society and the process of modernisation will take a specific pattern, reiterating an adoption/ adaptation strategy (Abo 1994) that has been observed since the Meiji era. In other words, the internal and external pressures and opportunities will induce a hybridisation process not only of organisations (Boyer *et al.* 1998), but of economic and financial institutions (Tsuru 1995). The emergence of the Toyotist production system gives a good example of the power of such a strategy. After the Second World War, Japanese managers wanted to implement typical mass-production principles but were blocked by some structural incompatibilities with the prevailing domestic conditions: tiny markets, lack of saving and credit, little modern equipment and strongly organised workers fighting against the de-skilling typically associated until the so-called 'American methods' (Shimizu 1999). Out of this totally contradictory situation a series of seemingly marginal adaptations have finally led to an unprecedented production system that two decades later turned out to be quite efficient, while preserving some distinctive Japanese features.

The same pattern can be observed nowadays for the implementation of information technologies, the reform of labour contracts and possibly the introduction of financial innovations, in order to overcome the major structural weaknesses that have been inhibiting growth all through the 1990s. Thus, the MBS could be complemented by the control exerted by financial markets upon subsidiaries (Tsuchiya and Konomi 1996; Dirks *et al.* 1999). The opening to foreign financial innovation would be carefully managed in order to preserve the capacity of coordination that has been so efficient within the *keiretsu* structure. The strengthening of competition would be a slow process, in order to prevent the emergence and the persistence of mass unemployment, especially if a quick rationalisation were introduced into the low-productivity service sector. In this respect, the EU track is quite unattractive. Similarly, the companyist compromise would be restricted to the core, company-related competency, whereas the creation of a labour market for professionals would extend the degree of external mobility for some key expertise required by the new productive paradigm and transferable from one firm to another (Miyamoto 1998). The school system and universities could be reformed in order to cope with the need to be at the scientific and technological frontier and thus sustain Japanese competitiveness (Boyer 1999b).

Women could be brought more significantly into the labour force, both for their competence and in order to cope with the burden of an ageing population. Moreover a serious reconsideration of the family nexus and welfare system would be required for such an agenda to succeed. Simultaneously, the rise of the services could endogenously induce a shift from the primacy of the companyist compromise to a system of highly diversified and flexible labour contracts (Ribault 1999). Reduction of working time would go along with the possible emergence of a radically new growth regime governed by a better satisfaction of the social needs of Japanese citizens. Last but not least, following a long tradition, Japanese authorities would manage carefully the opening to innovations, technologies and organisations coming from the international system, in order to be sure that these adaptations benefit domestic groups while complying with the rules of the game set by the various international organisations (WTO, OECD, IMF, BIS). Opportunities of hybridisation would shift from manufacturing to finance, research and the organisation of social life.

It is quite difficult to forecast what will be the final *régulation* mode that might emerge from this trial-and-error process, since this scenario generates itself a whole spectrum of possible trajectories. Everything is up to the leading force and institutionalised compromise that will finally shape the whole socio-economic system. The episodes of the Meiji and post-Second World War reforms may deliver some guidelines for managers, politicians, unionists and citizens. But any relevant strategy has to be adapted to the context of the 21st century since there are no such things as Kondratief long waves and Schumpeterian clock which would set the pace of capitalist restructuring, that is not governed by pure technological nor economic determinism. Furthermore the issues are quite different.

Firstly, the dramatic episode of the Second World War had induced a complete redesign of past political coalitions and economic organisations; by contrast the powerful contemporary financial markets are leading and exert a daily control upon governments' choices and managers'strategies. Secondly, after 1945, drastic and rather coherent reforms could be introduced and synchronised, and they could overcome the obstacle of structural complementarity and inertia of political compromises. But nowadays the form of political governance and the larger complexity of financial, economic, and technological organisations, themselves the expression of an unprecedented deepening of division of labour, seem to allow only partial and marginal reforms. They will eventually lead to the emergence of a totally new *régulation* mode, one or two decades ahead, but it might be largely the unintended result of many trials and errors.

History never repeats itself . . . and history lasts long! This is a message of hope for the Japanese people who may thus find a way of modernising, once more, without losing either social cohesion or historical distinctiveness.

Notes

Chapter 1

1. A re-evaluation of the US–Japan labour-management compromises from the perspective of flexibility might be as follows. The institutionalisation of 'unlimited duties and job security' (in Japan) promotes flexibility in redesigning tasks and job content (internal and functional flexibility), but job security means restrictions are placed on flexibility in deciding the number of workers (external and quantitative flexibility). In contrast, 'limits on jobs – freedom of dismissals' (America) means that quantitative flexibility is guaranteed. In short, there is a mixture of flexibility and rigidity in either system, but unlike the 'flexible job content – rigid employee numbers' (for regular male employees of large firms) of Japan, the US features 'rigid job content – flexible employee numbers'. In general, enterprises must assure themselves some means of adjusting flexibly to external environmental change such as technological innovation or economic shifts, but the means of adjustment differ between the two countries. Miyamoto (1998) has identified institutional differences in corporate governance between management-dominated enterprises (Japan) and shareholder-dominated enterprises (US) as the basis for the differences between 'rigid employment adjustment and flexible job definition' (Japan) and 'flexible employment adjustment and rigid job definition' (US). This point will be emphasised in the latter part of this chapter.
2. On this point, see the excellent work of Kurita (1994), on which this chapter draws heavily.
3. From another point of view, regarding the dominant-subordinate personal relations of the employment relationship, Western workers have attempted to protect themselves by 'sectioning (clarifying) relations' or through 'contractual relations', while Japanese workers have, in contrast, tried to protect themselves by forming 'all personal character (long-term) relations' and 'trusting relations'. As explained in the following section, long-term and trusting relationships are not distinctive features of employment relations alone, but also of institutional structures such as interfirm relations and enterprise-bank relations. Grasping this phenomenon is essential to understanding the Japanese mode of *régulation*.
4. As can be hypothesised from Japan's distinctive capital procurement structure, the basis of the country's corporate governance lies within enterprise-bank and

interfirm relations. However, it should be noted that the structure of corporate governance does not lie within interfirm relations (cross-shareholdings and *keiretsu*) and enterprise-bank relations (MBS) alone, but extends to bank-government relations (the so-called convoy system) as well. According to the *régulation* approach, there is interpenetration among the various institutions, including forms of competition (interfirm relations), monetary constraints (enterprise-bank relations), and bank-government relations (forms of the state). This unusual feature means that the structure of governance is centred not at the level of the individual firm (micro level) nor at the national or state level (macro level), but at the group enterprise level implied in interfirm and enterprise-bank relations. It is from this structure that Japan derives its distinctive 'meso-corporatist' viewpoint.

5. Management security does not necessarily mean personal security for managers, and in fact stipulates that their retirement and replacement are necessary. As the terms 'long-term enterprise security' and 'management security' indicate, what is protected is the identity of the firm as a legal entity encompassing much more than its individual managers. It is only when this enterprise identity is protected that it becomes possible to establish among employees a sense of membership in and identity with the firm.

6. Many works have already indicated the complementarity of Japanese industrial relations (especially long-term employment), interfirm relations (cross-shareholdings), and company-main bank relations (Aoki 1988; Sheard 1994b; Aoki and Patrick, eds 1994; Uemura, Isogai, and Ebizuka 1998).

7. In this manner, Japanese companyist *régulation* functioned as a superb productivity-raising mechanism in support of Japan's post-war productivity regime. However, it failed to stimulate the development of an adequate demand regime circuit, particularly with regard to consumption. From the mid-1970s, in fact, it functioned to hold real wages to relatively low levels. When productivity rises are accompanied by tight wage restraint, industry relies more heavily on exports, causing economic growth to become export led. The export-led nature of the Japanese economy became especially pronounced during the early 1980s when the strong dollar made Japanese exports to the US even cheaper (Uni 1998). As a result, Japan became labelled an 'export giant-lifestyle midget' (Kim 1994).

8. Cf. 'An episode in which the mechanisms associated with the prevailing mode of *régulation* prove incapable of overcoming unfavourable short-term tendencies, even though the regime of accumulation was at least initially viable, will be defined as a crisis of the system of *régulation*. . . . [This crisis] within a regulatory system may [. . .] stem from any of its components: the inadequacy of existing forms of competition, the wage relation, state intervention, monetary management, or a country's position in international relations.' (Boyer 1990a: 52–3)

Chapter 4

1. The institutional arrangements are complex since they are brought about by four sets of strategic interactions. The first set of interactions occurs between nation-wide organisations of employers and unions. The second set take place

between central organisations and the rank-and-file members, i.e. individual firms or unions. The third set of interactions occurs between bargaining units and the monetary authorities. The fourth sets take place between the banking sector and the monetary authorities.

2. For further details of *shunto* see Takagi 1976; Koshiro 1983 and Sako 1997. Negotiations in *shunto* are not concerned with the 'rate of each job' but with the employer's total bill. This formula is convenient for employers since the wage bill is directly linked with price competitiveness.

3. These views can be understood in union leaders' statements referring to a kind of social contract. On 28 August in 1974 Chairman Yoshiji Miyata of Tekko Roren (the Federation of Steel Workers Unions) said that he would seek wage hikes consistent with economic growth and also insisted that as long as employers sought to maintain employment, unions should make an effort to cooperate with employers and the government. Chairman Seiji Amaike of Domei (Japanese Confederation of Labour) also advocated that his federation would accept moderate wage increases in the 1975 *shunto* (IMF–JC 1984; Mori 1992; Garon and Mochizuki 1993; Ohmi 1994).

4. Sohyo was organised in 1950 as a democratic union federation in opposition to the communist-led union movement. It later mutated from democratic to leftist. It was the largest national federation in Japan until the national labour confederation, Rengo (Japanese Private Sector Trade Union Confederation), was established in 1987.

5. In the period of high economic growth, the competitiveness of metal-related industries such as steel, shipbuilding, electric machinery, automobile and precision machinery, significantly increased. On this basis, leading private-sector unions founded the moderate International Metalworkers Federation – Japan Council (IMF–JC) in 1964 that transcended the ideologically conflicting nation-wide labour centres. It can be viewed as a national centre for export-related industries.

6. In 1983, a Japan–US Yen/Dollar committee was set up under the pressure of the US government with a view to deregulating the Japanese financial system. In the committee, US government officials urged the Japanese government to remove exchange controls based on external trade transactions and restrictions on exchange transactions (Nihon Ginko Kin'yu Kenkyujo 1995). This removal made it possible for economic agents to speculate on exchange rates since money was not necessarily coupled with the flow of goods and services or investments.

7. Japanese banks are permitted to own up to 5 per cent of the outstanding shares of their client firms. Most Japanese firms maintain ties to a bank, which is typically the firm's largest lender and also has a substantial equity ownership stake. These ties make it easy for the bank to get information on firms and to monitor management. This bank is called a 'main bank'.

Chapter 5

1. While there are also services provided and organised by local bodies, unions and other non-profit organisations, it is very difficult to evaluate and quantify these services.

2. In Germany, indirect salaries are relatively low, but that is partly compensated by the high remuneration for non-working days.
3. Nordic countries such as Sweden and Denmark have also adopted this principle.
4. Until 1979 Italy was a member of this group.
5. The role of the family is far from negligible. It influences the lives of retired people, the provision of a guaranteed income, particularly modes of consumption, and the care necessary with the passing years. A more profound theoretical study of the triumvirate of state, company and family appears necessary.
6. The 1986 law relating to the stability of employment for elderly people simply states that companies must make efforts to ensure that retirement age should be sixty or more.
7. The notional basic wage for the pupose of calculating retirement allowances is derived from the actual base wage. In fact, the two are often identical. Since the actual base wage is calculated by meritocratic mechanisms, the retirement allowance will also be affected by the company-ist *régulation* mode.
8. See Seike (1994) for a study of the effect of the retirement allowance on the internal labour market.
9. The data for these calculations come from a 1995 Labour Management Research Institute (*romu gyousei kenkyujo*) survey.
10. These examples are taken from actual companies.
11. This system came into operation in Japan in 1962 following the introduction of the Qualified Pension Plan in the United States.
12. This system was introduced in Japan in 1966, inspired by the 'Contract Out' scheme of the 'Professional Pension' plan in the UK.
13. To obtain the full old-age pension, one must have contributed for forty years. For those who have contributed for a shorter time, the pension will be reduced.
14. 'Collective' does not necessarily mean state provided. One can imagine various frameworks for payment such as associations, the third sector or mixed enterprises.

Chapter 6

1. Both *régulation* theory and comparative institutional analysis share the idea that the plural institutions which compose an economic system complement each another, and that the evolution of an economic system is defined by the initial historical conditions. See Aoki (1996) for an outline of comparative institutional analysis
2. In an analysis of the structural change of the US financial system, Wolfson (1994: Ch. 14) presents the concept of a 'system of financial *régulation*'. The concept includes not only the arrangement for supervising and regulating financial institutions, but also the entire institutional structure of a financial system, including the various means of financing the demand for credit, the role of government in the financial system, the nature of financial institutions, and so on. In other words, a system of financial regulation may be viewed as the financial component of a social structure of accumulation. The concept of a 'financial mode of *régulation*' in this chapter is very similar to this one.

3. Because of the widespread practice of demanding compensating balances (*buzumi* and *ryodate*) during the high-growth period, effective loan rates may have been not much lower than equilibrium rates, but, as I argue below, regulatory rents accrued to the banking sector and/or the corporate sector in this case, too.

4. There is little evidence that the activities of public financial institutions fostered high growth. For example, Horiuchi and Otaki (1987) conducted a causality test to verify whether lending by the JDB induced lending by private financial institutions. They concluded that such an 'inducement effect' was ambiguous for basic industries in the high-growth period. But Horiuchi and Sui (1994) argue that the information production activity of the JDB may have worked effectively for individual firms, though it did not play a major role as a means of industrial policy. Namely, they say that the information produced by the screening and monitoring activity of the JDB was somehow transmitted to private financial institutions, and that this improved the reputation of firms which received the JDB loans, leading the private financial institutions to provide more loans to those firms, and the firms to increase capital investment. They call this effect an 'information effect'.

5. Studart (1993), arguing from a post-Keynesian perspective, advances a more fundamental criticism of financial liberalisation models of developing countries based on the Shaw-McKinnon framework. He points out that the financial liberalisation models are based on the loanable funds theory of the rate of interest. Thus, in this model, appropriate financial policy has to increase aggregate saving through a rise in deposit rates. In contrast, Keynes and post-Keynesians do not consider interest rates to be the adjustment variable in the saving-investment market. Since investment is financed not by saving but by bank credit in the modern financial system, investment is not constrained by the shortage of aggregate saving.

6. Aglietta (1995: Ch. 3) argues that financial systems in advanced countries such as Japan and Germany are not going to converge toward the American-type capital-market-based system because banks perform an important function, supplying risk capital, which capital markets cannot perform.

7. See Horiuchi and Sui (1992); Shikano (1994: Ch. 8); and Yabushita (1995: Ch. 5), for a review of the debate on the MBS.

8. Aoki (1994b) points out that, in Japan, the corporate finance structure entrusts management control to inside managers when the financial position of firms is favourable, but the main bank intervenes in or takes over firms in distress. He calls such a corporate governance structure the 'contingent governance structure'.

9. On the existence of regulatory rents in the banking sector and estimates of their scale, see Horiuchi (1994: 20–1) and Ueda (1994: 94–6).

10. The following description concerning this point is largely drawn from Teranishi (1993).

11. Another factor which has facilitated financial deregulation is the rapid innovation in information and communications technology. These technological innovations stimulate financial innovations such as the development of new financial products and the expansion of financial transactions. But competition-restrictive regulations have the effect of retarding financial innovation, so it is expected that the social costs which

accompany these regulations are increasing rapidly. See Horiuchi (1994) and Ikeo (1994a).

12. Noshita (1995) argues that the change in the relationship between firms and banks definitely transformed the Japanese financial structure, and this induced the intensification of the competition among financial institutions (ibid. 189–94). City banks went into the field of loans for small and medium-sized companies and individuals that they had not dealt with before. Further, regional banks and *sogo* banks whose corporate client bases were eroded by the loan offensive of city banks not only competed with city banks more fiercely, but also entered the market of lower-tier financial institutions such as *shinkin* banks and credit unions. Kitahara (1995) calls the intensification of competition among financial institutions generated by the city banks' behaviour a 'billiards phenomenon' of financial institutions (ibid. 71–4).

13. J. M. Keynes argued in the concluding chapter of *The General Theory*: 'The State will have to exercise guiding influence on the propensity to consume partly through its scheme of taxation partly by fixing the rate of interest, and partly, perhaps, in other ways. Furthermore, it seems unlikely that the influence of banking policy on the rate of interest will be sufficient by itself to determine an optimum rate of investment. I conceive, therefore, that a somewhat comprehensive socialisation of investment will prove the only way of securing an approximation to full employment' (Keynes 1936: 378). Basing on Keynes's recommendation for socialising investment, American radical economists present their own proposals for reforming the US financial system. See Dymski, Epstein and Pollin (eds) (1993).

Chapter 9

1. There is development of intra-industry commerce in this region. In certain key industries, machines, electronics, the exchange between Japan and NIEs, ASEAN is highly dominated by this type of commerce (Inoue 1997).
2. In other words, it was considered a result of the 'wild goose flying growth' (Akamastu 1961) model initiated by multinational firms. But we have already noticed that the success and limit of industrialisation in Asian NIEs should be analysed from a structural and endogenous point (Inoue 1997).
3. Concerning the concept of credit money, and the concept of antevalidation (Lipietz 1983).

Chapter 10

1. The authors wish to thank Masanori Hanada who, in spite of the distance, provided them with very valuable and updated information on the subject.
2. Krugman (1993), has notably insisted on the idea that competitiveness is a 'dangerous obsession' and defends the idea that the notion of productivity is sufficient to nurture the discussion on the joint improvement of GDP and standards of living. Reducing the discussion solely to productivity is not sufficient to define a competitive policy that would allow a nation's external

economic performance to improve while protecting and encouraging labour incomes.

3. Eiji Toyoda, who once chaired Toyota, recalls in his memoirs how he had to let banks, notably the Mitsui Bank, interfere with firm management, in exchange for their help when, in 1950, the firm faced a liquidity crisis. The banks insisted on severe downsizing, and Fukio Nakagawa was appointed top executive by Mitsui.

4. The banks' role may also be illustrated by Mazda, a member of the Sumitomo group. When Mazda first entered a difficult period, after 1973, they could obtain very low rate loans, which encouraged the firm to increase the number of its financial shareholders. The commercial firm of the Sumitomo *keiretsu*, Sumitomo Corporation, organised the distribution sector and part of the management of the firm. The member firms of the *keiretsu* also encouraged the firm's payroll to buy Mazda products at discount prices. On the other hand, when Chrysler was on the verge of bankruptcy, almost 400 banks increased their help and none of them was really aware of the gravity of the problem, until the crisis became official.

5. Most experts agree on the necessity to reassess this rate by 4 per cent, if it is to be compared to Western countries' rates.

References

Abo, T. (ed.) (1994) *Hybrid Factory: The Japanese Production System in The United States*, Oxford: Oxford University Press.

Aglietta, M. (1979) *A Theory of Capitalist Regulation: The US Experience*, London: NLB.

Aglietta, M. (1982) *Regulation and Crisis of Capitalism*, New York: Monthly Review Press.

Aglietta, M. (1995) *Macroéconomie financière*, Paris: La Découverte.

Aglietta, M. and Orléan, A. (eds) (1998) *La monnaie souveraine*, Paris: Éditions Odile Jacob.

Akamatsu, K. (1961) 'A Theory of Unbalanced Growth in the World Economy'. Volkswirtschaft Archiv no. 86.2, Publ. Japan 1937.

Amable, B., Barré, R. and Boyer, R. (1997) *Les systèmes d'innovation à l'ère de la globalisation*, Paris: OST/Economica.

Amable, B., Boyer, R. (1994) 'L'Europe est-elle en retard d'un modèle technologique?', *Economie Internationale*, revue du CEPII, no. 56, 4ème trimestre, La Documentation Française.

Amable, B. and Chatelain, J.B. (1995) 'Systèmes financiers et croissance: les effects du court-termisme', *Revue Economique*, 46(3), 827–36.

Aoki, M. (1988) *Information, Incentives, and Bargaining in the Japanese Economy*, Cambridge: Cambridge University Press.

Aoki, M. (1990) 'Toward an economic model of the Japanese firm', *Journal of Economic Literature*, 1.

Aoki, M. (1994a) 'The Japanese firm as a system of attributes: a survey and research agenda', in Aoki, M. and Dore, R. (eds), *The Japanese Firm: The Sources of Competitive Strength*, New York: Oxford University Press.

Aoki, M. (1994b) 'Monitoring characteristics of the main bank system: an analytical and developmental view', in Aoki, M. and Patrick, H. (eds) (1994).

Aoki, M. (1994c) 'The contingent governance of teams: analysis of institutional complementarity', *International Economic Review*, 35.

Aoki, M. (1996) 'Towards a Comparative Institutional Analysis: Motivations and Some Tentative Theorizing', *The Japanese Economic Review*, 47, 1: 1–19.

Aoki, M., Murdock, K. and Okuno-Fujiwara, M. (1996) 'Beyond the East Asian Miracle: Introducing the Market-Enhancing View'. In M. Aoki, Kim H.-K. and Okuno-Fujiwara, M. (eds) (1996).

Aoki, M. and Patrick, H. (eds) (1994) *The Japanese Main Bank System: Its Relevance for Developing and Transforming Economies*, New York: Oxford University Press.

Aoki, M., Kim, H-K. and Okuno-Fujiwara M., (eds) (1996) *The Role of Government in East Asia Economic Development: Comparative Institutional Analysis*, New York:

Oxford University Press.

Aoki, M., Patrick, H. and Sheard, P. (1994) 'The Japanese main bank system: an introductory overview', in Aoki, M. and Patrick, H. (eds) (1994).

Aoki, T. (ed.) (1995) *Kin'yu Zeijakusei to Fuanteisei: Baburu no Kin'yu Dainamizumu (Financial Fragility and Instability: Financial Dynamism of the Bubble)*, Tokyo: Nihon Keizai Hyoronsha.

Asanuma B. (1989) 'Manufacturer-Supplier Relationships in Japan and the Concept of Relation Specific Skill', *Journal of the Japanese and International Economy*, Mar., 3(1), pp. 1–30.

Asensio A., Mazier J. (1991) 'Compétitivité, avantages coûts et hors-coûts et spécialisation' *Revue d' Economie Industrielle*, no. 55, 1er trimestre.

Baba, H.(1997) 'Japanese companyism and the end of Cold War', in Banno J. (ed.) *The Political Economy of Japanese Society*, Vol. 1: *The State or the Market?* Oxford: Oxford University Press.

Beffa, J.-L., Boyer, R. and Touffut J.-Ph. (1999) 'Les relations salariales en France: Etat, entreprises, marchés financiers', *Note de la fondation Saint Simon*, no. 107, Avril.

Benassy, J.P. (1982) *The Economics of Market Disequilibrium*, Boston: Academic Press.

Blossfeld, H.P. (1986) 'Career Opportunity in the Federal Republic of Germany: a Dynamic Approach to the Study of Life-course, Cohort and Period Effects', *European Sociological Review*, vol. 2, no. 3.

Bourdieu, P. (1988) 'Qu'est-ce que comparer?' Communication aux Journées de l'EHESS, juin, Montrouge.

Bowles, S. (1985) 'The Production Process in a Competitive Economy: Walrasian, Neo-Hobbesian, and Marxian Models', *American Economic Review*, 75, 1, pp. 16–36.

Bowles, S. and Boyer, R. (1990) 'A Wage-led Employment Regime: Income Distribution, Labour Discipline and Aggregate Demand in Welfare Capitalism', in S. Marglin and J. Schor (eds) *The Golden Age of Capitalism: Reinterpreting the Post-war Experience*, Oxford: Clarendon.

Bowles, S. and Boyer, R. (1995) 'Wages, Aggregate Demand, and Employment in an Open Economy: a Theoretical and Empirical Investigation', in Epstein, G. and Gintis, H. (eds) *Macroeconomic Policy After the Conservative Era: Studies in Investment, Saving and Finance*, Cambridge Ma: Cambridge University Press, p. 143–71.

Bowles, S., Gordon, D.M. and Weisskopf T.E. (1983) 'Long Swings And The Non-Reproductive Cycle', *American Economic Review*, vol. 73, no. 2, May.

Boyer, R. (1979) 'Wage formation in historical perspective: the French experience', *Cambridge Journal of Economics*, no. 3, March, pp. 99–118.

Boyer, R. (1981) 'Les transformation du rapport salarial dans la crise: une interprétation de ses aspects sociaux et économiques', *Critiques de l' économie politique*, no. 15/16, avril-juin.

Boyer, R. (1986) *La flexibilité du travail en Europe: une étude comparative des transformations du rapport salarial dans sept pays de 1973 à 1985*, Paris: La Découverte.

Boyer, R. (1988a) 'Formalising Growth Regimes', in Dosi, G. *et al.* (eds) *Technical Change and Industrial Transformation*, London: Pinter Publishers.

Boyer, R. (1988b) *The Search for Labour Flexibility*, Oxford: Clarendon Press.

Boyer, R. (1990a) *The Régulation School: A critical Introduction*, New York: Columbia University Press.

Boyer, R. (1990b) *Nyumon Regyurashion (Introduction to the 'Régulation')*, Tokyo:

Fujiwara Shoten.

Boyer, R. (1992) 'Rapport Salarial et Régime d'accumulation au Japon: Emergence, Originalité et Prospective: Premiers Jalons', *Mondes en Développement*, Tome 20, no. 79/80, pp. 31–58.

Boyer, R. (1995a) 'Is the Japanese Wage-Labour Nexus Decaying or Evolving? Part I: Theoretical and Historical Background', paper presented to the International Seminar on the Regulation Approach to Japanese-style Capitalism, Hitotsubashi University, 28–29 January.

Boyer, R. (1995b) 'The Great Transformation of Eastern Europe: a "Regulationist" Perspective', *Emergo: Journal of Transforming Economies and Societies*, vol. 2, no. 4, Autumn, pp. 25–41.

Boyer, R. (1998) *Sekai Kyoto: Shindan to Shohosen (The Current Crisis and its Solutions* Tokyo: Fujiwara Shoten.

Boyer, R. (1999a) 'Le politique à l'ère de la mondialisation et de la finance: le point sur quelques recherches régulationnistes', *L'Année de la régulation 1999*, Vol. 3, p. 13–75.

Boyer, R. (1999b) 'Germany and Japan: Two Embedded Capitalisms, but Distinctive Features and Futures. The case of innovation systems', mimeograph prepared for the conference *'Germany and Japan in the 21st Century: Strengths Turning into Weaknesses?'*, Cologne, 24–26 June.

Boyer, R. and Juillard, M. (1995) 'Has The Japanese WLN Reached Its Limits?' Mimeograph prepared for the international seminar Japanese Economy and 'Régulation' Theory, Kumamoto, 14–16 September, 21 August.

Boyer, R. and Saillard, Y. (eds) (1995) *Théorie de la Régulation. L'état des Savoirs*, Paris: La Découverte.

Boyer, R. and Saillard, Y. (eds) (2000) *'Régulation' Theory. The State of Art*, London: Routledge.

Boyer, R., Charron, E., Jürgens, U. and Tolliday, S. (eds) (1998) *Between Imitation and Innovation: The Transfer and Hybridization of Productive Models in the International Automobile Industry*, Oxford: Oxford University Press.

Campbell, J.Y. (1994), 'Changing patterns of corporate financing and the main bank system in Japan', in Aoki, M. and Patrick H. (eds) (1994).

CERC (1986) Les compléments du salaire, *Documents du CERC* no. 86.

CERC (1987) Salaires et compléments de rémunération: analyse des pratiques d'entreprises, *Documents du CERC* no. 87.

Chartres, J.-A. (1995) 'Le changement des modes de régulation apports et limites de la formalisation', in Boyer, R. and Saillard, Y. (eds) (1995), pp. 273–81.

Chavance, B. (1990) 'L'analyse des systèmes économiques socialistes et la problématique de la régulation', *Revue d'Etudes Comparatives Est-Ouest*, (21), 2.

Chavance, B. (1998) 'Grand-route et chemins de traverse de la transformation post-socialiste', *Economies et Societés, Développement, Croissance et Progrès*, série F, no. 36, pp. 141–9.

Chen, Y. (1994) 'Conflicting interests in information disclosure and short-term orientation of firms', *International Journal of Industrial Organization*, pp. 211–25.

Chuma, H. (1997) 'Keizai Kankyo no Henka to Tyu-ko-nenreiso no Choki Kinzoku-ka (*Changes in the Economic Environment and the tenure prolongation of the middle-aged)*' in Chuma, H. and Suruga, T. (eds) *Koyo Kanko no Henka to Josei Rodo (Changing Employment Practices and Female Labour Force)*, Tokyo: Tokyo University Press.

Clark, K.B. and Fujimoto, T. (1989) 'Product Development and Competitiveness',

Paper presented to the International Seminar on Science, Technology and Growth, OECD, April.

Clark, K.B. and Fujimoto, T. (1991) *Product Development Performance*, Boston: Harvard Business School Press.

Contamin, R. and Lacu, C. (1998) 'Origines et dynamiques de la crise asiatique', *L'Année de la Régulation 1998*, Vol. 2, Paris: La Découverte, pp. 11–63.

Coriat, B. (1991) *Penser à l'envers: Travail et organisation dans l'entreprise japonaise*, Paris: Christian Bourgois.

Coriat, B. (1998) 'La grande crise de l'économie japonaise selon *Made in Japan* – Une vue régulationniste' in Yoshikawa (1994–98).

Delorme, R. and André, Ch. (1983) *L'Etat et l'économie*, Paris: Seuil.

Dirks, D. (1999) 'Limits and latitudes of labour adjustment strategies in Japanese companies', in Dirks, D., Huchet, J.F. and Ribault Th. (eds) (1999).

Dirks, D., Huchet, J.F. and Ribault Th. (eds) (1999) *A Comparative Perspective on Systems under Distress*, Berlin: Springer Verlag.

Dopfer, K. (1985) 'Reconciling Economic Theory and Economic History: The Rise of Japan', *Journal of Economic Issues*, vol. 19 (1), pp. 21–73.

Dore, R. (1994) 'Introduction' To Dore, R., Boyer, R. and Mars Z. (eds) *The Return To Income Policy*, London: Pinter Publishers.

Dornbusch, R.A. (1998) 'The Japanese Crisis and the Bureaucrats', *Far Eastern Economic Review*, 26 February.

Dymski, G.A., Epstein, G. and Pollin, R. (eds) (1993) *Transforming the U.S. Financial System: Equity and Efficiency for the 21st Century*, Armonk, New York: M. E. Sharpe.

Ebizuka, A., Uemura, H. and Isogai A. (1996), 'The "hierarchical market-firm nexus" and the post-war Japanese economy. Focusing on incentives and flexibiliy', *XLV congrès annuel de l'AFSE*, Paris.

Ebizuka, A., Uemura, H. and Isogai, A. (1997) 'L'hypothèse de "la relation hiérarchisée marché-firme" et l'économie japonaise d'après-guerre', *L'Année de la Régulation* vol. 1, Paris: La Découverte, pp. 297–315.

Elger, T. and Smith Ch. (eds) (1994) *Global Japanization?* London: Routledge.

EPA (1993) *Keizai Hakusho (The Economic White Paper)*, Tokyo: Okurasho Insatsukyoku.

EPA (1994) *Keizai Hakusho (The Economic White Paper)*, Tokyo: Okurasho Insatsukyoku.

EPA (1998a) *Keizai Hakusho (The Economic White Paper)*, Tokyo: Okurasho Insatsukyoku.

EPA (1998b) *Sekai Keizai Hakusho (White Paper of World Economy)*, Tokyo: Economic Planning Agency.

EPA (1998c) *Ajia Keizai 1998 (Asian Economy 1998)*, Tokyo: Okurasho Insatsukyoku.

Epstein, G.A. and Gintis, H.M. (eds) (1995a) *Macroeconomic Policy after the Conservative Era: Studies in Investment, Saving and Finance*, Cambridge: Cambridge University Press.

Epstein, G.A. and Gintis, H.M. (1995b) 'Macroeconomic policy after the conservative era: a dual agency approach to state and market' in Epstein, G.A. and Gintis, H.M. (eds) (1995a).

European Commission (1994), *The European Report on Science and Technology Indicators 1994* Report EUR 15897, October.

Fagerberg, J. (1998) 'International Competitiveness', *Economic Journal*, 98: 355–74.

Garanto, A. (1994) 'Le mouvement syndical japonais: vers un redéploiment des stratégies', *Pouvoirs*, no. 71: Le nouveau Japon, pp. 73–90.

Garon, S. and Mochizuki, M. (1993) 'Negotiating Social Contracts' in Gordon, A. (ed.) *Postwar Japan as History*, Berkeley: University California Press.

Geoffron, P. and Rubinstein M. (1996) *La crise financière du modèle japonais*, Paris: Economica.

German Institute for Japanese Studies (1997) 'The Japanese Employment System in Transition. Five Perspectives', Arbeitspapier 97/3, Tokyo: Erscheinungsort.

Gibney, F. (1998) *Unlocking the Bureaucrat's Kingdom*, Washington: The Brooking Institution.

Glyn, A. (1995) 'The Assessment: Unemployment and Inequality', *Oxford Review of Economic Policy* 11,1, pp. 1–25.

Godement, F. (1999) *The Downsizing of Asia*, London: Routledge.

Gordon, D.M. (1995a) 'Putting the Horse (Back) before the Cart: Disentangling the Macro Relationship between Investment and Saving', in Epstein, G.A. and Gintis H.M. (eds). (1995a)

Gordon, D.M. (1995b) 'Growth, Distribution and the Rule of the Game: Social Structuralist Macro Foundations for a Democratic Economic Policy', in Epstein, G.A. and Gintis H.M. (eds) (1995a).

Hanada, M. (1992) 'Le mouvement syndical et rapport salarial au Japon: vers une relation de symbiose', *Mondes en Developpement*, Tome 20, no. 79/80, pp. 83–95.

Hanada, M. (1994) 'Modalités de la fixation des salaires au Japon et en France: Etude du bulletin de paye de Nissan et Peugeot', *Japon in Extenso*, no. 31, Mars-Avril, pp. 23–41.

Hanada, M. (1997) 'Syndicalisme japonais et gestion des conflits sociaux', in J.-M. Bouissou (ed.) *L'envers du consensus*, Paris: Presses de Sciences Politipus.

Hancock, M.D. and Shimada, H. (1993) 'Wage Determination in Japan and West Germany', Fukui, H. *et al.* (eds) *The Politics of Economic Change in Postwar Japan and West Germany*, New York: St. Martin's Press.

Hasegawa, H. and Hook, G.D. (1998) *Japanese Business Management: Restructuring for Low Growth and Globalisation*, London: Routledge.

Hashimoto, M. (1993) 'Aspects of Labour Market Adjustments in Japan', *Journal of Labour Economics*, vol. 11, no. 1, pp. 136–161.

Hashimoto, M. and Raisian, J. (1985) 'Employment Tenure and Earnings Profiles in Japan and the United States', *American Economic Review*, 75: 721–35.

Hatch, W. and Yamamura K. (1996) *Asia in Japan's embrace*, New York: Cambridge University Press.

Heilbroner, R.L. (1988) 'Capitalism', *New Pelgrave Dictionary*, London: Macmillan, pp. 347–53.

Hellmann, T., Murdock, K. and Stiglitz, J. (1996) 'Financial restraint: towards a new paradigm', in Aoki, M., Kim, H. and Okuno-Fujiwara, M. (eds) (1996).

Higuchi, Y. (1991) *Nihon Keizai to Shugyo Kodo (The Japanese Economy and Work Behaviours)*, Tokyo: Toyokeizai-shinposha.

Hirano, Y. (1993) 'Sengo Nihon no Keizai Seicho to Chinrodo Kankei (Economic Growth in Post-war Japan and the Wage-labour Nexus)', in R. Boyer and T. Yamada (eds), *Kiki: Shihon-shugi (Capitalism in Crisis)*, Régulation Collection, vol. 1, Tokyo: Fujiwara-shoten.

Hirano, Y. (1994) 'Une économie de partage à moyen terme et son altération', *Japon in Extenso*, no. 31, Mars-Avril, pp. 42–8.

Hirano, Y. (1996) *Nihonteki Seido to Keizai Seicho (Japanese Institutions and Economic Growth)*, Tokyo: Fujiwara Shoten.

Hollingsworth, J.R. and Boyer, R. (eds. (1997) *Contemporary Capitalism: The Embeddedness of Institutions*, Cambridge: Cambridge University Press.

Horiuchi, A. (1994) Nihon Keizai to Kin'yu Kisei' (The Japanese economy and financial regulation), in Horiuchi, A. (ed.) *Kin'yu (Banking, Security & Insurance)*, Tokyo: NTT Shuppan.

Horiuchi, A. (1995) 'Financial structure and managerial discretion in the Japanese firm: an implication of the surge of equity-related bonds', in Okabe, M. (ed.), *The Structure of the Japanese Economy*, Macmillan Press.

Horiuchi, A. and Fukuda, S. (1987) 'Nihon no Mein Banku ha dono yona Yakuwari o Hatashita ka?' (What role has the main bank played in Japan?), *Kin'yu Kenkyu* 6, pp. 1–27.

Horiuchi, A. and Otaki, M. (1987) 'Kin'yu: Seifu Kainyu to Ginko Kashidashi no Juyosei' (Finance: the importance of public intervention and bank lending), in Hamada, K., Kuroda, M. and Horiuchi, A. (eds) *Nihon Keizai no Makuro Keizai Bunseki (Macroeconomic Analyses of the Japanese Economy)*, Tokyo: University of Tokyo Press.

Horiuchi, A. and Sui, Q. (1992) 'Mein Banku Kankei no Keizai Bunseki: Tenbo' (Economic analyses of main bank relation: an overview), *Kin'yu Keizai Kenkyu*, no. 3, pp. 8–25.

Horiuchi, A. and Sui, Q. (1994) 'Joho Seisansha to shiteno Kaihatsu Ginko: Sono Kino to Genkai (The Japan Development Bank as an information producer: its functions and limits)', in Kaizuka, K. and Ueda, K. (eds) (1994).

Horiuchi, A. and Yoshino, N. (eds) (1992) *Gendai Nihon no Kin'yu Bunseki (Structural Analyses of the Japanese Financial System)*, Tokyo: University of Tokyo Press.

Hoshi ,T. (1994) 'The economic role of corporate grouping and the main bank system', in Aoki, M. and Dore, R. (eds), *The Japanese Firm: The Sources of Competitive Strength*, Oxford: Clarendon Press.

Hoshi, T., Kashyap A. and Scharfstein, D. (1990) 'Bank *monitoring* and investment: evidence from the changing structure of Japanese corporate banking relationship', in Hubbard G. (ed.), *Asymmetric Information, Corporate Finance and Investment*, University of Chicago Press.

Hoshi, T., Kashyap, A. and Scharfstein, D. (1991) 'Corporate structure, liquidity and investment: evidence from Japanese industrial groups' *Quarterly Journal of Economics* 106(1), pp. 33–60.

Ikeo, K. (1994a) Shin'yo Chitsujo to Ginko Kisei' (The order of the credit system and banking regulation), in Horiuchi, A. (ed.) (1994).

Ikeo, K. (1994b) Zaimumen kara Mita Nihon no Kigyo' (Japanese firms seen from the aspect of financing), in Kaizuka, K. and Ueda, K. (eds) (1994).

Ikeo, K. and Hirota, S. (1992) Kigyo no Shihon Kosei to Mein Banku' (The capital structure of firms and main banks), in Horiuchi, A. and Yoshino, N. (eds) (1992).

Imai, K. and Komiya R. (1994) *Business Enterprise in Japan*, Cambridge: MIT Press.

IMF-JC 20 Nenshi Hensan Iinkai (Editing Committee of IMF-JC 20-Year History) (1984) *IMF- C 20 Nenshi: 21 Seiki wo Tenboshita Aratana Hatten wo (The 20-Year History of IMF-JC: Toward New Development for Prospects for the 21st Century)*, Tokyo: Zen Nihon Kinzoku Sangyo Rodo Kumiai Kyogikai.

Inoki, T. (1995) 'Kigyonai Fukurikosei no kokusai hikaku ni mukete' ('For the international comparison of company welfare'), in Inoki T. and Higuchi, Y., *Employment System and Labor Market in Japan*, Tokyo: Nihon Keizai Shinbunsha.

Inoue, Y. (1992). 'L'économie japonaise – compétitivité, exportation, globalisation', *Mondes en développement*, t. 20, no. 79-80.

Inoue, Y. (1994) 'Trajectoires nationales d'industrialisation de la Corée du Sud et de Taiwan'. *Japon in extenso*, no. 32/33.

Inoue, Y. (1996a) *'Seikimatsu Daitenkan' wo Yomu (Reading the 'Great Transformation fin de siècle')*, Tokyo: Yuhikaku.

Inoue, Y. (1996b) 'East Asia's Industrialization: past and present', unpublished.

Inoue, Y. (1997) 'The Development of the Intra-industrial commerce in East-Asia and its impact for the European MNF'. Communication au séminaire international de recherche sur les Economies d'Asie de l'Est, Nîmes, 19-20 juin.

Inoue, Y. and Yamada, T. (1995) 'Démythifier la régulation' in Boyer R. and Saillard Y. eds. *Théorie de la Régulation l'Etat des savoirs*, Paris: La Découverte.

Ishikawa, T. and Deshima, T. (1994) 'Rodoshijo no Nijusei' (Dual Structures in the Japanese Labour Market) in T. Ishikawa (ed.) *Nihon no Shotoku to Tomino Bunpai (Distribution of Income and Wealth in Japan)*, Tokyo: Tokyo University Press.

Isogai, A. and Uemura, H. (1996) '"Seido no keizaigaku" to kahei-rodo no dainamikusu' ('"The economics of institutions" and the dynamics of money and labour'), *Keizaigaku Kenkyu* (Kyushu University), 63(2).

Isogai, A., Uemura, H. and Ebizuka (1999) 'Sengonihonkeizai no Seidobunseki: "Kaisoteki Shijo-kigyo Nekusasu" Ron no Kanten kara' ('The Institutional Analysis of Post-war Japanese Economy: From the Viewpoint of "the Hierarchical Market-Firm Nexus")' in T. Yamada and R. Boyer (eds.) (1999).

Ito, O. (1995) *Nihongata Kin'yu no Rekishiteki Kozo* (The Historical Structure of Japan's Financial System), Tokyo: University of Tokyo Press.

Itoh, M. (1990) *The World Economic Crisis and Japanese Capitalism*, London: Macmillan.

Iversen, T. (1996) 'Power, Flexibility, and the Breakdown of Centralized Wage Bargaining: Denmark and Sweden in Comparative Perspective', *Comparative Politics*, 28,4: 399–436.

Iwata, R. (1977) *Nihonteki Keiei no Hensei Genri (The Organizational Principles of Japanese Management)*, Tokyo: Bunshindo.

Japan Institute of Labour (1994): *White Paper on Labour 1994*, Tokyo: Ministry of Labour.

Jaussaud, J. (1996), 'Gestion des ressources humaines: l'adaptation des effectifs dans la grande entreprise japonaise', *Ebisu*, no. 12, janvier–mars.

JETRO (1998) *JETRO Hakusho: Boeki-hen (White Paper of Foreign Exchange)*, Tokyo.

Johnson, C. (1995) *Japan: who governs? The rise of the Developmental State*, New York: W.W. Norton.

Juillard, M. (1995) 'Une analyse économétrique des changements de régime de croissance aux Etats-Unis', *Revue Economique*, Mai.

Kaizuka, K. and Ueda, K. (eds) (1994) *Henkakuki no Kin'yu Shisutemu (The Japanese Financial System in Transition)*, Tokyo: University of Tokyo Press.

Kaldor, N. (1966) *Causes of the Slow Rate of Economic Growth of the United Kingdom*, Cambridge, Cambridge University Press.

Kaldor, N. (1978a) 'The effects of Devaluations on Trade in Manufactures' in Kaldor, N. (1978b).

Kaldor, N. (1978b) *Further Essays on Economic Theory*, London: Duckworth.

Keizai Kikakucho (Economic Planning Agency of Japan) (1997) *Kokumin Keizai Keisan Nenpo (Annual Report on National Accounts)*, Tokyo: Okurasho Insatsukyoku.

Keynes, J. M. (1936) *The General Theory of Employment, Interest and Money*, reprinted as *Collected Writings of John Maynard Keynes*, Vol. 7, London: Macmillan, 1973.

Kim,Y.-H. (1994) 'Nihon keizai no kaikaku to higashi ajia (The reform of Japanese economy and East Asia)', *Sekai*, 593.

Kitahara, T. (1995) 'Baburu to Ginko Kodo' (The bubble and bank behavior), in Aoki, T. (ed.) (1995).

Kline, S. and Rosenburg, N. (1986) 'An Overview of Innovation', *National Academy of Engineering in 'the Positive Sum Strategy'*, Washington: National Academy Press.

Kodama, F. (1991) *Emerging Patterns of Innovation: Sources of Japans Technological Edge*, Boston: Harvard Business School Press.

Koike, K. (1988) *Understanding Industrial Relations in Modern Japan*, London: Macmillan.

Koike, K. (1995) *The Economics of Work in Japan*, Tokyo: LTCB International Library Foundation.

Komiya, R. (1987) 'Japanese firms, Chinese firms: problems for economic reforms in China', Part I, *Journal of the Japanese and International Economies* 1; Part II, 3, pp. 97–145.

Koshiro, K. (1983) 'Development of Collective Bargaining in Postwar Japan', in Shirai, T. (ed.) *Contemporary Industrial Relations in Japan*, Madison: University of Wisconsin Press.

Krugman, P. (1993) *Pop Internationalism*, Cambridge: MIT Press.

Krugman, P. (1998) 'What happen to Asia?', Web/DISINTER.

Kurita, K. (1994) *Nihon no Rodo Shakai (The Society of Labour in Japan)*, Tokyo: Tokyo University Press.

Kwan, C.H. (1994) *Economic Interdependence in the Asian-Pacific region: towards a yen bloc*, London: Routledge.

Lafay, G. and Herzog, C. (1989) *Commerce international: la fin des avantages acquis*, Paris: Economica.

Lafay, G., Herzog, C. and Richemond, A. (1991) 'Effort d'innovation et spécialisation: comparaisons internationales', *Economie Prospective Internationale*, no. 48, 4e trimestre.

Lazear, E.P. (1979) 'Why Is There Mandatory Retirement?', *Journal of Political Economy*, Vol. 87.

Lichtenberg, F. and Pushner, G. (1992) Ownership structure and corporate performance in Japan, *NBER Working Paper*, 4092.

Lipietz, A. (1979) *Crise et inflation, pourquoi?*, Paris: Maspéro-La Découverte.

Lipietz, A. (1983) *Le monde enchanté*, Paris: La Découverte/Maspero,

Lipietz, A. (1985) *Mirages et miracles*, Paris: La Découverte,

Lipset, S.M. (1996) *American Exceptionalism: A double-edged sword*, New York: WW Norton & company.

Lordon, F. (1999) 'Croyances économiques et pouvoir symbolique', *L'Année de la Régulation 1999*, Vol. 3, Paris: La Découverte, pp. 169–210.

McKinnon, R.I. (1973) *Money and Capital in Economic Development*, Washington DC: Brookings Institution.

McKinnon, R.I. (1999) 'Wading in the yen trap', *The Economist*, 24 July, pp. 77–9.

Marglin, S. and Bhaduri, A. (1990) 'Profit Squeeze and Keynesian Theory', in Marglin, S. and Schor, J. (eds.) *The Golden Age of Capitalism: Re-interpreting the Post-war Experience*, Oxford: Clarendon.

Mincer, J. and Higuchi, Y. (1988) 'Wage structures and labor turnover in the United

States and Japan', *Journal of the Japanese and International Economies*, 2, June.

Ministry of Labour (1996) *Shugyo Keitai no Tayoka ni kansuru Sogo Jittai Chosa (Report on Diversifying Firm-workers)*, Tokyo: Labour Policy Bureau.

Ministry of Labour (1998a) *Rodo Hakusho (White Paper of Labour)*, Tokyo: Nihon Rodo Kenkyu Kiko.

Ministry of Labour (1998b) *Chingin-kozo Kihon Tokei Chosa (Basic Survey on Wage Structures)*, Tokyo: Ministry of Labour.

Ministry of Labour (various years) *Maitsuki Kinro Tokei Chosa (Monthly Labour Statistics)*, Tokyo: Ministry of Labour.

Miyamoto, M. (1996) 'Gino Keisei to Rodo-shijo no Kozo' (Skill Formation and the Structure of the Labour Market)' *Senshu Keizai-gaku Ronshu*, 30, 3, 67–130, Senshu University.

Miyamoto, M. (1998) 'Nihon-gata koyo shisutemu ni towareteiru mono: kokusai hikaku no kanten kara' (The Japanese-style employment system in question: from the point of view of international comparison), Tominaga, K. and Miyamoto, M. (eds), *Mobiriti Shakai heno Tenbo (Towards a Mobile Society)*, Tokyo: Keio Gijuku University Press.

Miyazaki, Y. (1985) *Nihonkeizai no Kozo to Kodo (Structures and Behaviours in the Japanese Economy)* Chikuma-shobo.

Miyazaki, Y. (1992) *Fukugo Fukyo (The Complex Depression)*, Tokyo: Chuo Koronsha.

Mizoguchi, T. and Matsuda, Y. (1997) *Ajia ni okeru Shotoku Bunpai to Hinkonsitsu no Bunseki (Distribution of National Income and Poverty Rate in Asia)*, Tokyo: Tagashoten.

Mjoset, L. (1995) 'Pays Scandinaves: des regulations originales en crise', In Boyer R. and Saillard, Y. (eds) *Théorie de la Régulation. L'état des Savoirs*, Paris: La Découverte, pp. 398–407.

Mori, T. (1992) 'Rodo Kumiai to Kokumin Seikatsu (Labour Unions and the Life of the People)', in Kurita, K. (ed.) *Gendai Nihon no Roshi Kankei: Koritsusei no Baransu Shito (Contemporary Industrial Relations in Japan: The Balance Sheet of Efficiency)*, Tokyo: Rodo Kagaku Kenkyujo Syuppanbu.

Morishima, M. (1982) *Why has Japan 'succeeded'? Western technology and the Japanese ethos*, Cambridge: University Press, Ma.

Morishima, M. (1995) 'Embedding HRM in a Social Context', Mimeograph University of Illinois and Keio University, prepared for the conference 'Labour Relations: Themes for The 21st Century', 29–31 May, Washington, DC, *Journal of British Industrial Relations*, 33(4), December, pp. 617–40.

Murakami, Y. (1996) *An Anticlassical Political-Economic Analysis: A Vision for the Next Century*, Stanford: Stanford University Press.

Muramatsu, H. (1995) 'Nihon no Koyo Chosei' (Employment adjustment in Japan), in Inoki, T. and Higuchi, Y. (eds.) *Nihon no Koyo Shisutemu to Rodo Shijo (The Employment System and Labour Market in Japan)*, Tokyo: Nihonkeizai-shinbunsya.

Nabeshima, N. (1997) 'La tranformation du système financier et la crise contemporaine: le mode de régulation financière dans le capitalisme japonaise', *Revue d'economie financière*, no. 43: 37–79.

Nakamura, T. (1981) *The Postwar Japanese Economy*, Tokyo: University of Tokyo Press.

Nakatani, I. (1984) 'The economic role of financial corporate grouping', in M. Aoki ed., *The Economic Analysis of the Japanese Firm*, Amsterdam: North Holland.

Nippon Ginko (Bank of Japan) (various years) *Syuyo Kigyo Keiei Bunseki* (Analysis of Financial Statements of Principal Enterprises), Tokyo: Nihon Shin'yo Chosa

Kabushiki Gaishya Syuppanbu.

Nippon Ginko Kin'yu Kenkyujo (Bank of Japan, Institute for Monetary and Economic Studies) (1995) *Wagakuni no Kin'yu Seido (The Japanese Financial System)*, Tokyo: Nihon Shin'yo Chosa Kabushiki Gaishya Syuppanbu.

Nishiguchi, T. (1994) *Strategic Industrial Sourcing: The Japanese Advantage*, New York: Oxford University Press.

Nitta, M. (1995) 'Roshi kankei no hen'yo to "futatsu no moderu" (Transformation of industrial relations and the "two models")', in Hashimoto, J. (ed.), *20 Seiki Shihonshugi (20th Century Capitalism)*, vol. 1, University of Tokyo Press.

Noshita, Y. (1995) 'Kin'yu Kozo to Kin'yu Fuanteisei no Shoruikei' (Varieties of financial structure and financial instability), in Aoki, T. (ed.) (1995).

Odagiri, H. (1992) *Growth through Competition: Competition through Growth*. Oxford: Clarendon Press.

Odagiri H. and Goto A. (1993) 'The Japanese system of innovation: past, present and future' in Nelson R. (ed.), '*National innovation systems – a comparative analysis*', New York: Oxford University Press.

Odaka, T. (1984) *Rodo-shijo Bunseki* (The Analysis of the Labour Market: The Evolution of Dual Structures in Japan), Tokyo: Iwanami-shoten.

OECD (1985 to 1998) *OECD Economic Studies: Japan*, Paris: OECD.

OECD (1995), The Labour Market and Older Workers, *Social Policy Studies* no. 17.

Ohmi, N. (1994) 'Gendai Nihon no macro-corporatism' (Macro-corporatism in Contemporary Japan), in Inagami, T., Whittaker, H., Ohmi, N., Shinoda, T., Shimodaira, Y. and Tsujinaka, Y. (1994) *Neo-Koporatizumu no Kokusai Hikaku (International Comparative Research on Neo-corporatism)*, Tokyo: Japan Institute of Labour.

Okazaki, R. and Horiuchi, A. (1992) 'Setsubi Toshi to Mein Banku' (Capital Investment and Main Banks), in Horiuchi, A. and Yoshino, N. (eds) (1992).

Okina, K. (1999) 'A Risky Prescription', *Financial Times*, 12 August.

Okina, K., Takeuchi, Y. and Yoshikawa, H. (1989) 'Waga Kuni ni okeru Jisshitu Chingin no Kettei' (The Determination of Real Wage in Japan), *Keizai Ronshyu*, 55, 2, pp. 77–85, Tokyo University.

Okurasho (Ministry of Finance) (various years) *Hojinkigyo Tokei (Financial Statement Statistic of Corporations by History)*, Tokyo: Okurasho Insatsukyoku.

Okurasho Zaisei Kin'yu Kenkyujo (Ministry of Finance, the Institute of Fiscal and Monetary Policy) (1993) 'Shisan Kakaku Hendo no Mekanizumu to sono Keizaikoka (The Mechanism of Fluctuations in Assets Prices and their Economic Effects), *Financial Review* 30.

Ominami, C. (1986) *Le tiers monde dans la crise*, Paris: La Découverte.

Ono, A. (1989) *Nihonteki Koyo Kenko to Rodo Shizo (Japanese Employment Practices and Labour Market)*, Tokyo: Toyo Keizai Shimposha.

Ozaki, R. (1991) *Human Capitalism*, New York: Penguin Books.

Palombarini, S. (1997) 'La crise italienne de 1992, une lecture en terme de dynamique endogène', *L'Année De La Régulation 1997*, Paris: La Découvert, pp. 229–261.

Palombarini, S. (1999) 'Vers une théorie régulationniste de la politique économique', *L'Année de la Régulation 1999*, vol. 3, Paris: La Découverte, pp. 97–126.

Pasinetti, L.L. (1973) 'The Notion of Vertical Integration in Economic Analysis' *Metoroeconomica*, vol. 25, pp. 1–29.

Patrick, H. (1994) The relevance of Japanese finance and its main bank system', in Aoki, M. and Patrick, H. (eds) (1994).

Pollin, R. (1995) 'Financial structures and egalitarian economic policy', *New Left Review*, no. 214: 26–61.

Pontusson, J. (1992) 'Introduction: Organization and Political Economic Perspective on Union Politics', in Golden, M. and Pontusson, J. (eds) *Bargaining for Change: Union Politics in North America and Europe*, Ithaca, N.Y.: Cornell University Press.

Pontusson, J. and Swenson, P. (1996) 'Labour Markets, Production Strategies, and Wage Bargaining Insititutions', *Comparative Political Studies* 29,2: 223–50.

Ribault, Th. (1999) 'Flexible Employment in Japanese Retailing: Toward a Just-in-Time Employment Model', in Dirks, D., Huchet, J.F. and Ribault Th. (eds) *A Comparative Perspective on Systems under Distress*, Berlin: Springer Verlag.

Riel, B. van (1995) *Unemployment Divergence and Coordinated Systems of Industrial Relations*, Bern: Peter Lang.

Rowthorn, R.E. (1982) 'Demand, Real Wages and Economic Growth', *Studi Economici*, 18.

Saguchi, K. (1991) *Nihon ni okeru Sangyo Minshushugi no Zentei (Preconditions of Industrial Democracy in Japan)*, Tokyo: University of Tokyo Press.

Sako, M. (1997) 'Shunto: The Role of Employer and Union Coordination', in Sako, M. and Sato, H. (eds) *Japanese Labour and Management in Transition: Diversity, Flexibility and Participation*, London: Routledge.

Sapir, J. (1998) *Le krach russe*, Paris: La Découverte.

Schoenholtz, K. and Takeda, M. (1985) 'Joho Katsudo to Mein Banku Sei' (Information activities and the main bank system), *Kin'yu Kenkyu* 4: 1–24.

Seike, A. (1994) 'Social Security Benefits and the Labor Supply of the Elderly in Japan', in Noguchi, Y. and Wise, D.A. (eds) *Ageing in the United States and Japan*, Chicago: University of Chicago Press.

Shapiro, S. and Stiglitz, J. (1984) 'Equilibrium unemployment as a worker discipline device', *American Economic Review*, 74 (3), pp. 433–44.

Shaw, E. S. (1973) *Financial Deepening in Economic Development*, New York: Oxford University Press.

Sheard, P. (1989) 'The main bank system and corporate monitoring and control in Japan', *Journal of Economic Behavior and Organisation* 11: 399–422.

Sheard, P. (1994a) 'Main banks and the governance of financial distress', in Aoki, M. and Patrick, H. (eds) (1994).

Sheard, P.(1994b) 'Interlocking shareholdings and corporate governance', in Aoki, M. and Dore, R. (eds) (1994).

Shikano, Y. (1994) *Nihon no Ginko to Kin'yu Soshiki (Banks and the Financial System in Japan)*, Tokyo: Toyo Keizai Shimposha.

Shimizu, K. (1994), 'Rapport salarial toyotien: hier, aujourd'hui et demain', *Japon in Extenso*, mars-avril, pp. 68–85.

Shimizu, K. (1999) *Le Toyotisme*, Repères, Paris: La Découverte.

Shimizu, K. and Horiuchi, A. (1997) 'Nihon no Seifuthi Netto to Kin'yu Shisutemu no Anteisei' (Japan's safety-nets and the stability of the financial system), in Asako, K., Fukuda, S. and Yoshino, N. (eds) *Gendai Makurokeizai Bunseki: Tenkanki no Nihon Keizai (The Japanese Economy in Transition: A Macroeconomic Analysis)*, Tokyo: University of Tokyo Press.

Shinkawa, T. (1984) '1975nen Shunto to Keizaiteki Kiki Kanri' (The 1975 Shunto and the Management of Economic Crisis), in Ohtake, H. (ed.) *Nihon Seiji no Ronten (Issues on Japanese Politics)*, Tokyo: San'ichi Shobo.

Shinohara, M. (1982) *Industrial Growth, Trade, and Dynamic Patterns in the Japanese*

Economy, Tokyo: Tokyo University Press.

Soskice, D. (1990) 'Wage Determination: The Changing Role of Institutions in Advanced Industrialized Countries', *Oxford Review of Economic Policy*, 6: 36–61.

Stiglitz, J. (1987) 'Dependence of Quality on Price', *Journal of Economic Literature*, Vol. XXV, Mars, pp. 1–48.

Studart, R. (1993) Financial repression and economic development: toward a post-Keynesian alternative', *Review of Political Economy* 11: 277–98.

Takagi, I. (1976) *Shunto Ron: Sono Bunseki, Tenkai to Kadai (On Shunto: An Analysis on Shunto, Its Development and Problems)*, Tokyo: Rodo Junpo sya.

Takezawa, S.-I. (1995) *Japan Work Ways*, Tokyo: The Japan Institute of Labour.

Taylor, L. (1991) *Income Distribution, Inflation, and Growth: Lectures on Structuralist Macroeconomic Theory*, The MIT Press.

Teranishi, J. (1993) 'Mein Banku Shisutemu' (The main bank system)', in Okazaki, T. and Okuno, M. (eds) (1993) *Gendai Nihon Keizai Shisutemu no Genryu (The Origins of the Modern Japanese Economic System)*, Tokyo: Nihon Keizai Shimbunsha.

Teranishi, J. (1994) 'Loan syndication in war-time Japan and the origins of the main bank system', in Aoki, M. and Patrick, H. (eds) (1994).

Teranishi, J. (1998) 'Nihon to Buraziru no Shotoku Bunpai' (Distribution of National Income in Japan and Brazil) in Minami, R., Nakamura, M. and Nishizawa, T. (eds) *Demokurashi no Hokai to Salsei (Decline and Renaissance of Democracy)* Tokyo: Nihonkeizaihyorousya.

The Economist (1994 to 1998): various issues.

The Economist (1999a) 'The new Economy. Work in progress', 24–30 July, pp. 19–21

The Economist (1999b) 'Economic Indicators', 21–27 August.

Théret, B. (1999) 'L'effectivité de la politique économique: de l'autopoïèse des systèmes sociaux à la topologie du social', *L'Année de la Régulation 1999*, Paris: La Découverte, pp. 127–68.

Tohyama, H. (1990) 'Kodo seicho-ki niokeru chinrodo keitai: regyurashion apurochi no shiten kara' (Wage-labour forms in the high growth period: from a viewpoint of the régulation approach), *Keizaigaku Zasshi* (Osaka City University), 91(1).

Tohyama, H. (1994) 'Company-ism Regulation: Hypothesis and the Wage-Formation in Postwar Japanese Economy', Mimeograph Shizuoka University, Japan, 12 November.

Topel, R.H. (1982) 'Inventories, Layoffs, and the Short-Run Demand for Labour', *American Economic Review*, Vol 72, no. 4, September, pp. 769–87.

Tsuchiya, M. and Konomi, Y. (1996) *Shaping the Future of Japanese Management: New Leadership to Overcome the Impending Crisis*, Tokyo: LTCB International Library Foundation.

Tsuda, M. (1987) 'Shin-Nijukozo Jidai ha Torai Suruka' (Is the Dual Structure Being Renewed?), *Nihon Roudo – Kyokai Zasshi*, no. 331, pp. 33–43.

Tsuru, K. (1995) *The Japanese Market Economy System: Its Strengths and Weaknesses*, Tokyo: LTCB International Library Foundation.

Tsuru, T. (1992a) 'Shunto ni okeru Sangyo-kan Chingin-hakyu-koka no Henka' (Changes in the Interindustry Wages Spillover Effect under Shunto), *Keizai Kenkyu*, 43, 3, 214–24, Hitotsubashi University, Institute of Economic Research.

Tsuru, T. (1992b) 'Wage spillovers under the Spring Offensive system in Japan', *Mondes en développement*, 20 (79/80).

Ueda, K. (1994) Institutional and regulatory frameworks for the main bank system', in Aoki, M. and Patrick, H. (eds) (1994).

Uemura, H. (1992) 'Growth and distribution in the post-war regime of accumulation: a theory and realities in the Japanese economy', *Mondes en développement*, 20(79/80).

Uemura, H. and Ebizuka, A. (1994) 'Incentives and Flexibility in the Hierarchical Market-Firm Nexus: A Prelude to the Analysis of Productivity Regimes in Japan', *Japan in Extenso*, no. 31, March–April.

Uemura, H., Isogai, A. and Ebizuka, A. (1996) 'A Regulation Approach to the Post-war Japanese Economy: The Hypothesis of the Hierarchical Market-Firm Nexus', *International Economic Conflict Discussion Paper*, no. 91, Nagoya University.

Uemura, H., Isogai, A. and Ebizuka, A. (1998) *Shakai-keizai Shisutemu no Seido-bunseki: Marukusu to Keinzu wo koete (The Institutional Analysis of Socio-economic Systems: Beyond Marx and Keynes)*, Nagoya: Nagoya University Press.

Uni, H. (1998) *Kozo Henka to Shihon Chikuseki (Structural Change and Capital Accumulation)*, Tokyo: Yuhikaku.

Weinstein, D.E. and Yafeh, Y. (1994) 'On the Costs of a Bank Centered Financial System: Evidence from the Changing Main Bank Relation in Japan', *Working Paper*, Cambridge MA: Harvard University, June.

Wolfson, M.H. (1994) *Financial Crisis: Understanding the Postwar U.S. Experience*, 2nd edn, New York: M. E. Sharpe.

Womack, J.P., Jones, D.T. and D. Roos (1990) *The Machine that Changed the World*, New York: Harper Perennial.

Womack, J.P., Jones, D.T., Roos D. and Sammons Carpenter, D. (1990) *The Machine That Changed the World*, New York: Macmillan Publishing.

World Bank (1993) *The East Asian Miracle: Economic Growth and Public Policy*, Washington DC: World Bank.

Yabushita, S. (1995) *Kin'yu Shisutemu to Joho no Riron (Japan's Financial System: Markets, Banks, and Their Stability)*, Tokyo: University of Tokyo Press.

Yamada, T. (1992) 'Heurs et malheurs du mode de régulation japonais', *Mondes en développement*, 20(79/80).

Yamada, T. (1994) *20 Seiki Shihonshugi (The 20th Century Capitalism)*, Tokyo: Yuhikaku.

Yamada, T. and Boyer, R. (1999) (eds) *Sengo Nihon Shihonshugi: Chosei to Kiki no Bunseki (Post-war Japanese Capitalism: An Analysis of 'Régulation' and Crisis)*, Tokyo: Fujiwara-Shoten.

Yamamoto, E. (1998) 'Sekai Defure Kaihi no tameni Nihon ga Subekikoto' (What Japan should make to avoid the world deflation), *Sekai*, August, Tokyo.

Yamamura, K. and Yasuba, Y. (eds) (1987) *The Political Economy of Japan, Vol. 1: The Domestic Transformation*, Stanford: Stanford University Press.

Yokoyama, K. (1999) 'Companies move to tap female talent', *The Nikkei Weekly*, 9 August, pp. 1 and 19.

Yoshikawa, H. (1994) *Made in Japan*, édition française Paris: Hachette, Livre de poche (1998).

Yoshikawa, H. (1995) *Macroeconomics and the Japanese Economy*, New York: Oxford University Press.

Yoshikawa, H. (1996) (ed.) *Kin'yu Seisaku to Nihon Keizai (Financial Policy and The Japanese Economy)*, Tokyo: Nihon Keizai Shinbunsya.

Zysman, J. (1983) *Government, Markets and Growth: Financial Systems and the Politics of Industrial Change*, Ithaca, New York: Cornell University Press.

Index